QUIET ON THE SET!
CELEBRITY TRIVIA

has arrived. Crammed with gossip galore, this book was written with the name-dropper in all of us in mind. It's loaded with public and private memorabilia on actors, writers, rock stars and tyrants and the scandalous facts they probably wouldn't want you to know. From Napoleon to Alice Cooper, anyone who has caught the public eye is fair game! For example, the answers to those cover questions are:

1. Ryan O'Neal   2. Jack Kerouac   3. John Wayne
4. Lou Costello   5. Gerald Ford   6. Frank Zappa
    7. Lawrence Welk   8. Charlie Chaplin
      9. David Merrick   10. Zero Mostel.

*TQ—Your Trivia Quotient—is scored this way:
10 right—Someone turn on a blue spotlight!
7 to 9—Not bad, but you forgot a few lines.
5 to 6—Uh, we'll call you.
4 or less—It's curtains . . . unless you read

Celebrity
Trivia

ABOUT THE AUTHOR

Ed Lucaire, a former advertising executive, has been a chronic reader of almanacs, dictionaries, encyclopedias, and biographies since he was ten years old. From his readings, he collects all interesting and unusual facts. In addition to *Celebrity Trivia*, Mr. Lucaire has written *Hollywood Almanac, The Greatest Animal Book Ever, The Joy of Knowing Almost Everything About S*E*X*, and has been a contributor to *Esquire* and *New York* magazines, *The Book of Lists*, and *The Filmgoer's Companion*.

A graduate of Amherst College, Mr. Lucaire lives on Central Park West in New York City with his wife Lewise and two children, Laurin and Eddie. His current works-in-progress include a musical-comedy about Russian monk Rasputin (entitled *Hello Grigori!*) and a definitive biography of television announcer Don Pardo.

Celebrity Trivia

A Collection of Little-known Facts About Well-known People

Edward Lucaire

WARNER BOOKS

A Warner Communications Company

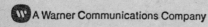

For my wife Lewise and
our children, Laurin and Eddie,
who tolerate my idiosyncrasies and
endure the long hours I spend
delving into the obscure . . .

Acknowledgments

In addition to the authors and publishers acknowledged in the Sources section of this book, I would like to thank the following friends and associates:

To Tony Gonzalez, Aubrey Hawes, Peter Ognibene, Ed Stein, Steve Strauss, and Luis Villegas for encouraging me to put some of my ideas and *shticks* on paper.

To my friends John Gabriel, Gary Gold, and Dave Galbreath and their respective families for their support.

To various people who helped in some way somewhere along the line: Eric Brettschneider, Van Brokaw, David Brown, Tom Caskanett, Don Challis, Rusty Clowes, Mort Cooperman, Nancy Crawford, Tom Derderian, Cathy Di Libero, Robert Eaton, Joni Evans, Richard Evans, John A. Gambling, Don Gilbert, Bill Heaney, Frank Henderson, Murray Hysen, Fredda Isaacson, Ed Jewett, Jim Janowitz, Mike Keiser, Tom Laughlin, Ed Madden, Tom Madden, Pat McGinnis, John Moeling, Dick Mumma, Charlie Partington, the David Roberts, Ruth Salevouris, Maurice Sculfort, Bernard Shir-Cliff, Peter Spivey, Brooks Stanwood, Steve Stefenhagens, the Marcus Strocks, Stu Tomey, Richard Willoughby, and to the pleasant people at the New York Public Library system, especially Mrs. Leonard Jackson.

And to the rest of my family—the William Lucaires, the Maynard Hesses, and the Hager clan—who provided additional support and encouragement.

Celebrity
Trivia

Introduction to Celebrity Trivia

Are you fascinated by celebrities? Famous people like movie and television stars, professional athletes, authors, composers, poets, kings, queens, U.S. presidents, tyrants—even stripteasers and movie porn queens—those remarkable individuals who have achieved fame or infamy in this world? This book is a comprehensive collection of legitimate but little-known facts and tasty tidbits about those famous people.

I culled these facts from biographies, autobiographies, almanacs, encyclopedias, interviews, talk shows—every non-fiction source that I could find.

I was intrigued not by the obvious facts about well-known people but by the ironies, the contradictions, the unusual backgrounds, and the eccentricities of celebrities, living and dead. For example, I was surprised to learn that:

A great opera singer drank a shot of whiskey before his performances.

A handsome movie star, famous for his penetrating blue eyes, is color-blind.

A conservative Republican congressman kept a pet boa constrictor in his dormitory room during his college days at Yale.

A well-known billionaire regarded as his most important moment not when he made his first million or billion dollars but when he became an Eagle Scout.

As an Alfred Hitchcock fan, for example, I enjoyed finding out how the crafty director managed to make his obligatory appearance in the movie *Lifeboat* which featured only eight actors and took place on a small lifeboat. (No, he was not in drag playing Tallulah Bankhead!)

A few of the facts in *Celebrity Trivia* are not funny but are nevertheless interesting. These facts are included not to be mean or malicious but to show the public that celebrities have their share of woes and miseries and are basically like you and me. Problems such as drug addiction, alcoholism, suicides, etc., are sad realities that seem to affect most people in our society. My purpose in including these items is to encourage commiseration, not to foster gossip.

Other facts were amusing because they were out-of-character or totally unexpected of the particular person:

One quite masculine Academy Award-winning actor's first stage job was as a dancing female impersonator!

A Pulitzer Prize-winning novelist was a cook in the U.S. Army and loved the job. (He subsequently taught all his wives how to cook!)

Another famous actor, once a romantic lead in his native Europe, was able to play only ghouls and fiends in Hollywood films.

This kind of trivia is hard not to enjoy or find interesting. Drop a few of these gems in your chatter at the next cocktail party and you'll find people intrigued with what you have to say—which is surely better than having them yawn in your face.

If you have fun reading this book and learn a lot of things you didn't know before, then the book has accomplished its mission. Having fun and learning at the same time are no trivial matters!

A

Abbott, Bud

The straight-man in the Abbott and Costello comedy team was an epileptic and alcoholic.

Abbott and Costello made only one movie in which they were not the stars. The movie was *One Night in the Tropics,* released in 1939.

Abdul-Jabbar, Kareem

At birth, Kareem weighed 13 pounds and was 22 inches tall. His parents were not exactly short —his father was six feet four inches and his mother six feet one inch tall.

Before converting to the Islamic faith, Kareem was a member of the Roman Catholic Church.

He and ex-wife Habiba (nee Janice Brown) loved kosher food. He once said, "Thank Allah for the Jews in Milwaukee—we live on kosher food."

Abzug, Bella

The ex-congresswoman's father owned the Live and Let Live meat market in New York City.

13

Miss Abzug's first job was modeling turbans at a department store.

Adams, Edie

Born Elizabeth Edith Enke in Kingston, Pennsylvania, the singer-comedienne adopted her mother's maiden name, Adams, as her stage name.

Adams, John

John Adams, the first U.S. president to live in the White House, was the first U.S. Ambassador to England and is credited with founding the U.S. Marine Corps in 1798.

Of all the U.S. presidents, John Adams lived to be the oldest—he was 90 years, 247 days old when he died and was ex-president longer than any other president—25 years and 4 months.

Adams was also married longer than any other president. His marriage to Abigail Smith Adams lasted 54 years and 3 months.

Adams, John Quincy

During his presidency, John Quincy Adams used to "skinnydip" in the Potomac River every day (weather permitting).

Adams published a book of poetry in 1832 and is the only president to have published his poems.

Because of a childhood accident, the sixth U.S. president's right arm was malformed and was smaller than the left one.

Adams was the only president to name a son after George Washington. The son, an erstwhile poet, died at the age of 28, victim of an apparent suicide.

Two of Adams's four children were born outside the United States. His son George Washington Adams was born in Berlin, Germany in 1801 and his daughter, Louisa Catherine Adams, was born in St. Peterburg, Russia in 1811. Adams was on official government missions at the time. Adams's wife was also foreign-born and was the only presidential wife to have this distinction. Louisa Catherine Johnson Adams was born in London, England in 1775.

Adams was the first president ever to be photographed (1843), although he was not president at the time. (Six years later, President James Polk was the first president to be photographed while in office.)

In the 1820 presidential election John Quincy Adams received only one electoral vote, versus James Monroe's 231—the most lop-sided presidential election defeat on record.

John Quincy Adams was the only president whose father was also president.

Not only was John Quincy Adams a U.S. Ambassador to England but so was his father, John Adams, and his son, Charles Francis Adams.

Adams, Maude

Born Maude Kiskadden, the actress adopted the stage surname of her mother Annie Adams, also an actress.

Adams, Samuel

Samuel Adams, one of the leaders of the American Revolution, was the second person to sign the Declaration of Independence.

Addams, Charles

The ghoulish cartoonist's sense of humor not only appears on the pages of *The New Yorker* magazine but also pervades his home life too. In his living room Addams has a human skeleton displayed in a glass case, a human skull on his bedroom dressing table, and strange looking bottles labeled "Arsenic" in his liquor cabinet.

Adderley, Cannonball

As a young schoolboy in Florida, the future jazz musician had a reputation for eating anything in sight so his classmates called him "Cannibal." Adults, not understanding the nickname, started calling him "Cannonball." The name died out around 1943 but in 1955 Adderley (Julian was his real first name) ran into an old school friend who revived the nickname.

Adler, Mortimer

The educator and author (*The Great Books*) never graduated from high school. At DeWitt Clinton High School in New York City where Adler was editor of the school newspaper, the principal objected to Adler's trying to run the school as well as the newspaper and didn't let him graduate. Later at Columbia University, Adler was elected to Phi Beta Kappa but did not receive his B.A. degree because he refused to take the swimming test.

Aesop

The fabulist is believed to have been a dwarf.

Agnew, Spiro

Distrustful of the press, the former vice-president of the United States once commented, "Some newspapers dispose of their garbage by printing it."

Despite his penchant for alliteration and long words, Agnew did not major in English at college. He studied chemistry for three years at Johns Hopkins University before switching to law.

Agnew was the first vice-president of the U.S. of Greek origin. The family name was originally Anagnostopoulos, then shortened to Anagnost, and finally became Agnew.

Aiken, Conrad

When the poet and author was 11 years old, his father shot his wife and then committed suicide. Aiken related the episode in his book *Ushant*, published in 1952.

Albee, Edward

The playwright (*Who's Afraid of Virginia Woolf?*) was a Western Union delivery boy in his early writing career.

Albert, Eddie

Early in his career, Edward Albert Heimberger (his real name) became a "song, dance, and patter man" in a trio appearing on a Minneapolis radio station but was always introduced as Eddie *Hamburger* so he dropped his last name and used his easy-to-pronounce given names.

Albertson, Jack

Actor Jack Albertson originally became a "hoofer" instead of an actor because he suffered from stage fright and he knew that as a dancer audiences would look at his feet and not at him.

Alcott, Louisa May

The former dolls' dressmaker despised her book *Little Women* and the subsequent fame it brought her.

Miss Alcott began her writing career as the author of "potboiler" stories, using the pen names A.M. Barnard and Flora Fairfield.

Alda, Alan

The star of the television "M.A.S.H." series is the son of actor Robert Alda whose original name was Alfonso D'Abruzzo. The senior Alda created his stage surname by taking the first two letters of his given name, *Al*fonso, and combining it with the first two letters of his family name, *D'*Abruzzo.

Alexander, Shana

Miss Alexander's father, Milton Ager, wrote the song "Ain't She Sweet."

When Shana, an anthropology major in college, became a reporter her first job was to interview Gypsy Rose Lee on her pregnancy.

Alger, Horatio

The son of a Unitarian minister, Alger was a graduate of Harvard Divinity School. His famous stories starting with *Ragged Dick* were not "rags-to-riches" stories, as popularly believed, but were about people who through honesty and perseverance improved their lives, not necessarily making lots of money.

According to writer George Juergens, "Horatio Alger wrote the same novel 135 times and never lost his audience."

Ali, Muhammad

At Central High School in Louisville, Kentucky, Ali was graduated 376th in a class of 391 students but very likely he is the most successful student ever to come out of that class or that high school.

Usually the appearance of Muhammad Ali in the ring guarantees a large attendance but his fight with Sonny Liston on May 25, 1965 in Lewiston, Maine was an exception. The attendance was only 2,434—a record low for a world heavyweight title fight.

In an interview with *Sport* magazine, Howard Cosell highly praised Ali but revealed that "he has one of the shortest attention spans of any human being I've ever known—20 seconds at best."

Ali's first wife Khalilah (formerly Belinda) appeared in the movie *China Syndrome* as the television news team stage manager.

The heavyweight champ's father, a signpainter with a flair for show business, named Ali's younger brother Rudolph Valentino Clay. (Rudolph is now known as Rahaman Ali.)

Ali's great-great-grandfather was a slave owned by Cassius Marcellus Clay, the American ambassador to Russia in the 1860s and early abolitionist. A great-grandfather was an Irishman named Grady.

Allen, Fred

In his teens, John Florence Sullivan started in vaudeville as a juggler who told jokes while he juggled. He first used the stage name Fred St. James but later shortened it to Freddy James. As Fred's jokes got better, he did less juggling and more joke telling until he finally graduated to big-time vaudeville as a stand-up comedian, with the new and final stage name of Fred Allen.

Allen, Gracie

George Burns's wife and partner was really named Grace Allen—it was not a stage name.

Originally Gracie Allen was supposed to be "straight man" to Burns but she drew so many laughs during their act that he became the straight man.

Allen, Steve

The talented television personality has published 22 books and written over 4,000 songs.

Allen's youngest son, Brian Allen, now goes by the name Logic Israel. He underwent a religious conversion and is now an elder of the Church of Jesus Christ at Armageddon in Seattle, Washington and lives there in the church commune.

Allen, Mel

The "Voice of the Yankees" was born Melvin Allen Israel but was advised to change his last name when he started his first broadcasting job in New York. The sports announcer agreed to the suggestion and merely dropped his surname.

Allen, Woody

It is not easy to get a straight story on how Allen Stewart Konigsberg became Woody Allen but . . . some sources say that Woody's real name is Heywood Allen but if that were true, why did he once say that "when other kids learned my name, they'd beat me up. So I'd tell them my name was Frank, but they'd still beat me up." Actually, his new last name is his old first name and the name Woody probably comes from his talent on the clarinet and his not-so-secret ambition to be a great clarinetist like Woody Herman.

Allyson, June

June Allyson's real name is Ella Geisman and, despite her midwestern appearance, she was born and raised in the borough of Bronx, New York.

When June was eight years old, a tree limb fell on her and a friend, killing the friend and hurting June badly enough for her to wear a leg brace for four years.

Alpert, Herb

With his back to the camera, Herb Alpert appeared in the movie *The Ten Commandments* as the man who drummed while Moses descended from the mountain.

None of the seven original Tijuana Brass band members was of Spanish-American or Mexican-American descent.

Alpert's son, Dore, was named after the first two notes of the musical scale.

In 1966 Herb Alpert's Tijuana Brass albums sold 13,700,000 copies, making the group "the greatest recorded success in a single year," according to the *Guinness Book of World Records*, prior to the Bee Gees' success in 1978–79.

Ambler, Eric

The British novelist and screenplay writer studied engineering at London University and apprenticed in electrical engineering for two years before becoming a writer.

In addition to writing the screenplays for movies like *A Night to Remember* and *The Wreck of the Mary Deare*, Ambler also worked on the script of the Marlon Brando *Mutiny on the*

Bounty. Ambler's job was to beef up Fletcher Christian's part (Brando) and cut down Captain Bligh's part (Trevor Howard).

Ameche, Don

Don Ameche was the host of the first national television broadcast in color, the Tournament of Roses parade on the NBC television network, January 1, 1954.

Ameche's name was originally spelled Dominic Felix Amici.

Amin, Idi Dada

In the summer of 1973, Amin sent President Richard M. Nixon a get-well card wishing him "a speedy recovery from Watergate."

From 1951 to 1960 Idi Amin was Uganda's heavyweight boxing champion.

Idi Amin, a known anti-Semite, received his military training in Israel.

The "Dada" sometimes used in Amin's name has an interesting origin. In the early 1960s in the Ugandan army, Amin kept two wives in his quarters (regulations permitted one wife). When a British officer questioned Amin's practice, he explained that one woman was his wife and the other was an elder sister or "dada" in Swahili. From then on, he became known as Idi Amin Dada.

Amos 'n' Andy

The comedy team first appeared on radio station WGN in Chicago as "Sam 'n' Henry" in 1925.

Anders, William

The *Apollo 8* astronaut was born in Hong Kong where his father was a navy commander and executive officer of the United States gunboat *Panay*.

Andersen, Hans Christian

The Danish storyteller was literally a stuffed shirt. He was so self-conscious about his "sunken-chest" that he used to stuff paper under his shirt.

Hans Christian Andersen didn't have any problem writing or telling stories but he did have trouble reading them—he was a dyslexic.

Anderson, Marian

On January 7, 1955 Marian Anderson became the first black to sing with the Metropolitan Opera. The contralto appeared as Ulrica, the fortune teller, in Verdi's *Un Ballo in Maschera*.

Anderson, Sherwood

The author of *Winesburg, Ohio* died of peritonitis in 1941 after swallowing a toothpick.

Andrews, Dana

Andrews was a gas station attendant in Van Nuys, California for four years before he entered show business.

Carver Dana Andrews (his full name), the son of a Baptist minister, was named after Mssrs. Carver and Dana, two professors under whom his father had studied in a theological seminary.

Angeles, Victoria de los

The opera singer has an angelic voice and name but she was born Victoria Gamez Cima and adopted her new name, meaning "of the angels" or "angelic" in Spanish, for stage purposes.

Angeli, Pier

The late movie actress (*Somebody Up There Likes Me, Teresa*) was born Anna Maria Pierangeli on the island of Sardinia. Her surname split in two became her stage name.

Pier's twin sister, Maria Luisa Pierangeli, also became an actress, using the name Marisa Pavan. Marisa appeared in the movies *The Rose Tattoo* and *Solomon and Sheba*, among others.

Anka, Paul

As a favor, singer and songwriter Paul Anka wrote the musical introduction to Johnny Carson's "The Tonight Show." Thinking the show might not last very long, he didn't expect to make any money on the music. Anka was wrong, however, and is $300,000 richer—which is what the music has earned in residuals since Johnny Carson has been hosting the show.

Anka is only five feet five inches tall.

Annabella

The French movie actress, once married to Tyrone Power, was born Suzanne Georgette Carpentier. After reading Edgar Allan Poe's *Anna-*

bell Lee, however, she decided to adopt the name Annabella.

Anne, Princess

Princess Anne's full name is Anne Elizabeth Alice Loving Windsor.

Ann-Margret

Ann-Margaret and her family once lived in a funeral parlor in Wilmette, Illinois, where her mother worked as a receptionist. Her father, an electrician, was very ill at the time and was not able to work, creating financial and housing problems for the family.

Ann-Margret's full name is Ann-Margret Olsson and she was born in Valsjobyn, Sweden.

Antoine

The late hairdresser, whose real name was Antek Cierplikowski, created his first hairdo when he was only eight years old. He cut and dressed his younger sister's hair and set her curls with honey. The curls were perfect except for one problem—they attracted swarms of bees.

Antoine got the idea for bobbed hair by accident in 1910. He was hired to make actress Eve Lavalliere look younger and while he was trying to figure out a solution, a young girl with bangs walked in front of him—giving him the idea to use a similar hairdo for his actress client.

Antonioni, Michelangelo

The Italian movie director (*Blow-Up*, *Zabriskie Point*) earned a doctorate in economics and commerce at the University of Bologna.

Apollinaire, Guillaume

The French poet and art critic's real name was Wilhelm Apollinaris de Kostrowitsky.

Arafat, Yasir

When Arafat first joined the militant Palestinian organization Al Fatah, he used the alias Abu Amar.

Al Fatah is an Arabic acronym for "Harakat al tahrir al-Falastin" which means "The Movement for the Liberation of Palestine." Arafat is a civil engineer by training.

Arden, Elizabeth

Florence Nightingale Graham started a Fifth Avenue beauty salon in 1909 with Elizabeth Hubbard, but the partnership was dissolved within a year because of differences between the two women. Miss Graham opened up her own salon and gave it the name Elizabeth Arden, inspired by Tennyson's poem *Enoch Arden* and her mother's first name, Elizabeth.

Elizabeth Arden's horse Jet Pilot won the 1947 Kentucky Derby.

Arden, Eve

In 1933 when Eunice Quedens was appearing in the Leonard Sillman revue *Lo and Behold* in

Los Angeles, she was seen by Broadway producer Lee Shubert and was immediately signed up for the Billy Burke show "Ziegfeld Follies." At that time the actress adopted the name Eve Arden, which she said was a combination of the two names of cosmetics she was using at the time—Elizabeth *Arden* and *Eve*ning in Paris.

Aristotle

The Greek philosopher stuttered.

Arkin, Alan

Alan Arkin majored in drama at an all-woman's college, Bennington College in Vermont. He was one of few men recruited specifically for their drama and dance departments. (He never was graduated because of a dispute over transfer credits from two California colleges.)

Arkin's first movie was *The Russians are Coming* in 1966.

Arlen, Harold

The composer of great hits like "Stormy Weather," "Over the Rainbow," and "That Old Black Magic" also composed his own name. His name at birth was Hyman Arluck.

One of Arlen's songs, "We're Off to See the Wizard" (from *The Wizard of Oz*), was used as the marching song of Australian troops during World War II.

Arlen, Michael

The author of *The Green Hat, May Fair* and *The London Venture* was born with the name

Dikran Kouyoumdjian but was advised by publisher William Heinemann to change his name. He made up the name Michael Arlen and checked the telephone book to make sure no one else had the same name.

While staying at the Imperial Hotel in London, Arlen once poured a martini on Paul Joseph Goebbels, the German Nazi propaganda leader.

Armstrong, Henry

In 1938 Armstrong held three world boxing titles simultaneously—the featherweight, lightweight, and welterweight titles.

"Hurricane Hank" Armstrong's real name was Henry Jackson but there was already another boxer by that name so he changed his name. He took the name Armstrong from his trainer Harry Armstrong who helped him improve his boxing technique.

The ex-boxer is now a preacher and is known as Reverend Henry Jackson.

Armstrong, Louis

If Louis Armstrong had not been arrested on New Year's Day in 1913, he might not have become a famous trumpet player. But he was in fact arrested for shooting off a gun and sent to reform school, where he learned to play the bugle and trumpet.

Armstrong's nickname "Satchmo" was really a contraction of the nickname "Satchelmouth" which he got from an editor of the *London Melody Maker*. Eventually the nickname became shortened to "Satchmo." (Note: Louis's friends called him "Pops.")

Satchmo started "scat" singing, the singing of nonsense syllables instead of words.

Armstrong was born on the Fourth of July in 1900.

Arness, James

On the long-running television program "Gunsmoke" it was Chester (played by Dennis Weaver) who had the limp but it was James Arness who should have been limping—he was wounded in the leg at Anzio in World War II.

The six foot six actor's last name was originally spelled "Aurness" but was simplified to Arness when he became an actor. His brother Peter, also an actor ("Mission Impossible"), abandoned the name altogether and adopted the surname Graves.

James Arness's first movie role took advantage of his size but not his acting ability—he played the monster in the Howard Hawks's film production *The Thing,* released in 1952.

Arno, Peter

The Yale educated *New Yorker* magazine cartoonist was born Curtis Arnoux Peters.

Arnold, Benedict

The infamous American traitor owned a drug and book store in New Haven, Connecticut for 13 years before joining the militia during the Revolutionary War.

Arquette, Cliff (Charlie Weaver)

Cliff Arquette's parents were the vaudeville team, Arquette & Clark, billed as "The Funny Hebrew and the Singing Soubrette"—an unusual name, considering that his father was French and his mother Irish.

Arroyo, Martina

Opera singers are often asked what his or her favorite role is. With a good sense of humor, soprano Martina Arroyo once answered the question with, "Madame Butterball," acknowledging her weakness for high calorie and spicy foods.

Arthur, Chester

Chester Arthur, the 21st president of the United States, was the first president to indulge in the harmful practice of smoking cigarettes.

About Chester Arthur, someone once said that he was "first in ability on the list of second-rate men."

Arthur knew the way to a woman's heart. He gave flowers to his wife every day of their marriage and even after her death had flowers placed under her portrait every day until he died.

Arthur, Jean

The petite movie actress (*Mr. Smith Goes to Washington, Shane*) was born Gladys Green.

Ashe, Arthur Jr.

Tennis-great Arthur Ashe is of Negro, Mexican, and American Indian ancestry.

Ashley, Elizabeth

Born Elizabeth Ann Cole, she changed her name in the early 1960's to avoid confusion with another actress named Elizabeth Cole.

The actress once toured New York State as Miss Genny for Genesee beer and was also the "Chiffon-light Jell-O Pudding and Pie Filling Girl" on *The Price is Right* television quiz show.

Asner, Edward

The popular television actor ("The Mary Tyler Moore Show") is the father of twins, Liza and Matthew.

Asner's father was a scrap iron dealer in Kansas City, Missouri, but was sometimes less euphemistically called a "junk man."

Astaire, Fred

Women aren't the only people who watch soap opera television serials. Astaire is addicted to "As the World Turns" and "The Guiding Light" shows and whenever he misses the programs he calls his housekeeper to find out what happened.

Astaire's first screen test report read: "Can't act. Slightly bald. Can dance a little." After the test, he learned to act, bought a toupee, and danced a lot.

Astaire's last name was originally Austerlitz—a great name for a "storm trooper" but not for a vaudeville "trouper."

Astor, Mary

Although Mary Astor used to be a heavy drinker, it never seemed to affect her ability as an actress. In fact, on the MGM lot she was known as "One-Take Astor."

Her first sound movie in 1930 was appropriately titled *Ladies Love Brutes*.

After she published her memoirs *My Story* in 1959, Mary Astor started a second career as a writer and wrote five novels and another book of memoirs, *A Life in Film*.

Her real name was Lucile Vasconcells Langhanke but was changed to Mary Astor by Jesse Lasky, Louella Parsons, and Walter Wanger when she won a six-month contract with the Famous Players-Lasky movie production company. Miss Astor liked her new name, unlike many actresses being renamed, because it had a "sound of affluence."

Atlas, Charles

Someone told muscular Angelo Siciliano that he looked like the statue of Atlas in front of a Brooklyn bank. Rather than shrug off the remark he decided to adopt the name Charles Atlas and sell his "dynamic tension" muscle-building technique by mail.

Attila the Hun

The only Hun ever to become famous was a dwarf.

Audubon, John James

The famous ornithologist, naturalist, and painter was born in Cayes, Haiti. He emigrated to the United States when he was 18 years old.

Austen, Jane

The working title of Jane Austen's *Pride and Prejudice* was *First Impressions*.

Autry, Gene

As a telegraph operator working the nightshift in the Chelsea, Oklahoma railroad station, young Gene Autry passed the time by strumming a guitar and singing to himself. One night, a stranger stopped by the station to send a telegram, heard Gene singing, and told him that he ought to be on the radio. If the man hadn't been Will Rogers, Autry might not have taken the advice seriously and might still be pounding out Morse code in Chelsea.

At the peak of his popularity, Gene Autry sold more records than Bing Crosby by a three-to-one margin and his fan mail was greater than that of Clark Gable or Shirley Temple.

It is fairly well known that Gene Autry is a millionaire but he is very much a millionaire. He is worth $100,000,000! The singing cowboy wisely invested his movie and record earnings in oil wells, radio and television stations, real estate, and athletic teams and is now worth over $100 million, putting him in the same league as some of the Rockefellers and Duponts.

Avalon, Frankie

The star of the movie *Beach Blanket Bingo* is the father of *eight* children.

Born Francis Avalonne in Philadelphia, the singer Anglicized his name to Avalon which, incidentally, is a New Jersey seashore town visited by many Philadelphians during summer vacations.

Avedon, Richard

The great model and portrait photographer was originally destined to become a poet. At DeWitt Clinton High School in the Bronx, New York, Avedon was the class poet laureate. He was an avid reader of Carl Sandburg, T. S. Eliot, and William Butler Yeats and even as a teenager had his poetry published in the *New York Sun* and *Journal American* newspapers. However, as a Merchant Marine in World War II, Avedon was assigned to a photography unit and spent most of his time taking ID photos of service personnel. This service experience sparked his interest in photography as a profession.

At DeWitt Clinton High School, one of Avedon's friends was writer James Baldwin and they both served, at various times, as editor-in-chief of *The Magpie*, the school literary magazine. Many years later in 1964, they collaborated on the book *Nothing Personal* which was a collection of photographs and prose based on their impressions of life in America.

Avila, Bobby

The ex-Cleveland Indian second baseman is now the mayor of Veracruz, Mexico.

Axton, Hoyt

The country and western singer's mother, Mae Boren Axton, a schoolteacher, co-wrote the Elvis Presley hit "Heartbreak Hotel."

B

Bacall, Lauren

Lauren Bacall's real name is Betty Perske. After her mother divorced her father, Lauren and her mother took the name Bacall which was part of her mother's maiden name (Weinstein-Bacal) with an "l" added to avoid having the name rhyme with "crackle." The name Lauren was an extra touch given to her in Hollywood when she went there to appear in the movie *To Have and Have Not*, opposite future husband Humphrey Bogart.

Lauren hasn't seen her father William Perske in over 49 years. He is 91 years old, is retired, and living in Chevy Chase, Maryland. In her autobiography, Miss Bacall said that her father "flew the coop" but he denies the allegation.

To make her voice deeper, the actress used to park on Mulholland Drive in Beverly Hills and read aloud from the book *The Robe*.

Bach, Johann Sebastian

In Bach's 65 years, he not only produced many concertos, cantatas, sonatas, etc. but also produced many children—he had 7 children by his first wife and 13 children by his second one —a total of 20 children!

Bacharach, Burt

Burt's first name sounds just like his newspaper columnist father's name but it is spelled differently. His father's first name is spelled with an "e"—Bert.

Baer, Max

When Max Baer fought Lou Nova in 1939 it was the first televised prize fight. After Nova knocked Baer out in the first round, it became one of the shortest televised fights in boxing history.

Baez, Joan

On the day folksinger Joan Baez's husband David Harris was released from jail, she marked the occasion by getting a tattoo of a flower put on the small of her back.

Bailey, Pearl

Joan Baez isn't the only singer with a tattoo. On the inside of Pearly Mae's thigh is a tattoo of a heart.

Baker, Howard

At the University of Tennessee, Baker majored in electrical engineering until his senior year when he switched to law because the law school registration lines were shorter, according to Baker.

As a lawyer, Baker earned the nickname "Old Two-to-Ten" by winning light sentences for his clients.

The Republican senator married Joy Dirksen, daughter of Illinois Senator Everett Dirksen, in 1952.

When Baker won the senatorship in 1966 he was the first popularly elected Republican senator in Tennessee's history.

Baker, Wee Bonnie

Singer Wee Bonnie Baker's real name was Evelyn Nelson but when bandleader Orrin Tucker gave her a job as a vocalist with his band, he renamed her Bonnie Baker. The "Wee" was added soon thereafter by members of the band who kidded her about being so short (four feet five inches).

Balanchine, George

As a dancer with the Soviet State Troupe touring Europe, Georgi Melitonovitch Balachivadze met Sergei Diaghilev of the Ballet Russe in Paris and was asked by Diaghilev to stay in Paris with the Ballet Russe. Having political problems with the Russian government at the time, Balanchivadze accepted the offer but, at Diaghilev's request, adopted the name Balanchine, a Gallicized version of his real last name.

Baldwin, James

When James Baldwin, the son of a clergyman, was only 14 years old, he became a "holy roller"

39

preacher in the Fireside Pentecostal Church in Harlem. He preached "the Word" for three years before deciding to become a professional writer.

Ball, Lucille

Although Philip Morris was the sponsor of the "I Love Lucy" television series, Lucille Ball always smoked Chesterfield cigarettes. The chairman of the board of Philip Morris, not liking but tolerating her brand preferences, made Lucy keep her Chesterfields in Philip Morris packages.

On the same night (1/19/53) Lucille Ball really gave birth to Desi Arnaz IV, Lucy Ricardo gave birth to Ricky, Jr. on the "I Love Lucy" show. (The segment was actually filmed several months before.)

Ball is Lucille's real last name although she once used the name Diane Belmont as a model and aspiring actress in New York City.

The actress and comedienne was once paralyzed from an automobile accident and was never supposed to walk again.

According to ex-husband Desi Arnaz, Lucille Ball was once fired as a soda jerk in a New York drugstore because she always forgot to put the bananas in the banana splits.

Lucy's middle name Desiree is coincidentally similar to the first name of ex-husband Desi Arnaz.

Desi Arnaz says that he and Lucy were divorced for one day in 1944 but they made up the next day. In 1960 they split up for good.

Ballard, Kaye

Comedienne Kaye Ballard (nee Gloria Katherine Balotta) has been deaf in one ear since she was 12 years old.

Balzac, Honore de

The French novelist's family name was originally Balssa.

Balzac also wrote under the pseudonyms Lord R'hoone (an anagram of Honore) and Horace de Saint Aubin.

The author of *Le Pere Goriot* was originally a lawyer and was a graduate of the law school at Paris University.

Balzac was a coffee addict and drank as much as 60 cups a day.

Bancroft, Anne

Actress Anne Bancroft, born Anne-Marie Italiano, first used the stage name Anne Marno (the first three letters of *Mar*ie and the last two letters of Italia*no*) when she appeared on "The Goldberg's" television series. She changed her name again after winning a movie contract with Twentieth Century-Fox, choosing the name "Bancroft" from a list submitted to her by Darryl F. Zanuck, then head of Fox production.

Her first movie as Anne Bancroft was *Don't Bother to Knock* in 1952.

Bankhead, Tallulah

At New York's famous Stork Club one night, Tallulah sat down with Otto Preminger, Marlene Dietrich, and some friends and proceeded to open her blouse and bare her big but firm breasts, boasting of the plastic surgery that had just been performed.

The uninhibited, gravel-voiced actress was the daughter of a Speaker of the House of Representatives, William Brockman Bankhead, the niece of John Hollis Bankhead, U.S. Senator from Alabama, and was related to other prominent American politicians.

An acquaintance of Miss Bankhead once remarked that "A day away from Tallulah Bankhead is like a month in the country."

Banky, Vilma

The silent movie star, discovered by Samuel Goldwyn on a vacation in Europe, was born Vilma Lonchit.

Bara, Theda

The silent screen vamp's real name was Theodosia Goodman but the rumor spread by the studio publicity men was that she was the daughter of an Eastern potentate and that her name was an anagram of "Arab Death." Actually, she was from Cincinnati, Ohio and started her acting career as Theodosia de Coppet (de

Coppet was her mother's maiden name) but when she was signed to do her first movie for producer William Fox, she and Frank Powell, a movie director, picked the new stage name for her . . . Theda Bara.

Barbeau, Adrienne

In 1971 the television ("Maude") and movie actress appeared in the New York nude review *Stag Movie* for three months. (Her acting *looked* very good!)

Barber, Red

The pioneer sports announcer, born Walter Lanier Barber, received his middle name from the Southern poet Sidney Lanier, to whom Barber was related.

Barnard, Dr. Christiaan

In 1960, before the South African became known for his heart transplant surgery, he received international publicity for successfully transplanting a second head onto a dog.

When Dr. Barnard came to the United States in 1955 to study at the University of Minnesota Medical School, he mowed lawns, washed cars, and did other odd jobs to support himself before winning a grant from the Danzian Foundation for Medical Research.

Barnes, Clive

Drama critic Clive Barnes's ability to dissect a play was probably acquired at the London

School of Medicine, where he was once a student. Barnes had hopes of becoming a psychiatrist but a tour in the Royal Air Force in 1946 interrupted his medical studies. Upon being discharged Barnes, rather than resume his medical studies, became a ballet critic, later expanding into theatre criticism.

Barnes is such an avid dance enthusiast that he named his daughter Joanna Rosemary Maya Barnes after Maya Plisetskaya, the Russian ballerina, who danced her last *Swan Lake* in London on the night Joanna was born.

Barnum, Phineas T.

A businessman to the end, Barnum's final words were reported to be, "How were the receipts today at Madison Square Garden?"

The famous showman was the mayor of Bridgeport, Connecticut in 1875.

Barrett, Rona

As a token of his feelings toward Hollywood gossip reporter Rona Barrett, actor Ryan O'Neal once mailed her a live tarantula.

As a chubby thirteen-year-old girl, Rona Burstein fell in love with singer Eddie Fisher and started a fan club for him. When she visited Fisher's manager she introduced herself as Rona Barrett because, in her words, "Burstein would never make it in the world of glamour" and was a name "for the grocery business."

Barrymore, Elaine Barrie

After seeing actor John Barrymore for the first time in the movie *Svengali*, Elaine Jacobs fell in love with the screen idol and started calling herself Elaine Barrie. Later when she found out that Barrymore was a patient at a nearby hospital, she sent him get-well notes and then made frequent visits to his room. These visits developed into a love affair and she subsequently married the great actor.

Barrymore, John

John Barrymore's real name was John Sidney Blythe. Maurice Barrymore, his father, was born Herbert Maurice Blythe but never legally changed his last name.

According to actor Anthony Quinn, Barrymore called women "cunts" or "twittering vaginas" and called men he liked "shits." Some of his other favorite words were "defecation," "eleemosynary," "expectoration," "glorious," and "wonderful."

Barrymore was seduced at age 15 by his stepmother Mamie Floyd.

Even though "the Profile" usually knew his speaking lines, he insisted that the studios always have the lines written on blackboards positioned in his view. Even simple one word lines like "Yes." Barrymore likened the practice to a tightrope walker who had nets set up but didn't necessarily use them.

Barrymore, Lionel

Lionel Barrymore (*Grand Hotel, Key Largo*) was partially responsible for the invention of the boom microphone. As a director of sound tests at MGM studios, the celebrated actor was inhibited by stationary microphones so he tied one to a fishing pole and held it above the actors.

Bart, Lionel

The British composer, lyricist, and playwright (*Stop the World, I Want to Get Off*) was born Lionel Begleiter.

Barthelme, Donald

The surrealistic writer could not have written it better—after being drafted into the U.S. Army during the Korean War, he was shipped to the war-torn country—the day the truce was signed.

Bartholdi, Frederic Auguste

The French sculptor, creator of the Statue of Liberty in the New York harbor, used his mother as a model for the statue.

The statue (*Liberty Enlightening the World* was its official name) was originally copper-colored, being made from large sheets of copper, but with the passage of time it turned the pale green color it is now.

Barton, Clara

The founder of the Red Cross was born on Christmas Day in 1821.

Batista y Zaldivar, Fulgencio

The Cuban leader had an unusual racial heritage. He was of white, Negro, Chinese, and Indian descent.

Baudelaire, Charles

For reasons unknown, the French poet used to dye his hair green.

Baum, Lyman Frank

The author of the popular children's Oz stories also wrote under the pen names Schuyler Stanton, Floyd Akers, and Dith Van Dyne.

Bauman, Jon "Bowzer"

The lanky bass singer for the singing group Sha Na Na was graduated magna cum laude from The Columbia University School of Music.

Bayes, Nora

The vaudeville singer was born Dora Goldberg in Los Angeles, California.

Beame, Abe

The first Jewish mayor of New York City was born Abraham David Birnbaum in London, England.

Beame was nicknamed "Spunky" as a youth because of his high energy level and enthusiasm.

Abe graduated first in his high school class and was the only member to score 100 on the New York State Regents bookkeeping exam. He also graduated cum laude at New York's City College evening sessions in four years by registering at both the uptown and downtown campuses in order to take twice the number of courses normally permitted to evening students. (During the day Beame worked a full shift at a local paper factory!)

Bean, Orson

The television personality and raconteur's real name is Dallas Frederick Burrows. He adopted the name Orson Bean when he was a child magician appearing at night clubs in the Boston area. He "looked around for a pretentious first name and a plain last name and came up with the most incongruous combination" he could conjure up.

Orson Bean, whose father was a campus policeman at Harvard University, is a third cousin of Calvin Coolidge, the 30th president of the United States.

Beatty, Warren

Warren Beatty's favorite word for his girlfriends is "pussycat" and in fact the movie *What's New Pussycat?* was written especially for him. However, when the producers would not give the woman's role to Leslie Caron, Beatty's love at the time, he turned down the role and it was then given to British actor Peter O'Toole.

According to columnist Sheilah Graham, Warren Beatty could be president of the United States if he wanted to be ". . . with the votes of all the women he has made love to! Good authorities say that he's a great 'roll in the hay'!"

John F. Kennedy wanted Warren to play him in the movie *PT-109* but the producers felt that Beatty's image was "too mixed up." (Cliff Robertson eventually won the part.)

According to most sources, Carly Simon wrote her 1972 hit record "You're So Vain" with Warren Beatty, a onetime boyfriend of hers, in mind.

At Washington and Lee High School in Arlington, Virginia, Warren was class ('55) president, center on the football team, and was voted "Best All Around" male.

The spelling of Warren's last name was originally "Beaty" (one "t") but apparently the name did not suit him "to a tee" so he added another one.

Beardsley, Aubrey

Beardsley's last words were, "I am imploring you—burn all the indecent poems and drawings." Someone either did not hear or heed the artist or had a different definition of the word "indecent."

Becket, Thomas à

The Archbishop of Canterbury was born Thomas Becket, son of Gilbert Becket, in England. He was never known as Thomas á Becket in his lifetime. No one knows how the letter "a" became a part of his name.

Beckett, Samuel

In 1934 the British playwright published a collection of short stories entitled *More Pricks than Kicks.*

Beene, Geoffrey

The noted dress designer attended Tulane Medical School but dropped out during his first year because he "wasn't dedicated enough to dissect cadavers."

Beery, Wallace

The Academy Award-winning actor (*The Champ,* '31) was an elephant trainer for the Ringling Brothers circus before he became a movie actor.

Beethoven, Ludwig van

During the entire period Beethoven spent composing his Ninth Symphony, he never bathed.

Plagued by hearing problems, Beethoven was completely deaf by the time he wrote his Ninth Symphony and as supervisor of the first performance of the symphony, he could not hear the music or hear the audience's reaction to it. Only when one of the singers turned Beethoven around to face the audience did he see their reaction. The audience loved the symphony— enough to give Beethoven five ovations!

Behan, Brendan

Brendan Behan was not the only writer in his family. An uncle, Peadar Kearney wrote the

"Soldier's Song"—which eventually became the Irish National Anthem.

The talented but dissipated writer was an alcoholic, a diabetic, and bisexual.

Bejart, Maurice

The Belgian ballet dancer and choreographer's real name is Maurice Jean de Berger.

Bell, Alexander Graham

Bell was not the first person to invent a telephone. A German, Philip Reis, in 1861 invented a primitive sending-receiving device which he called a "telephone." Reis's ill health and lack of funds prevented him from commercially exploiting his invention. He died in 1874, two years before Bell received his patent. Bell's telephone, in any event, was an improvement in that it could transmit human voices.

The inventor was one of the original founders of *National Geographic* magazine. Using the pseudonym H. A. Largelamb (an anagram of A. Graham Bell) he once wrote an article on lizards and turtles for *National Geographic*.

By his friends and family, the distinguished inventor was known as Alec.

Belli, Melvin

The prominent trial attorney's first direct experience with law was in high school when he was expelled two weeks before graduation for participating in a beer party in the school newspaper offices. Belli's father initiated a suit against the principal to give his son a diploma and won the suit.

Belmondo, Jean-Paul

As an amateur boxer, the French movie actor won 15 bouts, lost 5, and tied 3.

Belmont, August

The American banker and financier's real name was August Schonberg. Born a German Jew, he decided to change his German name (which meant "beautiful mountain") so he picked the distinguished-sounding French translation of his German name, *bel mont.*

Belushi, John

At Wheaton High School (Illinois), Belushi was co-captain of the football team and was homecoming king in his senior year.

Bench, Johnny

At Binger High School in Oklahoma, Bench was not only a great baseball star (batting average: .675; pitching record: 29 wins, 1 loss) but the future Cincinnati Reds catcher was also a scholar—he was the valedictorian of the class of 1965.

Benchley, Peter

Before the author of *Jaws* wrote his first book, he was a reporter and obituary writer for *The Washington Post.*

Benchley also was a speech writer for President Lyndon B. Johnson in 1967. One of his major contributions was the phrase "On Your Knees, America" as a slogan for the National Day of Prayer.

Benchley, Robert

At Phillips Exeter Academy in New Hampshire, Benchley made a name for himself when he wrote a paper entitled "How to Embalm a Corpse" in response to a class assignment to write a "How to do . . ." article. A few years later at Harvard, Benchley strengthened his literary reputation by writing a scholarly thesis on the Newfoundland Fisheries case from the point of view of the fish!

Bendix, William

William Bendix was once a bat boy for the New York Giants at the Polo Grounds. (At the time the New York Yankees played at the Polo Grounds too and Bendix claimed that he once took an order of hot dogs to Babe Ruth, whom he later played in the 1948 movie *The Babe Ruth Story*.)

Benedict, Ruth

Before Ruth Benedict became an anthropologist she was a poet. She wrote under the pen name of Anne Singleton and was published in *The Nation, Poetry,* and other periodicals. To help occupy her spare time, Miss Benedict took courses in anthropology under Franz Boas at Columbia University. She became so interested in anthropology that she earned a Ph.D. in 1923 and eventually became one of the world's most recognized anthropologists—and least recognized poets.

Ben-Gurion, David

Ben-Gurion's real name was David Green. The late Israeli statesman took the name Ben-Gurion because he thought it had a good Old Testament sound. (A Ben-Gurion was one of the last defenders of Jerusalem against the Roman legions.)

Bennett, Tony

Born Anthony Dominick Benedetto, he started his career as a singing waiter at Riccardo's in Astoria, Queens, but he went from "rags to riches" when he was discovered by comedian Bob Hope in 1949. It was Hope who suggested that he use the name Tony Bennett, a shortened, "Americanized" version of his real name.

Benny, Jack

A thoughtful man to the end, Jack Benny designated in his will that a rose be delivered to his widow every day of her life.

Benny's reputation for being cheap was strictly for stage purposes. Actually he was considered a generous man by his friends and relatives . . . and by the U.S. government who took $885,680 in estate and inheritance taxes out of his appraised $5,852,025 estate.

Jack never ate Jell-O or smoked Lucky Strikes, two major sponsors of his shows. He was addicted to ice cream, however, even though he was a diabetic.

In 1939 the comedian was convicted of smuggling and fined $10,000 after admitting that a friend brought him $2,131 worth of jewelry into the United States from France without declaring it.

Born Benjamin Kubelsky, the comedian's first stage name was Ben K. Benny, a playful variation of his real name, but he was often confused with Ben Bernie, a comedian and bandleader popular at that time, so he changed his name to Jack Benny.

Benson, Robby

The young actor and screenwriter, son of Jerry and Ann Benson Segal, adopted his mother's maiden name to "avoid anti-Semitism."

Bentham, Jeremy

When the English philosopher and jurist died at the age of 84, his body was dissected by friends in accordance with his will. His skeleton was then reconstructed, given a wax head, dressed in his former clothes, and put along with his mummified head in a glass case on display at University College in London where it has stood for over 145 years.

Benton, Thomas Hart

The American painter was named after a great-uncle, Thomas Hart Benton (1782–1858), Missouri's first senator.

Bergen, Candice

Miss Bergen is not only an actress, model, photographer, and writer but also a playwright. Her play *The Freezer* was included in *The Best Short Plays of 1968* and was considered by many internationally-known critics and dramatists to be an important new work.

Bergen, Edgar

Ventriloquist Edgar Bergen (whose family name was originally spelled Bergren) borrowed the name for his dummy partner Charlie McCarthy from the carpenter who made Bergen's first white pine dummy. The carpenter's name was Theodore Mack. The ventriloquist added a Celtic suffix to the name Mack and tacked on a nice first name—presto, Charlie McCarthy.

Berkeley, Busby

The movie musical director (*Forty-Second Street, Golddiggers of 1933, 1935*) acquired his mania for large-scale, choreographed extravaganzas as a serviceman in World War I. Berkeley, an officer, used to lead his battalion through elaborate maneuvers on the parade grounds and liked it so much that he applied his skill to moviemaking.

The director was born William Berkeley Enos to Gertrude B. Enos, an actress, and Wilson Enos, the director of Frawley's Stock Company in Los Angeles. His father nicknamed him Busby after Amy Busby, the Frawley Company's leading lady. He became Busby Berkeley later when he adopted his mother's maiden name, Berkeley, as his professional surname.

Berle, Milton

In the movie *Tillie's Punctured Romance*, the baby Marie Dressler clutched to her heart was Milton Berle, making his screen debut.

Until her death in 1954, Uncle Miltie's mother saw every live performance her son ever gave. Berle even lived with his mother until he got married at age 33. He picked up some unusual habits from his mother. He puts butter on his radishes and he won't touch anything with ice in it.

Milton Berle's nose is no joke. He had it fixed by a plastic surgeon.

In his autobiography, Berle admitted that he fathered an illegitimate child, a son, as a result of an affair he had with a movie actress (now married to a Hollywood producer).

The comedian's last name was originally Berlinger but not wanting the name to linger on, he shortened it to Berle. (His mother, Sadie, even changed her first name to Sandra.)

Berlin, Irving

Although his famous song "Easter Parade" first appeared in a show *As Thousands Cheered* in the 1930s, Berlin actually wrote it during World War I when it was then titled "Smile and Show Your Dimple."

The Jewish songwriter, born Israel Baline in Temum, Russia, wrote two songs most strongly identified with the two most important *Christian* holidays—"White Christmas" and "Easter Parade."

Bernhardt, Sarah

The French-born actress, born Henriette Rosine Bernard, used to sleep in a coffin.

Bernhardt tried to commit suicide after her first three stage appearances.

The actress was an illegitimate child.

Bernstein, Leonard

Unlike many conductors and classical musicians, Bernstein was not considered a "child prodigy" and did not demonstrate any interest or talent in music until he was ten years old—when his mother volunteered to store an old upright piano for a relative and young Bernstein started to plink away at the keys.

Berry, Chuck

After Berry's incredible success ("Maybelline," "Roll Over Beethoven," etc.) in the 1950s, he soon found himself sentenced to two years at the federal penitentiary in Terre Haute, Indiana, for transporting a 14-year-old girl across state lines for immoral purposes. Although the 14-year-old, a hat-check girl at Berry's nightclub in St. Louis, was found to be a prostitute and had willingly traveled with him, the jury still found Berry guilty. Later in 1979, the rock and roll singer pleaded guilty to evading nearly $110,000 in income taxes for the year 1973 (in which his total income was $374,982—not a bad income for someone not in his prime.)

Beymer, Richard

The male lead in the movie *West Side Story* is now teaching Transcendental Meditation in Los Angeles, California.

Bierce, Ambrose

The satirical short-story writer was severely wounded twice during the Civil War.

Bierce went to Mexico in 1913 and never returned. To this day, no one knows what happened to him, although it was rumored that he was killed by Mexican revolutionaries.

Billingsley, Sherman

Before owning the world-famous Stork Club in New York City, Billingsley owned a chain of drugstores in the Bronx and Westchester areas of New York and also built apartment houses (Billingsley Terrace in the Bronx).

One technique Billingsley used to help develop a rich, sophisticated clientele was to advertise in Ivy League magazines and pay for the advertising space with due bills entitling the students to charge their tabs to the club.

Billy the Kid

Billy the Kid, whose real name was William H. Bonney, was not born in the West but in New York City.

At the age of twelve he killed his first victim. Nine years later and after 20 more victims, he was shot and killed by Sheriff Pat Garrett.

Birdseye, Clarence

The founder of frozen food started out as an explorer. He discovered the new method of preserving vegetables while on a wildlife expedition to Labrador in 1916. Fresh vegetables were not always available so Birdseye kept his vegetables in barrels of frozen water and found that they could be preserved for extended periods of time.

Birmingham, Stephen

The chronicler of the rich (*Our Crowd, The Right People*) won the annual poetry prize at Hotchkiss, the Connecticut preparatory school, and subsequently attended Williams College on a literary scholarship.

Bishop, Joey

In an interview with Tom Snyder, comedian Joey Bishop said that he weighed 2 pounds, 14 ounces at birth.

Bisset, Jacqueline

The British actress's mother was a lawyer.

Black, Karen

The movie actress (*Five Easy Pieces*) has a colorful family. Her name at birth was Karen *Blanche* (French for "white") Ziegler; she dropped out of high school to marry Charles *Black;* and her older sister, also an actress, is named Gail *Brown.*

Blackwell, Earl

As a boy in Atlanta, Georgia, Earl Blackwell caddied for professional golfer Bobby Jones, ran errands for Rosa Ponselle, the Metropolitan Opera singer on tour at the time, and has been fascinated with famous people ever since.

Blake, Eubie

The pianist and composer wrote the music to "I'm Just Wild About Harry" for the musical comedy *Shuffle Along* in 1921. It was originally written as a waltz but he changed it to a fox-trot.

Blake, William

Romantic poet William Blake never attended school because he had such an irascible temper and would have been an unruly student.

Blatty, William Peter

Before Blatty became nationally-known for his novel *The Exorcist* he was a screenplay writer and one of his scripts was for *A Shot in the Dark*, the hilarious Peter Sellers movie.

Good ideas often take time to incubate. In 1950 at Georgetown University in Washington, D.C., Blatty wrote a speech on demonic possession for the senior oratorical contest, after reading a *Washington Post* account of an alleged exorcism.

As a contestant on Groucho Marx's television show *You Bet Your Life*, Blatty won $10,000.

The writer's wife is Linda Tuero, once a top-ranked women's tennis player. They met during the filming of *The Exorcist* in which she appeared as an extra.

Blatty has a doctorate degree in English literature from George Washington University in Washington, D.C.

Bloom, Claire

The British actress's (*Look Back in Anger*) last name was spelled Blume when she was born in London but she changed it to Bloom as a young actress in B.B.C radio plays.

Blue, Ben

The vaudeville comedian's real name was Benjamin Bernstein.

Bly, Nelly

The peripatetic newspaper woman who went around the world in less than 80 days (72 days, 6 hours) was born Elizabeth Cochrane. She used the by-line "Nelly Bly" in order to protect her identity while writing controversial exposés.

Bocuse, Paul

The internationally-known chef maintains that "Women are good cooks, but they are not good chefs."

Bogarde, Dirk

In his autobiography, the British actor (*The Damned, Death in Venice*) revealed that as a young boy he was picked up in a movie theater by a man who offered to show him books about

Egyptian mummies. Fascinated by the unusual proposal, Bogarde went to the man's flat but was tied up and seduced . . . .

Of Dutch descent, the actor's real name is Derek Niven van der Bogaerde.

Bogart, Humphrey

Humphrey Bogart, who died of throat cancer, smoked about five packs of cigarettes a day. (His brand was Chesterfields.)

Bogie and Spencer Tracy both made their movie debuts in the movie *Up the River*, released in 1930.

As an actor, Bogart appeared on television only once—in a 1955 live television production of *The Petrified Forest* which also featured Lauren Bacall and Henry Fonda in the Bette Davis and Leslie Howard roles. Bogart was discouraged by Hollywood studio executives from doing any television work on the theory that the public would stop going to see his movies in theaters if they could see him free on television. The Duke Mantee role, however, was a sentimental favorite (the original Broadway play and movie were turning points in his career) and he was offered $50,000 for the appearance so he accepted the part.

An expert chess player, Bogart used to earn rent money by hustling fifty-cents a match in Sixth Avenue chess parlors in New York.

Bogie's tough-guy demeanor and gangster screen image belied his real background. He came from a well-to-do New York family—his

63

father was a successful doctor and his mother, Maude Humphrey, was a well-known magazine illustrator. He attended private schools: Trinity in New York City and Phillips Academy in Andover, Massachusetts. In fact, Bogie was supposed to go to Yale and then to medical school but after he was expelled from Phillips Academy for poor grades his career plans were changed.

Bogie's slight but famous lisp was not caused by a shrapnel wound suffered in World War I as Warner Brothers indicated in their press releases. It was the result of a childhood accident in which a splinter wound on his upper lip was poorly stitched together by an inept doctor.

Bogdanovich, Peter

Unlike many new movie directors who are products of Los Angeles or New York film schools, Bogdanovich not only did not go to college or film school, he did not even graduate from high school. He attended prep school (Collegiate School in New York City) but did not graduate because he failed to take his final examination in algebra.

Boleyn, Anne

Anne Boleyn, the second wife of Henry VIII and mother of Queen Elizabeth I, wore gloves most of the time to cover up an unusual physical defect—she had an extra finger on her left hand.

Bonanno, Joe "Bananas"

The retired Mafia chieftain, now in his mid-70s, was arrested 12 times during his career in crime and was convicted only once—for a labor law violation. His punishment was a $450 fine.

Bonanno claims to be related to Charles Bonanno, the man who designed the Leaning Tower of Pisa.

Bonaparte, Napoleon

Napoleon was graduated 42nd in a class of 51 at military school in Paris.

He supposedly lost the battle of Waterloo because he had hemorrhoids. He was unable to sit on his horse because of considerable rectal pain and therefore was not able to adequately survey the battle area.

The whites of Napoleon's eyes were actually yellow.

Napoleon's family name was originally Buonaparte. He began using the new spelling in 1796.

Bono, Sonny

Sonny Bono and Cher made their first professional appearance and first recording ("The Letter") under the name Caesar and Cleo to capitalize on the publicity that the movie *Cleopatra* was then receiving.

Sonny and Cher's daughter, Chastity, was not named after Cher's long-lost virtue but after a movie entitled *Chastity* which the couple produced in 1969. The movie about a runaway girl searching for the meaning of life lost $500,000 and nearly bankrupt the Bonos.

Boone, Debby

Debby Boone's hit record "You Light Up My Life" was not only the biggest singles hit of 1977—it was the biggest single in twenty years!

Boone, Pat

While filming the movie *April Love* in 1957 Pat Boone at first refused to kiss Shirley Jones because of his "religious beliefs" and then telephoned his wife to find out if it was okay.

The singer's full name is Charles Eugene Boone and he claims to be a descendant of the American pioneer Daniel Boone.

Pat's not just another pretty face. He graduated magna cum laude from Columbia University in 1958.

Boone's wife Shirley, whom he met in high school, is the daughter of country and western singer Red Foley.

Boone, Richard

The veteran movie and television actor was expelled from Stanford University in the late 1930s for throwing a painted dummy in front of a moving car and yelling, "My brother! My brother! You've killed my brother!" One of the passengers in the car was Mrs. Herbert Hoover who was "much shaken."

Booth, Edwin

A few years before John Wilkes Booth assassinated Abraham Lincoln, his actor-brother Edwin saved the life of Robert Lincoln, the president's son, when he was almost crushed by an oncoming train in Jersey City's (N.J.) Pennsylvania Station.

Booth, Shirley

Before joining a New Haven stock company, Thelma Booth Ford dropped her last name at her father's request (he didn't even want her in show business) and took the name Shirley from the part of Shirley Rossmore in *The Lion and the Mouse*, a play which she particularly liked.

Borg, Bjorn

To help him learn English, the young Swedish tennis champion likes to read American comic books.

Borg, only 23 years old, earned $3 million in 1979—which isn't a bad income for someone who quit school at age fourteen.

Borge, Victor

The pianist-comedian's real name is Borge Rosenbaum.

Borgia, Cesare

Cesare Borgia was made a cardinal at the age of 17.

Borgnine, Ernest

Although Ernest Borgnine's image is to the contrary, he actually has some aristocratic blood in him. His maternal grandfather was Count Paolo

Boselli, a financial adviser to King Victor Emmanuel of Italy.

Borgnine's full name at birth was Ermes Effron Borgnine. The family name was originally spelled Borgnino.

His car license plates read: BORG9

Borodin, Aleksandr

The Russian composer was the illegitimate son of an Imeretian prince and an army doctor's wife.

Borodin was a professor of chemistry by trade. His accomplishments in music were strictly avocational.

Botticelli, Sandro

The Italian painter's real name was Alessandro Filipepi. He borrowed the nickname of his eldest brother Giovanni Botticello. "Botticello" in Italian means "Little Barrel."

Bow, Clara

After appearing in the movie *It* as a sexy department store clerk, Clara Bow became known as the "It" girl.

About her new image, Miss Bow commented, "Being a sex symbol is a heavy load to carry, especially when one is tired, hurt and bewildered."

Bowdler, Thomas

The man best remembered for "doctoring up" Shakespeare's plays (*The Family Shakespeare*) by omitting "those words and expressions . . . which cannot with propriety be read aloud in a family" was in fact a medical doctor who quit his practice because he could not stand the sight of blood nor bear to see people in pain.

Bowie, David

David Bowie once said that Adolf Hitler "was one of the first rock stars" because he "staged a country."

Bowie, an admitted bisexual, met his wife, Angel, when they were both going out with the same *man.*

An illegitimate child, Bowie was named David Jones at birth. His son, born in 1971, is named Zowie.

As a result of a childhood street brawl, Bowie's left eye is partially paralyzed.

Boyd, Malcolm

Before he became an Episcopal priest and best-selling author (*Are You Running With Me, Jesus?*), Malcolm Boyd was an advertising man and Hollywood producer. After leaving college, Boyd joined the Foote, Cone and Belding advertising agency in Hollywood, California, then became a partner in P.R.B., Mary Pickford's production company. He also was the first president of the Television Producers Association. In 1951 Boyd decided to enter the ministry and went to the Church Divinity School of the Pacific in Berkeley, California.

Boyd, Stephen

Actor Stephen Boyd, best remembered for his role as Messala in the 1959 movie *Ben Hur*, was born William Millar and used that name until 1953 when he adopted his mother's maiden name, Boyd, and also took a new first name (two William Boyds had already preceded him).

Boyer, Charles

In response to mimics who used to imitate Boyer by saying the line, "Come with me to the Casbah," the French actor said, "Well, I never said that line in *Algiers*, and it certainly would have been strange, since the Casbah was a kind of no-man's-land where, as the film's hero, I was hiding out."

Boyer's only child, Michael, died of a self-inflicted gunshot wound at the age of 22. Two days after Boyer's wife of 44 years died of cancer, Boyer was found dead, presumably a suicide caused by despondency over his wife's death.

Bradbury, Ray

The science fiction writer (*Martian Chronicles*) lives in Los Angeles, California but does not own or drive a car. He rides a bicycle or uses public buses, commenting that he couldn't afford a car until he was 33 years old and at that age decided that driving was a "waste of time."

Bradshaw, Terry

At Woodlawn High School in Louisiana the Pittsburgh Steeler quarterback set an American high school record by throwing the javelin 244 feet, 11 inches.

Brady, "Diamond Jim"

The flamboyant millionaire ate so much food in his lifetime that after he died, an autopsy performed at Johns Hopkins Hospital in Baltimore revealed that his stomach was six times the size of a normal stomach.

Brae, Tycho

In a sword fight, the Danish astronomer lost the tip of his nose and subsequently replaced it with a prosthetic device made of gold.

Brand, Max

The "King of the Pulp Writers" wrote 530 full-length books, mostly westerns (and the Dr. Kildare stories), averaging a book every two weeks of his writing career. Born Frederick Schiller Faust, he also used the pen names Evan Evans, Frank Auston, George Owen Baxter, and Walter C. Butler.

Brando, Marlon

Despite Brando's dramatic nonappearance at the 1973 Academy Awards ceremony, he never did go to Wounded Knee as his spokesperson Sacheen Little Feather implied he would, according to Hollywood biographer Bob Thomas.

According to reporter James Bacon, Omaha-born Brando once made "a slight reference to a friendly romp with a goat back on the farm in

Nebraska," seemingly validating what Kinsey said farm boys did in their spare time.

The role of Stanley Kowalski in the movie *A Streetcar Named Desire* was first offered to John Garfield who was a proven box-office draw, but Garfield turned down the role because it was smaller than the Blanche Du Bois part. After two other movie actors rejected the role, director Elia Kazan finally gave Brando a chance.

Brando's nose is a bit flattened because actor Karl Malden hit him too hard in a boxing match during their run in the Broadway production of *A Streetcar Named Desire*. When Brando later went to Hollywood for a screen test the studios didn't want to view him unless he had his nose straightened and his name changed.

Brando often uses earplugs when shooting movie scenes to keep his concentration and to screen out noises on the set.

As a kindergarten student, Brando wandered so much on the way to school that his sister Jocelyn eventually had to take him to class on a leash.

Brando received $10,000,000 for his appearance in *The Godfather*, the highest pay an actor has ever received for one movie.

Brando is not Italian, contrary to popular belief. He comes from the French line of Brandeau's.

When checking into a hotel, Brando occasionally uses the name Lord Greystoke. (Lord Greystoke was Tarzan's real name in the Edgar Rice Burroughs Tarzan books.)

Brando was supposed to be in *Butch Cassidy and the Sundance Kid* with Paul Newman but the assassination of Martin Luther King upset him so much he turned down the part thereby giving Robert Redford his first big break.

Marlon Brando's mother, once an amateur actress in Omaha, gave Henry Fonda his start in acting by persuading him to try out for the Omaha Community Playhouse productions. Later, when Fonda was a star at Twentieth Century-Fox, the Brandos visited him at the studio and Marlon became intrigued with the idea of becoming an actor.

Brandt, Willy

The German leader's real name is Herbert Ernst Karl Frahm. He was the illegitimate son of Martha Frahm, a salesgirl in a German cooperative store. He adopted the pseudonym Willy Brandt in his teens when he wrote articles for the Social Democratic newspaper *Volksbote*.

Brazzi, Rossano

The Italian movie actor (*South Pacific*, *Three Coins in the Fountain*) studied law at the University of San Marco in Florence.

Brennan, Walter

When folksy actor Walter Brennan won the 1940 Oscar for Best Supporting Actor in *The Westerner*, he became the first three-time Oscar winning actor in the history of the Academy and was the only three-time winner until 1968 when Katharine Hepburn won her third award. Brennan's previous Oscars were for Best Supporting

Actor in *Come and Get It* (1936) and *Kentucky* (1938).

Brennan lost all his teeth in World War I and wore as many false teeth as his movie roles required. His lack of teeth enabled him to play the roles of older men at a relatively young age.

Brice, Fanny

The vaudeville and radio comedienne was born Fannie Borach but changed her name because she hated being called "Bore act" and "More ache" by wags and critics. She changed "Fannie" to "Fanny" later in her career but now she is remembered as the "Funny" girl.

Bronson, Charles

Charles Bronson got his first break when he was given a part in the movie *You're in the Navy Now* (1951) starring Gary Cooper. He won the role because of his unusual ability to belch on cue!

Bronson's family name was originally Bunchinsky which evolved into Buchinsky and finally became Buchinski when he arrived in Hollywood. He decided to change his name to Bronson (after Bronson Street off Hollywood Boulevard) because he noticed that Senator Joseph McCarthy was giving people with Russian-sounding names a bad time. His first movie as Charles Bronson was *Drum Beat* in 1954, starring Alan Ladd.

Brooke, Edward

According to Brooke's grandparents, the Massachusetts senator is a descendant of Thomas Jefferson, of Sir Philip Bowen Broke, a British admiral, and of Ruport Brooke, the English poet.

Brooks, Albert

The young comedian's real name is Albert Einstein—seriously. His father was Harry Einstein, better known as Parkyakarkus, the radio comedian of the 1930s and 1940s. One of Brooks's favorite lines is that the real Albert Einstein changed his name to sound more intelligent.

Brooks, Mel

As a combat engineer in World War II, Mel's job was to deactivate land mines to clear the way for the infantry. He first saw action in the Battle of the Bulge in 1944.

One of Brooks early ambitions was to be a pilot. Would you want to fly in a plane piloted by the director of *Blazing Saddles*?

Mel Brooks's real name is Melvin Kaminsky. As a drummer at a Catskills resort, he said his real name couldn't fit on the drums so he changed it to Brooks, an abbreviated version of his mother's maiden name, Brookman. Mel also didn't want to be confused with Max Kaminsky, a saxophonist already popular on the "Borscht Circuit."

Brown, Helen Gurley

If Helen's husband, movie producer David Brown, had not discovered some love letters Helen wrote to an old boyfriend, she might still be an advertising copywriter. Brown thought her writing style was so good that he encouraged her to write a book. She did and it became a bestseller in 1962—*Sex and the Single Girl*.

Bruce, Nigel

Best known for his portrayal of Dr. Watson in the Basil Rathbone Sherlock Holmes movies, Nigel Bruce also had the distinction of appearing in the first 3-D movie *Bwana Devil* in 1953.

Brummel, Beau

George Bryan Brummel, once nicknamed "Beau" for his neatness and good grooming, was plagued by gambling debts, crippled by two strokes, and died ragged and slovenly at a charitable asylum in Caen, France.

Brynner, Yul

In the movie version of *The King and I* when Yul is singing "Puzzlement" he can be seen wearing an earring in some shots but not in others.

Brynner was born Taidje Khan on Sakhalin, an island north of Japan and near the Soviet Union. His father was Mongolian and his mother, who died at Yul's birth, was a gypsy. When his father, a Swiss citizen, obtained Swiss citizenship for Yul, he changed the family name to Brynner.

Brynner's fame for his portrayal of the King of Siam in the Broadway musical and movie *The King and I* overshadows the fact that he made his Broadway debut as an oriental prince in

Lute Song opposite Mary Martin and he received the Donaldson Award for best debut performance in the 1945–46 theater season.

Brzezinski, Zbigniew

Presidential aide Hamilton Jordan calls the National Security Adviser "Woody Woodpecker" because of his crewcut hair and machine-gun speech delivery.

Buchanan, Edgar

The late movie (*Shane*) and television ("Petticoat Junction") character actor was not really the rustic he pretended to be. Prior to his becoming an actor he was a dentist and from 1929 to 1937, as Dr. William Edgar Buchanan he was head of oral surgery at Eugene (Oregon) Hospital. His wife, Dr. Mildred Spence, was also a dentist.

Buchanan, James

Although Buchanan was the only president to remain a bachelor his whole life, he was once engaged to Ann Caroline Coleman but she committed suicide after a "lover's quarrel."

Buchanan had unusual eye problems. He was farsighted in one eye and nearsighted in the other—and one eye was higher than the other.

In his book *It All Began With Columbus*, Richard Armour observed that "President James Buchanan is known as 'The President Who Never Married' and thus has become extremely useful in quizzes and crossword puzzles."

Buchwald, Art

The satirical columnist was raised in six foster homes as a child and left high school at age 16 to join the Marines in World War II.

Buck, Pearl

Pearl Sydenstricker Buck, who learned to speak Chinese before she learned English, was the first woman to win a Nobel Prize in literature (1938).

Miss Buck's manuscript for *The Good Earth* was turned down fourteen times before it was finally accepted for publication by the John Day Company.

Buckley, James

While a student at Yale, James Buckley achieved fame as the owner of a pet boa constrictor named Martha.

In 1958 Buckley inherited $17 million, as did his brothers and sisters, when his oil executive father William F. Buckley, Sr. died.

Buckley, William F. Jr.

Conservative William F. Buckley, Jr. became a political gadfly at an extremely early age. At six years of age he wrote a letter to King George V demanding that England pay her war debt to the United States.

Bulfinch, Thomas

The famous mythologist was a bank clerk with the Merchant's Bank of Boston. He liked the job because it was a sinecure and gave him time to write books on history and mythology—like *The Age of Fable*, now known as *Bulfinch's Mythology*.

Bumbry, Grace

Miss Bumbry won first prize on *Arthur Godfrey's Talent Scouts* television program in 1954. The 17-year-old sang the aria "O don fatale" from Verdi's opera *Don Carlo*.

Bunny, Bugs

Bugs Bunny was originally named Happy Rabbit and first appeared in the 1935 Disney cartoon *The Tortoise and the Hare*. As Bugs Bunny, his first appearance was in *The Wild Hare*, also released in 1935.

Mel Blanc, the voice of Bugs Bunny and many other cartoon characters, gave the rabbit the nickname of its creator—Ben "Bugs" Hardaway, a cartoonist for the Disney organization.

Bunyan, John

The English Puritan minister, imprisoned for preaching "illegally," wrote most of his famous allegory *The Pilgrim's Progress* while in jail.

Burpee

The family that founded the famous seed company comes from Huguenot ancestors named Beaupré and is also descended from William Pitt, Earl of Chatham.

Burns, Arthur

Arthur Burns's real name is Arthur Frank Burnseig (some sources indicate Burnzweig). The Federal Reserve Board chairman was born in Stanislau, Austria. He and his family moved to the United States, settling in Bayonne, New Jersey, where one of his teachers convinced him to shorten his name to Burns.

Burns, George

George Burns started carrying a cigar when he was only 14 years old. In his words, "I was afraid to go on stage without something to hold on to. For seven cents you could buy a cigar so big you'd have to wear a supporter."

Burn's early vaudeville acts were so bad that he frequently changed his name to get booked again. Some of the names he used were Captain Betts, Willie Delight, Jed Jackson, Buddy Links, Jimmy Malone, Harry Pierce, and Willy Williams. When he finally became confident that he could get rebooked he adopted the name George Burns. His real name is Nathan Birnbaum.

Gracie Allen wasn't Burns's only wife. He had a previous marriage to a vaudeville partner but the marriage lasted as long as the act—36 months.

Burns, Robert

The Scottish poet was the first person to use the now-cliché'd phrase "Man's inhumanity to man." It appeared in stanza seven of his *Man*

Was Made to Mourn. The full line is "Man's inhumanity to man makes countless thousands mourn."

Burnside, Gen. Ambrose E.

The Civil War general, after whom "sideburn" whiskers were named, was governor of Rhode Island from 1866 to 1869 and was a Republican congressman from Rhode Island from 1875 until his death in 1881.

Burr, Aaron

Aaron Burr's grandfather was the first president of Princeton University (then College of New Jersey), his father was the second president of Princeton, and Burr himself enrolled at Princeton at the age of 13. He graduated first in his class at age 16.

Burr, Raymond

In the 1940s Raymond Burr weighed as much as 340 pounds.

While working for the Oregon Forest Service, the future Perry Mason spent five months by himself when he was snowed in.

Burroughs, Edgar Rice

Before writing the Tarzan books, Edgar Rice Burroughs's first literary effort was a short story entitled "Under the Moon of Mars," published in a science fiction magazine in 1912 under the pseudonym Normal Bean.

Burroughs, William

William Burroughs, author of the surrealistic book *Naked Lunch*, is the grandson of the man who invented the adding machine (or, as Burroughs put it, "the gimmick that made it work").

Naked Lunch was originally titled *Naked Lust* but Burroughs's friend Jack Kerouac misread the word "lust" and called it Naked Lunch— which Burroughs liked better.

Burstyn, Ellen

The Academy Award-winning actress has had more names than most vaudeville comedians. Born Edna Rae Gillooly, she became Keri Flynn as a chorus dancer in a Montreal nightclub. In a 1944 Hollywood screen test she was named Erica Dean. As a regular on the "Jackie Gleason Show" in the mid-50s she was Edna Rae. In 1969, after her last movie (*Pit Stop*) as Ellen Rae, she married Neil Burstyn and planned to abandon her career when she received an offer to appear in the movie *Tropic of Cancer*. She took the job and made her first professional appearance as Ellen Burstyn.

Burton, Richard

Burton does not like to be called Dick. He claims that Dick is not a name but an "appendage."

Burton's pet cure for a hangover is a breakfast of chili and beer.

In a discussion with a reporter, talking about Elizabeth Taylor's conversion to Judaism, Burton said, "I'm more Jewish than she is, you know. My great-grandfather was a Polish Jew named Jan Ysar—and that was the family name until they changed it to Jenkins. It's true. I'm one-eighth Jewish. Elizabeth doesn't have a drop of Jewish blood in her."

Burton's real name is Richard Jenkins. He took the last name of Philip Burton, the man who taught him to speak English without a Welsh accent and encouraged him to become an actor.

Buttons, Red

Long before comedian Red Buttons won an Academy Award for his supporting role in *Sayonara*, he was a waiter named Aaron Chwatt at Dinty Moore's Tavern in the Bronx. With his *red* hair and a uniform full of *buttons* he found himself a catchy stage name.

Byington, Spring

Actress Spring Byington (*You Can't Take It With You*, "December Bride" TV series) was born in Colorado *Springs*, Colorado, perhaps accounting for her unusual first name.

Byrd, Robert

The West Virginia senator was born Cornelius Calvin Sale, Jr. in North Carolina. His mother died in the flu epidemic of 1918–1919, after which his father sent him to live with an aunt and uncle, Titus Dalton Byrd, in West Virginia.

In the late 1930s Byrd was a butcher in Crab Orchard, West Virginia.

Byron, Lord

The great poet was seduced when he was nine years old by the family nurse.

Lord Byron attended Harrow, the venerable English public school, and in fact played in the first soccer match between Eton and Harrow in 1805.

C

Caan, James

Said to be of mixed Dutch, German, and Jewish ancestry, movie actor James Caan recently clarified that he is "100% Jewish."

Cabot, John

The British navigator and explorer's real name was Giovanni Caboto and he was born in Genoa, Italy. His name was Anglicized when he was commissioned by King Henry VII to seek out new "isles, countries, regions or provinces of the heathen and infidels."

Cahn, Sammy

Sammy Cahn's first song, written at the age of 16, was "Like Niagara Falls, I'm Falling for You."

Explaining to columnist Martin Burden how he went from Sammy Cohen to Sammy Cahn, the four-time Oscar winning lyricist said, "But there was a comic named Sammy Cohen. I didn't want him getting credit for my work. I changed it to Cohn. He still got the credit. I changed it to Kahn. Composer Gus Kahn got the credit. Finally, Cahn." Not to be outdone, Sammy Cahn's son Steve, a guitar player, changed his last name to Khan.

Cagney, James

Cagney's first professional stage job was as a chorus *girl* in a female impersonation act at Keith's Eighty-first Street Theatre in New York City.

The vaudeville dancing act "Parker, Rand and Leach" became "Parker, Rand and Cagney" when James Cagney replaced "hoofer" Archie Leach who left to become a Broadway actor. Leach eventually made his mark as a comedic movie actor under a different name—Cary Grant.

The famous grapefruit scene in *Public Enemy* was based on a real incident in which a Chicago hoodlum, tired of hearing his girlfriend talk at the breakfast table, shoved his freshly cooked omelet in her face. In the movie Cagney used a grapefruit half because it was not as messy as an omelet. Thirty years later, in the movie *One Two Three*, Cagney threatened another woman with a grapefruit—a tongue-in-cheek cinema "quotation."

Cagney has a reputation of being short but he isn't that short. He's five feet eight inches tall, only two inches below the average height for an

American male. Once, however, opposite the tall actress Claire Dodd in *Footlight Parade*, Cagney needed some extra inches so he stood on a two-inch apple box for close-up scenes to avoid looking shorter than Miss Dodd.

Impressionists doing a Cagney imitation always say "All right you guys" and "You dirty rat" but the truth is that Cagney never uttered those lines in any of his movies.

Cagney's sister Jeanne, after graduating from college, wanted to be an actress and she did in fact become one. In the movie *Yankee Doodle Dandy* she appeared as Josie Cohan, sister of George M. Cohan who, of course, was played by James Cagney.

Caine, Michael

Born Maurice J. Micklewhite, the actor changed his name to Michael Caine just before landing a job on the West End stage in 1955. The "Michael" was from "Mickle" and the "Caine" was from a theater marquee he noticed advertising the movie *The Caine Mutiny*.

Michael Caine's younger brother, Stanley Hunter, is a British television actor.

As a youth, Caine attended a Jewish parochial school in the East End slums of London because it was the school nearest to his house. Consequently he has an excellent knowledge of Yiddish and knows enough Jewish dialect jokes to make Myron Cohen *kvell*.

Calamity Jane

Born Martha Jane Canary, her married life was a veritable calamity—she married 12 times!

Calder, Alexander

Calder became interested in mobiles at the circus where he marveled at seeing the performers in motion while maintaining perfect balance.

It is not surprising that Calder became a master at making mobiles, stabiles, and mobile-stabiles. His grandfather, Alexander Milne Calder, spent 40 years creating bronze and marble works for the city of Philadelphia (including the 37-foot statue of William Penn on top of City Hall), his father, Alexander Stirling Calder, was also a sculptor, his mother, Nanette, was an artist, and Calder himself earned a Masters of Engineering degree from Stevens Institute of Technology in Hoboken, New Jersey.

Calder was an illustrator for the *Police Gazette* in 1923 in order to help earn tuition money for his studies at the Art Students League in New York City.

"Sandy" Calder used to invent action toys for the Toddler Toys company in Oshkosh, Wisconsin.

Calhern, Louis

Born Carl Henry Vogt, he took a stage name at his family's request when he became an actor. He combined his given names into "Calhern" and took his new first name from the city of St. Louis where he was raised.

Caligula

The Roman emperor's last words were "I am still alive!" He was right but not for long.

Callas, Maria

The Metropolitan Opera diva, born Maria Calogeroupoulos, had such a strong international reputation and image as a volatile and temperamental Greek that it obscured the fact that she was born in New York City.

At age 14, Maria weighed about 210 pounds! She eventually slimmed down to avoid getting typecast for roles requiring girth.

Calvet, Corinne

The French actress, born Corinne Dibos, was made to change her name by her aristocrat father when he found out that Corinne was going to become an actress.

Cambridge, Godfrey

Before Cambridge became a successful comedian, he entered a laughing contest and was voted one of the top laughing champions of 1956. In fact that was his secret when he once appeared on the television program *I've Got a Secret*, before becoming famous.

Cameron, Rod

The Canadian-born actor (real name Nathan Cox) used to be Fred MacMurray's stand-in.

Camus, Albert

The Algerian-born French writer and Nobel Prize-winner received a free pair of shoes every year from the French government because his father died in the service of France.

Camus once worked as a meteorologist.

Cantinflas

Cantinflas's real name is Mario Moreno August. As a substitute announcer in a traveling tent show, he was so nervous that he garbled his speech and when he tried to correct himself he uttered incoherent words. His nonsensical gibberish amused most of the audience but one person stood up and yelled, "Callate (Shut up!) Cantinflas" (which was in itself a meaningless word). The audience thought that was his name and started calling him Cantinflas.

Cantinflas has inspired a new word in Mexican-Spanish: *Cantinflear* which means to talk in gobbledygook.

Cantor, Eddie

Born Isidore "Izzie" Itzkowitz, Cantor was raised by his grandmother, Esther Kantrowitz. When it came time for him to register for school she gave his name as Isidore Kanter. He later changed the spelling to Cantor. He received his new first name, Eddie, from his girlfriend, Ida Tobias, who thought the name was cute.

Capone, Al

On his business card, the infamous Chicago gangster listed himself as a "Second Hand Furniture Dealer."

According to the *Guinness Book of World Records*, Capone holds the record for the "highest gross income ever achieved in a single year by a private citizen." In 1927 Capone made an estimated $105 million from his many illegal activities.

Capote, Truman

Capote's name at birth was Truman Streckfus Persons but when he was four years old his mother divorced Truman's father and married a textile businessman named Joseph Garcia Capote who legally adopted young Truman.

Capote's inspiration for the character Holly Golightly in his book *Breakfast at Tiffany's* was Doris Lily, the gossip reporter and author of *The Fabulous Greeks, How to Marry a Millionaire*, and *How to Make Love in Five Languages*.

Having failed high school algebra three times, even with the help of a tutor, Capote once confessed, "I am a mathematical imbecile...." He also has trouble remembering the alphabet, "I can't recite the alphabet, at least not correctly or all the way through...."

Capp, Al

The cartoonist's real name is Alfred Gerald Caplin.

In his early twenties Capp did lettering for Ham Fisher, the creator of the "Joe Palooka" comic strip. In one strip, hillbilly characters were featured and it gave Capp the idea for his "Li'l Abner" strip.

Capp created what is now an American institution—Sadie Hawkins Day—in his "Li'l Abner" strip.

Capp also drew the "Abbie an' Slats" cartoon strip under the pseudonym Raeburn Van Buren.

The cartoonist lost his leg at age nine when he fell off an ice truck. During World War II he created a cartoon autobiography in which he stressed his progress in adapting to an artificial limb. The government distributed the booklet to all war amputees.

Capra, Frank

The Italian-American director has won two Oscars for Best Director (*It Happened One Night*, 1934; *You Can't Take It With You*, 1938) but it will always be one less than he wishes he had won. At the 1932–33 Academy Award ceremonies, he was a nominee for *Lady for a Day*. Emcee Will Rogers opened the envelope and said, "It couldn't happen to a nicer guy. Come up and get it, Frank!" Capra jumped up and rushed to the podium but just before he reached it, he heard Rogers say, "Frank Lloyd, the winner," and Capra retreated into the shadows, realizing that Frank Lloyd, the director of *Cavalcade*, had won.

Carlisle, Kitty

When Kitty (nee Katherine Conn) entered show business she took the stage name Carlisle, which she picked from the Manhattan telephone directory.

Carmichael, Hoagy

During the 1946 Academy Award ceremonies producer Samuel Goldwyn, exuberant over his movie *The Best Years of Our Lives* winning several Oscars, referred to Hoagy Carmichael, who appeared in the movie, as *Hugo* Carmichael.

Although Hoaglund Howard Carmichael was always musically inclined he really wanted to be a lawyer. He studied law at Indiana University (LL.B.1926) and was a lawyer with the Equitable Trust Company in New York City after graduation.

Carmichael, Stokely

As a youth in the Bronx, Carmichael was the only black member of the local white gang, the Morris Park Dukes.

Born in Port-of-Spain, Trinidad, the black activist has been living at his villa in Conakry, Guinea, West Africa, for the past ten years.

Carnegie, Andrew

Scottish-born Andrew Carnegie was no tightwad. In the last 18 years of his life he gave away the equivalent of $350 million—including 7,689 church organs.

Carnegie, Dale

Although his surname was spelled Carnegey, Dale Carnegie's father claimed that he was related to millionaire Andrew Carnegie. Dale changed the spelling of his last name in 1916 when he was about to give a lecture at—of all places—*Carnegie* Hall.

Dale Carnegie originally wanted to win friends and influence people by being an actor. He enrolled in the American Academy of Dramatic Arts in his early twenties and studied acting with classmates Howard Lindsay and Guthrie McClintic. However, after being in a road show, young Carnegie decided to change his act.

Carnera, Primo

Weighing 265 pounds, the Italian boxer was the heaviest world boxing champion on record but he also held the title for the shortest period of time—350 days, until Leon Spinks broke the record (212 days) in 1978.

Carney, Art

The television comedian and movie actor was wounded in World War II, shortly after landing at Normandy's Omaha Beach.

Carney started out in show business as a mimic specializing in political figures and his best showcase was a radio program called "Report to the Nation," a spoof on the *March of Time*. On the show, he did imitations of people like

Winston Churchill, Franklin D. Roosevelt, Al Smith, and Harry Truman.

Caron, Leslie

Although Leslie Caron was born in Paris, France, the actress and dancer is half-American. Her ballerina mother, Margaret Petit, was originally from Topeka, Kansas, but made her home in Paris when she married French chemist Claude Caron.

Carr, Allan

The caftan-clad movie producer (*Grease*), born Alan Solomon in Highland Park, Illinois, was nicknamed "Poopsie" in his school days.

Carroll, Lewis

Lewis Carroll's real name was Charles Lutwidge Dodgson. He created his pen name, according to some sources, by translating his given names into Latin (Carolus Ludovicus), reversing them, and then retranslating them back into English-sounding names. The resemblance of the pseudonym in rhyme and structure to the name Alice Liddell, a neighborhood girl on whom he later based his Alice stories, seems more than coincidental. He first used the name Lewis Carroll in 1856 when he published a poem in the magazine *The Train*.

Carradine, John

Born Richmond Reed Carradine, the character actor used the name John Peter Richmond from 1930 to 1935.

Carson's $5 million salary with NBC is modest when it is pointed out that his program generates 20 percent of NBC's profits.

The popular talk show host's first stage appearance was as a bumble bee in a grammar school health pageant.

After his high school graduation, Johnny hitchhiked to California, acquired a naval cadet's uniform and managed to do three noteworthy things: He danced with Marlene Dietrich at the Hollywood Stage Door Canteen; he was sawed in half by Orson Welles in a magic act (he volunteered from the audience); and he was arrested by the Military Police for impersonating a serviceman.

In an interview with Mike Wallace on television's "60 Minutes" it was revealed that Carson stole a ring from Woolworth's when he was 12 years old; he lets off steam by playing the drums given to him by Buddy Rich; he takes his lunch to the studio with him; and, according to his wife, he cried for two hours the day Jack Benny, his friend and idol, died.

On October 1, 1962, Carson became the new host of "The Tonight Show." His guests were Tony Bennett, Mel Brooks, Joan Crawford, and Rudy Vallee.

Carson's license plates read 360GUY, suggesting that he is an all-around guy.

Carter, Billy

Unlike his brother Jimmy Carter who was valedictorian of his high school graduating class, Billy "Buckshot" Carter was at the bottom of his class—26th out of 26 students.

Billy vomited in the men's room of a posh New York restaurant one evening when he found out that the paté he had been eating was actually goose liver.

Carter, Jimmy

Jimmy's father, owner of a farm-supply store, once ordered an oversupply of women's high-button shoes and rather than discard them, he encouraged family members to wear them, including Jimmy who wore a pair to high school!

Ex-peanut farmer Jimmy Carter is indebted to blacks for more than winning the 1976 presidential election—George Washington Carver, the Negro botanist and chemist, developed more than 300 products from peanuts.

Carter's father nicknamed Jimmy "Hot" because he thought young Jimmy was a "Hotshot" and would always succeed at anything he did.

Jimmy once shot his sister Gloria with a BB gun, hitting her in the rear end, after she threw a wrench at him.

When Carter entered college, according to his sister Gloria, he was only five feet three inches tall.

Carter, Rosalynn

Betty Ford received a lot of publicity for her facial plastic surgery but Rosalynn Carter, before her husband was elected president, underwent blepharoplasty, a medical procedure to correct drooping eyelids.

Cartland, Barbara

The prolific (230 books plus) writer of romance novels once commented, "I never specifically describe the sex act because it's such a bore laid bare."

Miss Cartland's name was originally Barbara McCorquodale.

Caruso, Enrico

Just before going on stage, Enrico Caruso used to take a nip of whiskey to get himself in the right spirit.

Caruso loved to play practical jokes on and off the stage. In one performance of *La Boheme*, for example, Marcello struggled unsuccessfully to put on his coat before exiting to get some medicine for the dying Mimi, only to find that the sleeves of the coat had been sewn closed—by Caruso, of course, before the performance.

Probably the greatest voice ever recorded, Caruso was the first singer to have his voice recorded for playback on a phonograph. Also, his recording of the aria "Vesti la giubba" from *I Pagliacci* in 1902 was the first record ever to sell a million copies and thus was the first "gold-record."

Caruso was not only the world's greatest tenor ("The man with the orchid-lined voice") but he was also an excellent caricaturist and took a lot of pride in his drawings. Once, when he found out that Mark Twain had not invited him to a dinner honoring eminent cartoonists, he said, "Mark Twain no invite me because he think of me as just a tenor."

Carver, George Washington

As a slave baby only a few weeks old, Carver and his mother were stolen from their plantation but the master ransomed them back for a race horse valued at $300.

Casanova, Giovanni Jacopo

The legendary Italian adventurer and lover is said to have invented the first diaphragm—a hollowed-out lemon.

Casanova was once a librarian at Dux Castle in Bohemia.

Cash, Johnny

Because Cash does many benefit performances at prisons (Folsom, etc.), people think that he has served prison time himself. Actually, he has never served a prison sentence but was jailed overnight seven different times years ago for drunkenness or possessing amphetamines. Also, his first prison concert occurred two years before his first arrest.

Cassidy, Butch

Cassidy's real name was George Leroy Parker. He earned the nickname, Butch, for being a cattle butcher and adopted the last name of the man who taught him how to steal horses and cattle.

Cassidy, David

If the young actor is anything like his father, the late Jack Cassidy, David should have a full head of gray hair by age 35.

Cassidy, Hopalong

When William Boyd appeared in the title role of the 1934 movie *Hopalong Cassidy* he became Hopalong Cassidy. Until that time he went by the name Bill Boyd to avoid being confused with William Boyd, the stage actor. The stage actor, to distinguish himself from the Hopalong Cassidy Bill Boyd, then started calling himself William "Stage" Boyd.

Cassidy, Shaun

The young singer takes a shot of Southern Comfort before every singing engagement.

Cassini, Oleg

Born Oleg Loiewski-Cassini in Paris, the fashion designer and socialite is the son of Alexander Loiewski, a Russian diplomat, and Countess Marguerite Cassini, the daughter of a Russian ambassador to the United States. To simplify the family name, Oleg and his brother Igor retained their mother's name and dropped their father's surname.

Castle, Irene and Vernon

The dancers' real names were Irene Foote and Vernon Blythe.

The only feature movie the couple made together was *The Whirl of Life* in 1915.

Castro, Fidel

At Colegio Belén, a Jesuit preparatory school in Havana, Castro was voted the best athlete in the class of 1944.

Cavett, Dick

As a gag writer for Jack Paar on "The Tonight Show" witty Cavett provided the following introduction for Jayne Mansfield: "And here *they* are ... Jayne Mansfield!"

Dick's full name is Richard Alva Cavett but he is not related to inventor Thomas Alva Edison.

Cavett's production company, Daphne Productions, is named after his dog Daphne.

Cervantes, Miguel de Saavedra

In the Battle of Lepanto in 1571, Cervantes was shot twice in the chest and once in his left hand, permanently maiming the hand but, in his words, "For the greater glory of the right" which he later deftly used to write his *Don Quixote*.

According to *McGill's Book of Quotations in Context,* Cervantes contributed the following phrases to Western civilization:

All is not gold that glitters
A bird in the hand is worth two in the bush
Born with a silver spoon in his mouth
Cry my eyes out
Every dog has his day
A finger in every pie
Give the devil his due
Honesty is the best policy
I'll turn over a new leaf
Let every man mind his own business
Mum's the word
No limit but the sky
Smell a rat
Split his sides with laughing
Strike while the iron is hot
There is no love lost
Thou hast seen nothing yet
When thou art at Rome, do as they do in Rome
With a grain of salt
A word to the wise is enough

All of the above phrases appear in Cervantes's *Don Quixote.*

Cezanne, Paul

Distrustful of most women, Cezanne once complained, "They're all scheming bitches."

Chaliapin, Feodor

The Russian opera singer once hit a low note when, fully clothed, he jumped off a yacht because he was bored with the host and his guests.

Chamberlain, Neville

Long before Chamberlain became the British Prime Minister (1937–1940), he invented the game of snooker pool while stationed in India with the Devonshire regiment. His new game was a combination of pocket billiards and carom billiards. The name "snooker" is a slang term for a new cadet at the Royal Military Academy.

Chambers, Marilyn

The girl "Behind the Green Door" and formerly on the Ivory Snow box was born Marilyn Briggs and raised in the affluent suburban town of Westport, Connecticut. She was given the "stage" name Marilyn Chambers because "it sounded very plain and nice and WASPish."

Marilyn's pornographic movie *Behind the Green Door* opened at the same time her Ivory Snow box started appearing on supermarket shelves.

Champion, Marge

Born Marjorie Celeste Belcher, the dancer and actress used the name Majorie Bell (short for Belcher) in her first movie *The Story of Vernon and Irene Castle* (1939) with Fred Astaire and Ginger Rogers.

Marge Champion modelled for Walt Disney's cartoon heroines in *Snow White and the Seven Dwarfs* and *Pinocchio* (as the Blue Fairy).

Chandler, Raymond

The author of *The Big Sleep* and *Farewell, My Lovely* was an oil company executive in the 1920s.

Chanel, Coco

Gabrielle Bonheur "Coco" Chanel's perfume "No. 5" is the best-known perfume in the world but its real significance is that it was the first synthetic-scent perfume ever produced and mass marketed. Prior to that time, all perfumes were made from animal products (e.g., civet, musk, ambergris) or plants (e.g., flower blossoms, barks, fruits).

Chaney, Lon

The "Man of a Thousand Faces" was once a guide at Pike's Peak, Colorado.

Chang Kai-Shek

The Chinese Nationalist leader was an habitual hummer and hummed incessantly while practising calligraphy or taking walks.

Channing, Stockard

The actress (nee Susan Stockard) trained for her earthly role as Rizzo in the movie *Grease* by growing up on the affluent East Side of New York City, attending Miss Chapin's and Madeira preparatory schools, graduating cum laude from Radcliff College, and by marrying Walker Channing, Jr., a Boston stockbroker.

Chapin, Harry

The singer and songwriter ("Cats in the Cradle") is the grandson of James Chopin, the artist who drew the illustrations for Robert Frost's first two books of poetry, *A Boy's Will* and *North of Boston*.

Chaplin, Geraldine

At age seven, Geraldine Chaplin made a brief appearance in her father's movie *Limelight*. Her one speaking line was, "Mrs. Alsop is out."

Miss Chaplin owes her first name to Geraldine Fitzgerald, the Irish-born actress whom her father especially admired.

Chaplin, Charlie

Chaplin once entered a Charlie Chaplin look-alike contest in Monte Carlo and came in *third* place!

Charlie Chaplin loved young women, if his four wives' ages at marriage were any indication. Mildred Harris, his first wife, was 16 years old, Lita Grey, his second wife, also was 16 years old, Paulette Goddard was relatively old—24 years old, and Oona O'Neil was 18 years old.

Chaplin, even when he was rich, never carried money with him.

Chaplin was supposed to be Alistair Cooke's best man in August of 1934 but Charlie never showed up. He was at Lake Arrowhead with Paulette Goddard and apparently was having too good a time to leave.

Both Charlie Chaplin and Adolf Hitler, the man Chaplin satirized in the movie *The Great Dictator*, were born in April, 1889.

Charisse, Cyd

Born Tula Ellice Finklea, the dancer and movie actress was nicknamed "Sid" as a child growing up in Texas by her younger brother in an attempt to say "sister." After marrying Nico Charisse, under whom she studied ballet, she changed the spelling of her nickname to go with her new last name . . . and became Cyd Charisse.

Charles, Prince

Prince Charles is the first heir to the British throne to earn a university degree. He received a Bachelor of Arts degree from Trinity College, Cambridge.

At the Cheam preparatory school in England, Prince Charles was captain of the football team (they never won a game). He played the malevolent Richard III in a school play and was reprimanded for playing practical jokes.

Prince Charles emptied the garbage every morning at the Gordonstoun "public school" in Australia and was considered a commendable "dustman."

Prince Charles's full name is Charles Philip Arthur George Windsor.

Charles, Ray

The singer's real name is Ray Charles Robinson but he dropped his last name to avoid being confused with boxer Sugar Ray Robinson.

The singer became blind at age five.

Chase, Chevy

The comedian's full name is Cornelius Crane Chase. The nickname "Chevy" was given to him by his paternal grandmother.

Chase, Salmon P.

Why does Salmon P. Chase appear on the U.S. $10,000 bill? Perhaps it was his reward for establishing a national banking system and for the issuance of a legal tender currency when he was Secretary of the Treasury under President Abraham Lincoln.

Chavez, Cesar

Because Chavez thinks that Christ wore one, the union leader wears a mezuzah or Jewish holy medal with the star of David on it. (He pointed out that "He certainly didn't wear a cross.")

Chayefsky, Paddy

The Academy Award-winning screenplay writer (*Marty, Hospital*) and playwright wrote his first play, *No Time Out for Love,* in a hospital, while recovering from wounds received in Germany during World War II.

Chayefsky's real first name is Sidney. He acquired the name Paddy in the U.S. Army when, to avoid K.P. duty on Sunday, the Jewish writer told his lieutenant that he had to go to mass—which prompted the lieutenant to call him Paddy, a good Irish Catholic name.

Cheever, John

The popular novelist's first published story was *Expelled,* based on the true story of his being expelled from Thayer Academy, a New England prep school, for smoking. He was 17 years old when the story was published.

For extra income during the Depression, Cheever summarized novels for MGM for $5 a piece.

The author used to be plagued by phobias, the most unusual of which was a fear of crossing bridges.

Chekhov, Anton

The Russian playwright and short-story writer was originally going to practice medicine but was forced into writing for a living. Chekhov went to medical school in Moscow on a scholarship but when his family suffered financial setbacks he was forced to become the family provider. To earn money he wrote humorous stories for Moscow and St. Petersburg magazines while still in medical school and became so popular that even after he received his medical degree in 1884, he devoted all his time to writing.

Cher

Cher's mother, an aspiring actress, was supposed to be in the movie *The Asphalt Jungle* but at the last minute the role was given to Marilyn Monroe.

The singer has a tattoo of flowers on her derriere.

Cher's name at birth was Cherilyn Sarkesian. She became Cherilyn La Piere when her divorced mother married bank manager Gilbert La Piere. In 1962 she met Salvatore "Sonny" Bono, a record promoter and aspiring singer, on a blind date, married him, and became Cher Bono.

Chevalier, Maurice

Chevalier, wounded and captured during World War I, was sent to a German prison camp at Altegrabow. He spent 26 months at the camp and spent most of his time learning to read English. Although Chevalier spoke English with a thick French accent on stage, he really knew and spoke English very well, almost without accent. He maintained the strong accent for the theatrical effect.

Child, Julia

As a child, Julia McWilliams (her maiden name) never did any cooking at home and never had any reason to—her family had a cook!

When Julia Child finally did learn how to cook, it wasn't French cooking she first learned. It was Chinese. During World War II, she worked in Ceylon as a file clerk and met Paul Cushing Child, a mapmaker for the O.S.S. Paul Child was a lover of fine wines and haute cuisine. When they were married and reassigned to China, he introduced Julia to Chinese cuisine. She became interested enough to seriously learn gourmet cooking and later studied the culinary art in France.

The gourmet cook would have made an excellent basketball player. She is six feet two inches tall!

Her favorite dish to cook is duck.

After graduating from Smith College, Julia spent two years writing advertising copy for a New York City furniture store.

Chisholm, Shirley

Representative Chisholm (nee St. Hill) was the first black woman ever elected to Congress when she was elected as the Democratic representative from the 12th Congressional District in Brooklyn in the fall of 1968.

Chopin, Frederic Francois

Because most of Chopin's audiences would see only one side of him during his recitals, the Polish pianist would sometimes shave only one side of his face.

Christie, Agatha

Dame Agatha Christie not only wrote 80 popular crime novels but also wrote the longest-running play, *The Mousetrap*, which has been playing in London since November 25, 1952.

In December, 1926 Miss Christie mysteriously disappeared from her home in England. She was later found, after a nation-wide search, in a hotel where she was living under another name. She apparently was the victim of amnesia.

Born Agatha Mary Clarissa Miller, she became Agatha Christie when she married Archibald Christie in 1912.

Christie, Julie

Julie Christie was born in Assam, India, where her father was a tea planter. She went to England when she was eight years old to get a "proper education."

Church, Frank

The Idaho senator was found to have cancer in 1948 and was expected to live only six more months.

Churchill, Winston

Winston Churchill and Franklin Delano Roosevelt were seventh cousins once removed, according to *Burke's Presidential Families of the United States of America*.

Churchill was born two months prematurely when he was delivered on November 30, 1874.

At twelve years of age, Churchill was admitted to Harrow School, despite his handing in a blank piece of paper for the Latin entrance examination.

The great British prime minister and statesman once proposed to Ethel Barrymore, the American actress.

Churchill failed the entrance examinations to Sandhurst, (the British equivalent of West Point) three times before coaching, cramming, and luck enabled him the pass the tests. He eventually graduated with honors and was 8 in a class of 150.

A chronic cigar smoker, Churchill is believed to have smoked about 300,000 cigars in his lifetime.

Churchill was an avid bricklayer and from 1928 until his death he was a dues paying member of the Amalgamated Union of Building Trade Workers. With this unusual skill, he built a swimming pool and treehouse for his children at Chartwell.

Cicero, Marcus Tullius

Everyone has his own cure for a hangover, even Roman philosophers. Cicero believed that eating cabbage the day after heavy wine-drinking would cure the hangover.

Clark, Dick

Dick Clark was not the first emcee of television's "American Bandstand." In 1956 the emcee who had been hired was involved in some misdemeanors and was fired. Looking for a replacement, the manager of WFIL-TV sought out a clean-cut, upright individual and selected the youthful Clark, who was already working for the station as a newscaster, to host the show.

After being graduated from Syracuse University in 1951, Clark became a newscaster at WKTV in Utica, New York. There he developed the technique of prerecording words on tape and synchronizing his lips with the recording, giving the impression of a live and spontaneous delivery. He later used this technique when doing commercials on "American Bandstand."

Dick Clark's older brother, Bradley Clark, was killed in action during World War II.

Clark, Kenneth

The educator and psychologist was born in the Panama Canal Zone where his father was a passenger agent for the United Fruit Company.

Clark, Petula

Most Americans never heard of Petula Clark until 1965 when her recording of "Downtown" became a hit but actually she had been in show business for about twenty years at the time. As a child she had her own radio show and also appeared in movies with Alex Guinness and Peter Ustinov in the 1940s and 1950s.

Cleland, John

Author John Cleland was in Newgate Prison in London when he wrote *Fanny Hill*. He was imprisoned for not paying his debts and to help pay the debts he wrote the racy classic.

Cleopatra

The Queen of the Nile married two of her brothers (Ptolemy XIII and Ptolemy XIV), not an unusual occurrence at the time, as it was an Egyptian custom in the royal dynasty for brother and sister to intermarry.

Cleveland, Grover

Grover Cleveland had an artificial jaw! Doctors found a cancerous growth on the roof of his mouth and the upper left part of his jaw had to be removed in 1893. He was then fitted with an artificial jaw made of vulcanized rubber. The operation was not made public at the time because it was feared that news of the operation would worsen an already poor economic situation prevailing in 1893.

Cleveland received more votes (5,540,365) in the 1888 presidential election when he lost than in 1884 (4,875,971) when he won.

He was born Stephen Grover Cleveland and was named after Stephen Grover, the minister of the First Presbyterian Church in Caldwell, N.J. where his father also preached. The first name Stephen, however, was dropped during his youth.

Cleveland was a 47-year-old bachelor when he became the 22nd president. In his second year of office he married 21-year-old Frances Folsom and became the only president ever to marry for the first time while in office.

Clift, Montgomery

Montgomery Clift had a twin sister named Roberta.

Clift once talked Frank Sinatra out of committing suicide (he was despondent over his relationship with Ava Gardner), after which Sinatra gave Clift an expensive gold cigarette lighter. (Sinatra later cooled his relationship with Clift when he found out that Clift was a homosexual.)

About Montgomery Clift, Marilyn Monroe once said, "He's the only person who's in worse shape than I am."

Clift loved caviar and ate it by the pound.

According to Patricia Bosworth in her biography of Clift, he had a small penis and was embarrassed about it.

Coca, Imogene

Imogene Coca is of Spanish and Irish descent —the family name at one time was Fernandez y Coca.

Coco, James

One of his earlier jobs was being a Santa Claus at Gimbels department store in New York City. He also played a plumber in a Drano commercial.

Coburn, James

Coburn's first major acting job was in a Remington shaver commercial for which he received $25,000 in residuals, not bad pay for a day's work in the late 1950s.

Cody, William F. (Buffalo Bill)

Writer Ned Buntline (E.Z.C. Judson) gave Cody the nickname "Buffalo Bill," acknowledging Cody's reputation as a buffalo hunter. He killed 4,280 buffaloes within a 17-month period. At the time, he was employed by the Goddard Brothers firm then under contract to supply food for the Kansas Pacific railroad construction crews.

Cohan, George M.

George M. Cohan was born on July 3, 1878, but his father changed the birthdate to July 4th.

In 1940 Congress gave Cohan a special Medal of Honor for writing songs like "Over There" and "You're a Grand Old Flag" which served as rallying songs during wartime.

Cohn, Roy

The prominent lawyer, son of a New York State Supreme Court judge, exchanged Christmas gifts with F.B.I. director J. Edgar Hoover for 20 years.

Colbert, Claudette

Actress Claudette Colbert didn't think that the right side of her face was attractive so she always insisted on being photographed on the left side, even if it required shifting the movie set around.

She was born Claudette "Lily" Chauchoin in Paris, France but when she was a child her parents moved to the United States. At the advice of playwright Anne Morrison she changed her name to "a shorter, catchier" one, Colbert, for her Broadway debut in *The Wild Westcotts* in 1923.

Cole, Nat King

Nat's full name was Nathaniel Adams Coles (with an "s"). After touring the country as a pianist with the Negro revue *Shuffle Along*, he settled in Los Angeles where a nightclub manager suggested that he form a quartet. Nat took the manager's advice but when the drummer never showed up the group was named the Nat Coles Trio. The manager made him wear a gold paper crown one night and the group then was renamed the "King Cole Trio," dropping the "s" to go along with the nursery rhyme name. Thereafter, the singer became known as Nat King Cole.

Coleman, Cy

At age 16 aspiring songwriter Seymour Kaufman was told by a music publisher that the name "Cy Coleman" was more salable than his real name. He adopted the new name and, with or without it, his songs like "Witchcraft" and "Hey, Look Me Over" would still have become hits.

Coleman, Gary

The diminutive (three foot seven inches) child star of the television series *Diff'rent Strokes* had a kidney transplant at age five. The kidney was donated by the family of a Greek boy who was killed in a car accident.

Collins, Michael

The former astronaut was born in Rome, Italy, where his father was the American military attaché.

Colt, Samuel

In order to help raise capital to make prototypes of his revolving-breech pistol, Colt toured the country as Dr. Coult, demonstrating "laughing gas" (nitrous oxide) and then taking collections.

Colt's company went out of business in 1842 but the outbreak of the Mexican War caused the U.S. Army to order 1,000 of Colt's revolvers and revived the company.

Comfort, Dr. Alex

Dr. Comfort did not write the best-seller *The Joy of Sex*—he *edited* it. It was written by a couple who preferred to remain anonymous.

The British-born doctor, a specialist in gerontology (the study of aging people and the decline of life), is missing all but the index finger on his left hand, the result of an accident when he was 14 years old.

Como, Perry

On an hourly basis, Perry Como is the highest paid television performer ever, according to the *Guinness Book of World Records*. NBC paid him $5,000,000 for four one-hour specials or $20,833 per minute.

Condon, Richard

In Condon's *The Manchurian Candidate*, all of the characters in Lt. Shaw's U.S. Army squad were based on characters from Phil Silver's television series "You'll Never Get Rich."

In another Condon book *A Talent for Loving*, the Chinese cook Mat Son was named after the author's literary agent, Harold Matson.

Before he started writing novels in 1958, Richard Condon was a theatrical producer and movie press agent. Among the people he worked for or with were Cecil B. DeMille, Samuel Goldwyn, Sam Spiegel, Otto Preminger, Darryl Zanuck, Walt Disney, and Howard Hughes.

Connally, John

Connally's oldest daughter Kathleen ("Kay-Kay") died "accidentally" when attempting to commit suicide with a shotgun. Her husband tried to stop her but the gun went off, killing her.

Connery, Sean

Sean Connery has two tattoos on his right wrist —one acknowledges his birthplace ("Scotland Forever") and the other is dedicated to his parents ("Mum and Dad") whom he left, at age 16, to join the Navy. (The tattoos have to be covered with make-up when he's filming a movie.)

Connery left the Navy at age 19 because he had ulcers and was given a nine-shilling-a-week pension.

Connery's real first name is Thomas, not Sean.

For his five James Bond movies, Connery was said to have received over $13,500,000 from his fees and percentage of the gross receipts, making him one of the highest paid actors in the history of movies.

Connors, Mike

In a special television movie several years ago, actor Mike Connors played a character named Kirk Ohanian—which is noteworthy only because his real name is Krekor "Kirk" Ohanian.

Conrad, Joseph

At age 21, Conrad became despondent and tried to commit suicide by shooting himself in the heart. He missed (!) his target, recuperated, and took a merchant ship to England, starting a 16-year adventure on the seas and in foreign lands, about which he eventually wrote in his novels (*Typhoon, Lord Jim*, etc.)

The writer's real name was Jozef Teodor Konrad Nalecz Korzeniowski. Although Poland already had a novelist named Jozef Korzeniowski in the first half of the nineteenth century, the reason Conrad changed his name was to make it easier for English-speaking people to read and pronounce it. Having spent many years in the British Navy, Conrad knew that the British had trouble pronouncing or remembering his Polish last name.

Conrad, Robert

The television actor's real name is Conrad Robert Falk.

Conway, Tim

In deference to Carol Burnett, on whose show Conway gratefully appeared, his license plates read 11 YEARS—which is how long "The Carol Burnett Show" was on the air.

Conway, Tom

Born Thomas Sanders, the British actor (*The Falcon's Brother, Cat People*) was the brother of actor George Sanders.

Coogan, Jackie

The former child movie star, 16 months old when he made his first movie, was a millionaire by age eight.

Cooke, Alistair

Alistair Cooke was named an honorary Knight Commander of the British Empire by Queen Elizabeth II in 1973 but because he is an American citizen he is not entitled to use "Sir" before his name.

Coolidge, Calvin

President Coolidge was born on the Fourth of July, 1872.

Teddy Roosevelt's daughter, Alice Roosevelt Longworth, said that Coolidge looked as though he were "weaned on a pickle."

Cooper, Alice

Regarding the choice of a female name, in an interview with Rex Reed, Cooper said that people are biologically both male and female and added, "I once studied under a hypnotist who taught me to become three equal parts—male for strength, female for wisdom, and child for faith. We integrated this thought into the act: a feminine image, rough masculine music and the 'toys' we play with onstage."

When Alice Cooper's Beverly Hills house burned down a couple of years ago, one of the items lost was a painting of Cooper done by Salvadore Dali. (The house, incidentally, was formerly owned by Nixon aide H. R. Halde-man.)

Cooper used to have a two-case a day beer (Budweiser) habit.

Cooper, Gary

Although Gary Cooper was raised in Montana, he lived in England (his father was a British lawyer) for four years and attended the Dunstable School. At age 13 he returned to the United States with a British accent but gradually lost it.

About Gary Cooper's acting ability, John Barrymore said, "That fellow is the world's greatest actor. He can do with no effort what the rest of us spent years trying to learn; to be perfectly natural." When asked to reveal his acting technique, Cooper admitted that he really didn't have one—all he did was try hard to think of his next line.

Although Cooper was right-handed, it was no problem for him to play left-handed Lou Gehrig in *Pride of the Yankees*. In throwing and batting sequences the photo laboratories printed the film on the reverse side, making Cooper appear left-handed.

Not always in the best of health, Cooper had four hernias and had impaired hearing from being too close to a dynamite blast.

Gary Cooper appeared in a few movies (*Tricks, Three Pals*) using his real given name (Frank James Cooper) but was advised by his newly acquired agent Nan Collins to change his first name. Cooper at first resisted the notion but gave in after reading that a Chicago man named Frank Cooper just killed his wife. Nan Collins, originally from Gary, Indiana, suggested that "Gary" would make a good first name. Cooper repeated the name several times and agreed to adopt the name, joking that he was lucky that she didn't come from Poughkeepsie, New York.

Cooper, James Fenimore

Cooper's father was born in Stratford-on-Avon, England (birthplace of William Shakespeare) but settled in New Jersey in 1679. The family later moved north to New York State and founded Cooperstown which later became well known as the site of the Baseball Hall of Fame.

Cooper entered Yale College at age 13 but was expelled for exploding a gunpowder charge in the lock of a tutor's door and for talking back to a professor.

Cooper, Peter

When Cooper ran for the U.S. presidency in 1876 as the Greenback Party candidate he was 85 years old—the oldest person ever to run for the office. He lost, of course, to a more youthful candidate—Rutherford B. Hayes who was 54 years old at the time.

In 1830 Peter Cooper invented the first passenger train in the United States. It was called the *Tom Thumb* and it followed a 13-mile route on the Baltimore and Ohio Railroad.

Copernicus

The Polish astronomer, born Mikolaj Kopernik, studied law and medicine as a student at the University of Padua and received a doctorate in canon law at Ferrara in 1503. He spent seven years as physician to the Bishop of Ermeland, his uncle.

Although Copernicus was smart enough to disprove the Ptolemaic theory that the earth was the center of the universe, he was not that smart —his IQ was estimated to be a modest 105 or slightly above average.

Copland, Aaron

The Brooklyn-born composer (*Appalachian Spring, Billy the Kid*) wrote the scores for the following movies, among others: *Of Mice and Men* (1939), *Our Town* (1940), *The Red Pony* (1948) and won an Academy Award for *The Heiress* in 1949.

Coppola, Francis Ford

The movie director (*The Godfather, Apocalypse Now*) was given the middle name Ford after the hospital in which he was born—the Henry Ford Hospital in Detroit.

Corbett, James John

"Gentleman Jim" Corbett was an assistant bank teller before he became a professional boxer.

Corbett was the first "actor" to have an exclusive contract for a single performance in a movie. In August 1894, the boxer was filmed by the Kinescope Exhibition Company in a six-round fight with Pete Courtney.

Cordobes, El

Born Manuel Benitez Perez, El Cordobes was originally known as El Renco ("The Cripple") which was his diabetic father's nickname. He was renamed by bullfight promoter Rafael Sanchez, acknowledging the province in which the bullfighter was born—Cordoba.

Prior to becoming a professional bullfighter, El Cordobes was a brick layer, the traditional trade of aspiring bullfighters.

Corelli, Franco

Franco Corelli, one of the world's greatest living tenors, never took a voice lesson in his life because he was told that voice coaches would ruin his voice.

Corelli once bit Birgit Nilsson on the neck in a performance of *Turandot* because she held a high note longer than he did.

Although Corelli has the image of being the "bad boy" of opera, he claims to be on good behavior, "I stay out of drafts, I don't go with women. That was the ruin for many singers, not me."

Cortez, Ricardo

The movie "Latin" lover was born Jacob Krantz in Vienna, Austria. He adopted a Latin name in Hollywood to take advantage of the success

Rudolph Valentino and Ramon Novarro were enjoying.

Cosell, Howard

The sportscaster's family name was originally Kosell but was changed to Cohen when they emigrated to the United States. After graduating from New York University Law School (Phi Beta Kappa; editor of the law review), he changed his name back to Cosell, adopting a new spelling of the name.

Costello, Elvis

The British rock singer who borrowed Elvis Presley's first name and Buddy Holly's eyeglass frames and built an act out of it was born Declan Patrick McManus.

Costello, Lou

After Costello split up with his partner Bud Abbott, he appeared in one movie by himself—*The Thirty Foot Bride of Candy Rock*, released in 1959, the year Costello died.

The drowning of his son in the family swimming pool is said to have precipitated Costello's heavy drinking and early death.

Cousteau, Jacques

Jacques Cousteau was co-inventor (with Emile Gagnon, a Parisian engineer) of the first aqualung, which they perfected in late 1942.

Coward, Noel

The very witty and clever playwright-actor-composer-director never graduated from grammar school.

Cox, Wally

Wally Cox was a silversmith and jewelry maker before his friends, including his roommate Marlon Brando, encouraged him to become a professional comedian and actor.

Cox's mother was a mystery story writer who used the pen name Eleanor Blake.

Crane, Hart

Poet Hart Crane (*The Bridge*) and Ernest Hemingway were both born on the same day, July 21, 1899, and both eventually committed suicide. Crane, also an alcoholic, took his life by drowning during a visit to Mexico where he was going to write an epic about Cortes and Montezuma.

Crawford, Broderick

Broderick Crawford acquired his Academy Award-winning (*All the King's Men*) acting ability and name from his stage actor parents, Helen *Broderick* and Lester *Crawford*.

Crawford, Christina

Her best-selling book *Mommie Dearest*, a revelational tale of horrors about her mother Joan

Crawford, was originally titled *The Hype* but the editor did not like the title.

Crawford, Joan

The actress appeared on "The Tonight Show" on October 1, 1962, the night Johnny Carson took over as host of the show.

Born Lucille Le Sueur in San Antonio, Texas, she became Lucille Cassin when her divorced mother married Henry Cassin and was nicknamed "Billie." In Hollywood she tried to use the name Lucille Le Sueur again but the studios felt that it sounded too much like the word "sewer" so they sponsored a contest to find her a new name. The winning name was Joan Arden but a bit player at MGM already had the name so the second choice name, Joan Crawford, (submitted by Mrs. Marie M. Tisdale, a crippled woman living in Albany, New York) was selected. The actress hated the name at first because it sounded like "crawfish" but soon grew to like it.

Cronyn, Hume

Stage and movie actor Hume Cronyn, once a law student at McGill University in Canada, was an excellent amateur boxer and was nominated for the Canadian Olympic boxing team in 1932.

Crosby, Bing

According to his wife Kathy, Bing Crosby was color blind.

Crosby's total worldwide record sales have been 400,000,000 copies, making him the "Most

Successful Recording Artist" by the *Guinness Book of World Records*. His biggest selling record was not "White Christmas" but "Silent Night," on which he never made any money because, in recognition of its being a religious song, he gave away all of the royalties to charity.

Crosby acquired his smooth "bub-bub-boo" style in college. Whenever he forgot lyrics to a song he was singing he would sing the notes and "bub-bub-boo" the lyrics. Eventually he became so famous for it that songwriters would write the non-lyrics into his songs.

When Bing did an occasional soft-shoe routine, it was really soft—he wore size 7½ shoes, a small size for a man.

Dinah Shore said that "Bing sings like all people think they sing in the shower."

The crooner was given the nickname "Bing" as a youth because of his fondness for the comic strip "The Bingville Bugle." The strip featured a character named Bingo who had big ears, prompting a friend to start calling him Bingo (the "o" was lost somewhere along the line.)

Crystal, Billy

The day the comedian started filming the movie *Rabbit Test*, in which he plays the first pregnant man, his wife found out that she was pregnant.

Crystal was captain of his high school baseball team and still tries to work out whenever he can, pretending that "the balls are William Morris agents."

Cugat, Xavier

Early in his career Cugat, a violinist, toured the United States with opera singer Enrico Caruso. They both had one pastime in common—they both loved to do caricatures of people. In fact, Cugat spent a year as a cartoonist for the *Los Angeles Times*.

Cullen, Bill

The perennial television quiz show host and panelist had a perilous childhood. At 18 months of age he was stricken with infantile paralysis (and still limps slightly because of it) and later was in an automobile accident that hospitalized him for nine months.

Cummings, E. E.

Edward Estlin Cummings spent six months in a French detention camp because of a misunderstanding with the French government. This experience is related in his first book *The Enormous Room*.

Cummings, Robert

When Robert Cummings abandoned his studies in aeronautic engineering at the Carnegie Institute of Technology, he studied acting at the American Academy of Dramatic Arts. Trying to get an acting job he found out that British actors were getting all the good parts so he went to England to study British speech and mannerisms. Returning to the states several months later with a newly acquired British accent, Savile Row clothes and the stage name "Blade Stanhope," Cummings won his Broadway debut role in J. K. Galsworthy's play *The Roof*. Later in Hollywood, Cummings noted that casting directors were looking for southern and western accents so he learned both accents and adopted the name "Brice Hutchens." It worked —his first movie was *Virginia Judge*.

Curie, Marie

Madame Curie and her daughter Irene both died from leukemia caused by overexposure to radiation.

Curie not only discovered radium but also discovered polonium which she named after her native country Poland.

Curtis, Cyrus

At age 13 Cyrus Herman Kotzchmar Curtis published his first magazine, a two-cent weekly called *Young America*. It was many years later that he founded *Ladies Home Journal* and the Curtis Publishing Company.

Curtis, Tony

Tony's second wife was German actress Christian Kaufmann whose father was an officer in the *Luftwaffe* during World War II.

Born Bernard Schwartz, the actor was given the last name Curtis by producer Bob Goldstein. In his first movie *Criss Cross* his name was Jimmy Curtis. He didn't like the name and suggested the name Anthony Adverse in honor of his "hungry childhood." The studio was not averse to changing the name Jimmy but they did want him to keep the last name Curtis.

Custer, George Armstrong

Custer may have graduated at the bottom of his West Point graduating class (1861; 35th out of 35 cadets) but he became a general in the U.S. Army at the age of 23, the youngest man ever to become a general.

At Little Big Horn, not only Custer died but also two of his brothers, a nephew, and a brother-in-law—in addition to the other 221 troops.

D

Dahl, Arlene

The ex-movie actress and current perfume company president (Dahlia Parfums, Inc.) has written 16 books, most of which are about health and beauty topics.

D'Amboise, Jacques

The choreographer and ballet dancer's full name is Jacques Joseph D'Amboise Ahearn. When he enrolled in the School of American Ballet, he dropped his surname and used his mother's maiden name D'Amboise as a stage name.

Among his children are a set of twin daughters, Charlotte and Catherine.

Dali, Salvadore

At age three the surrealist painter wanted to be a king and at age five he wanted to be Napoleon.

In his childhood Dali threw a little boy off a bridge, almost killing him; broke a doctor's pair of eyeglasses while he was about to pierce Dali's sister's ears; put a wounded bat in his mouth and almost bit it in two; and cut off his grandmother's hair—truly surrealistic acts.

Dali has admitted that he is not a faithful Catholic but he maintains that he is a faithful husband. As a demonstration of his faith, he has married his Russian-born wife, Gala, three times.

The artist has written more than 350 books, one of which weighed 100 pounds and costs $75,000.

Daly, John

The reporter and television personality ("What's My Line?") was born in Johannesburg, South Africa where his father was a mining engineer.

Damone, Vic

A name job and nose job transformed Brooklyn-born singer Vito Farinola into the handsome crooner Vic Damone.

Dare, Virginia

It is fairly well known that Virginia Dare was the first child born in America of English parents but that's about all that is known about her. Nine days after she was born her grandfather, John White, governor of the Virginia Colony, returned to England to get supplies. When he came back to the United States there was no trace of Virginia Dare or the rest of the colony.

No one has ever found out what happened to her.

Darin, Bobby

Born Walden Robert Cassotto, the late singer and actor began his career as a drummer playing at hotels in the Catskills. Fed up with that career, he went to New York City, changed his name to Darin (which he found in the Manhattan telephone book) and teamed up with Don Kirshner to write and sing commercials. In 1958 he recorded the song "Splish-Splash," and his career took off.

Darnell, Linda

As Monetta Eloyse Darnell, she and her family lived on Hollywood Street in Dallas, Texas but her mother seemed determined to have her daughter make it to Hollywood and Vine. After winning many Dallas talent contests, young Darnell was taken to the movie studios by her mother and was signed to a seven-year contract with Twentieth Century-Fox, where her first name was changed to Linda.

Darren, James

The Philadelphia born actor's real name is James Ercolani.

Darrow, Clarence

The great defense attorney once said, "I don't believe in God because I don't believe in Mother Goose."

Darwell, Jane

In the movie *The Grapes of Wrath*, Jane Darwell was so convincing as Ma Joad that she won the Oscar for Best Supporting Actress. In real life, however, Miss Darwell was far from being an impoverished "Okie." She was born Patti Woodard, daughter of railroad tycoon W.R. Woodard and attended the Dana Hall preparatory school in Boston before becoming an actress.

Darwin, Charles

Although Darwin is strongly identified with the phrase "survival of the fittest" it was not he who originated the phrase. It was Herbert Spencer in his scientific treatise *The Principles of Biology*.

Charles Darwin, the son of a country doctor, went to Edinburgh University in 1825 to study medicine but dropped out because he hated the sight of blood. He transferred to Christ's College, Cambridge to study for the ministry at his father's request but after graduating in 1831 Darwin signed up as a naturalist on the ship *Beagle* rather than become a minister.

Dassin, Jules

Jules Dassin, director of film classics like *Rififi* and *Never on Sunday*, is not French or Greek as some people think. Dassin was born in Middletown, Connecticut and was raised in the Harlem and Bronx sections of New York City. He moved to Europe during the McCarthy era.

Dassin appeared in both *Rififi and Never on Sunday* as an actor.

Davies, Marion

Marion Davies was born Marion Cecilia Douras. Her older sister Reine was the first to take the stage name of Davies. Marion related the story in her posthumously published autobiography *The Times We Had:* "My sister Reine wanted to have a stage name. One day, while driving from her place on Long Island, she saw a real estate sign: DAVIES REAL ESTATE. She thought, 'That's me.' We all took on the name automatically." (J. Clarence Davies, the real estate agent whose sign Reine Douras had seen, was from the Netherlands where his name was originally Davries!)

Davis, Adelle

The late nutritionist became interested in health foods at an early age and for an unusual reason. When Adelle was only ten days old her mother became paralyzed and could no longer breast-feed her. Adelle was then fed from an eyedropper (bottle feeding was unknown in 1904) which, according to her, caused a deprivation in her oral stage of development and created an abnormal interest in good nutrition in her adult life.

Davis, Angela

Angela Davis was the most decorated Girl Scout in the history of Alabama and also graduated

Phi Beta Kappa from Brandeis University in 1965.

Her brother Ben played professional football with the Cleveland Browns and Detroit Lions.

Davis, Bette

In 1953 doctors found that actress Bette Davis had osteomyelitis of the jaw and required surgery. Almost half of her jaw was removed but extensive plastic surgery enabled Miss Davis to recover with hardly a visible trace of the operation.

Her full name is Ruth Elizabeth Davis, but the Warner Bros. movie studio wanted to change her name to "Bettina Dawes." The actress complained that she did not want to go through life as "Between the Drawers" so they compromised with the name "Bette Davis."

Davis, Jefferson

Jefferson Davis was Zachary Taylor's son-in-law. The president of the Confederate States of America married Taylor's daughter Sarah who, incidentally, died three months after the day of their wedding.

Davis, Sammy Jr.

Movie mogul Samuel Goldwyn was not quite sure how to handle Sammy Davis: "Directors I can fight. Fire on the set I can fight. Writers, even actors I can fight. But a Jewish colored fellow. This I can't fight."

In 1933 eight-year-old Sammy Davis, Jr. made his movie debut in *Rufus Jones for President* in which he played a little boy who falls asleep in his mother's lap and dreams that he becomes president of the United States.

In an interview with *People* magazine, Davis admitted that he had an isolated homosexual experience at age 17 in the U.S. Army.

Dawber, Pam

The Mindy of the *Mork and Mindy* television series was asked to wear a padded brassiere for the show by the executive producer but she refused to comply.

The actress appeared in Neet hair remover and Tupperware television commercials earlier in her career.

Dawn, Hazel

Before her London stage debut in 1909, actress Hazel Letout was given her new name by impresario Paul Reubens. Like most Dawns she rose to the occasion and became a popular performer on the British stage.

Dawson, Richard

The television personality ("Hogan's Heroes," "Family Feud") joined the British merchant marines at age 14.

Day, Doris

Doris Day's frequent co-star Rock Hudson calls her Eunice and she calls him Ernie for reasons not known.

Doris Day (nee Kappelhof) was given her first name by her mother who admired silent screen actress Doris Kenyon. She was named Doris Day by nightclub owner Barney Rapp who felt that Doris needed a shorter name. He picked the name Day because Doris's rendition of the song "Day by Day" was very popular in her nightclub act and because it went well with her first name. (Barney's real name was Rappoport and the first name he suggested for Doris was Kapps!)

Day, Laraine

Born Laraine Johnson, the actress took the stage surname "Day" to honor Elias Day, the manager of the Long Beach Playhouse, under whom she apprenticed.

Laraine Day has a twin brother named Lamar.

Dean, Dizzy

Born Jay Hanna Dean, the baseball player was named Jay after mogul Jay Gould and Hanna after publisher Mark Hanna. He acquired the name Dizzy in 1930 from a major league manager who, after seeing Dean clown around on the baseball field, called him a "dizzy" kid.

James Dean's first professional acting job was in a Coca Cola commercial in the early 1950s. The commercial took place at a merry-go-round and in it Dean handed out Cokes to actors and actresses circling by him. Dean was picked for the commercial because he looked like a typical all-American boy.

Dean didn't have any front teeth and had to wear a special bridge to cover up the gap. Occasionally, to shock people, he would flash a smile without the bridge, revealing a strange, menacing look.

James Dean's first movie was *Has Anybody Seen My Gal?*, released in 1951, four years before *East of Eden.*

In 1953 Dean turned down a part in the movie *The Silver Chalice* in order to act in television plays. The role was given to Paul Newman who then made his movie debut.

In late 1955 James Dean filmed a television commercial about driving safety. Responding to questions posed by actor Gig Young, Dean told viewers, "People say racing is dangerous, but I'd rather take my chances on the track any day than on the highway.... Drive safely, because the life you save may be *mine.*" A few weeks later, James Dean died in a car crash while driving his Porsche Spyder to a racing competition in Salinas, California. Two hours before the accident, he was given a ticket for speeding.

Debs, Eugene V.

While in prison in 1920 for violating the Espionage Act, Debs ran for the U.S. presidency on the Socialist ticket and received 915,302 votes!

The Socialist, union leader and former locomotive engineer was an alcoholic.

Dee, Ruby

The actress's real name is Ruby Ann Wallace.

Defoe, Daniel

Daniel Defoe, author of *Robinson Crusoe*, was the son of James Foe, an English butcher and tallow-chandler. The writer added the "De" to his surname to avoid the negative connotations of the word "foe."

The original title of Defoe's most famous book was *The Life and Strange Surprising Adventures of Robinson Crusoe.*

DeGaulle, Charles

The great French leader, in a moment of frustration, once asked, "How can you govern a nation that has 350 kinds of cheese?"

De Havilland, Olivia

Olivia De Havilland and her sister Joan Fontaine were born in Tokyo, Japan where their British father, William Augustus De Havilland, was teaching law courses.

The two actresses are descendants of Sir Peter De Havilland, the supporter of Cromwell against Charles I of England.

In a fit of playful but misdirected ardor, actor Errol Flynn once put a dead snake in Miss De Havilland's panties.

Della Femina, Jerry

Although Jerry Della Femina is chairman of a $100 million advertising agency and a talented copywriter, he flunked the only copywriting course he ever took in college. To add insult to injury, the professor who flunked him applied for a job at Della Femina's agency several years ago. (He was not hired!)

Del Rio, Dolores

The Mexican-born actress, born Lolita Dolores Martinez Asunsolo Lopez, became Dolores Del Rio, not after a movie studio renamed her but after she married lawyer Jaime Del Rio in 1921.

DeMille, Agnes

The well-known choreographer was the daughter of film producer William DeMille, the niece of Cecil B. DeMille, and the granddaughter of American economist Henry George.

Demosthenes

The Athenian orator and statesman may have cured most of his speech problems by putting pebbles in his mouth but after all was said and done he was still unable to pronounce the Greek equivalent of the letter "r."

Dempsey, Jack

In his first fight, William Harrison Dempsey used the name "Kid Blackie."

The "Manassa Mauler" used to wash his face in brine to help make it tough.

Dempsey was not the only boxing champion named Jack Dempsey. In 1884 the middle-weight boxing champion was named Jack "Non-pareil" Dempsey, no relation to the other Dempsey.

Dempsey was rarely afraid of anybody but one fear object was not a big man. "There was one man—he was even smaller than I—I wouldn't fight because I knew he would flatten me. I was afraid of Sam Langford."

Dempsey's brother John, a drug addict, killed himself and his estranged wife three days before Jack fought Jack Sharkey.

De Niro, Robert

The movie actor is half-Italian, half-Jewish, and is married to a black woman.

De Niro's nickname in the Little Italy section of New York City, where he grew up, was "Bobby Milk" because he was thin and pale as milk.

De Niro's first movie, released in 1970, was *Hi Mom*.

Dennis, Patrick

Author Edward Everett Tanner III wrote under two pen names: Patrick Dennis and Virginia Rowans. As Patrick Dennis, he wrote his most famous book *Auntie Mame*. As Virginia Rowans, he wrote *Oh, What a Wonderful Wedding, House Party,* and *The Loving Couple*.

Dent, Bucky

Born Russell Earl O'Dey (O'Dey is his mother's maiden name—she divorced her husband before Bucky was born) in Savannah, Georgia, the future baseball player was sent to live with his aunt Sarah and uncle James Earl Dent in Florida. Bucky grew up thinking that his real mother was his aunt but when he found out the truth he spent 15 years searching for his real father—whom he finally found . . . Russell Stanford, an upholsterer in Savannah, Georgia.

Denver, John

The singer started off life on a high—he was born on New Year's Eve, 1943.

He shortened his name from Henry John Deutschendorf, Jr. because a record producer didn't think his real name would fit on a record label!

Denver revealed on "The Tonight Show" that he is missing two toes on his right foot but he didn't explain how he lost the toes.

Dern, Bruce

Dern was kicked off the track team at the University of Pennsylvania for wearing long sideburns.

Dern's grandfather George H. Dern was Secretary of War in Franklin D. Roosevelt's administration and was also governor of Utah. His father was a law partner of Adlai Stevenson.

The actor starred in the movie *The Incredible Two-Headed Transplant* in 1970 but was never paid for it. The movie was shot in six days, after which Dern was given a check for $1,700 but the check bounced. To this day he has never received any money for making the movie.

Dern's daughter accidentally drowned in the family swimming pool when a nurse left the child for a few minutes to answer a phone.

De Valera, Eamon

Eamon De Valera was not born in Ireland but in New York City. He and his family moved to Ireland when he was three years old.

Devane, William

When actor William Devane (*Family Plot, The Missiles of October*) was born, his father was a chauffeur for Franklin D. Roosevelt, then governor of New York.

De Vega, Lope

The Spanish poet and playwright started writing plays at age seven and wrote almost 1,800 plays in his lifetime. DeVega was a compulsive writer, averaging 20 pages of writing per day. He also claimed that 100 of his plays were staged within 24 hours of his writing them.

Dickens, Charles

Dickens's best friend in his youth was named Bob Fagin, a name he used in *Oliver Twist*.

Charles Dickens was such a devoted writer that he even named his sons after famous British writers. Among his sons were Henry Fielding Dickens, Alfred Tennyson Dickens, and Edward Bulwer Lytton Dickens.

Dickens coined the phrase "as good as gold." It appeared in *A Christmas Carol* but in the context it referred to Tiny Tim's behavior ("As good as gold . . . and better. Somehow he gets thoughtful, sitting by himself so much, and thinks the strangest things you ever heard.")

Dickey, James

Before James Dickey became a well-known poet and author (*Deliverance*) he was a copywriter at several Atlanta advertising agencies and heralded the virtues of products like Coca Cola, Delta Airlines, potato chips, and a fertilizer account.

Dickinson, Angie

Angie Dickinson's maiden name was Angeline Brown but at Glendale College (Calif.) she met and married Gene Dickinson, a star player on the Glendale football team.

Dickinson, Emily

The "Belle of Amherst" (also known as "The Nun of Amherst") wrote about 1,800 poems in her lifetime but only three of them were published while she was alive. Only after her death did her poetry become well known to the outside world.

Dietrich, Marlene

Marlene was born Maria Magdalene Dietrich and not von Losch as some sources erroneously report. She acquired the new last name von Losch after her father died and her mother married Colonel Edward von Losch, an army officer, a few years later. The name "Marlene" was a combination of the first part (Mar) of her first name and the last part (lene) of her middle name.

Dietz, Howard

The movie studio executive and songwriter created the MGM trademark of the roaring lion and the slogan "Ars Gratia Artis" (Art for Art's Sake). He got the idea from the laughing lion decoration on the cover of *The Jester*, a Columbia University humor magazine.

Dillman, Bradford

The movie actor (*Compulsion, Escape from Planet of the Apes*) never changed his name because, in his words, "Bradford Dillman sounded like a distinguished phony theatrical name so I liked it and kept it."

Di Maggio, Joe

Joe Di Maggio's marriage to Marilyn Monroe was so publicized that it tended to obscure the fact that the Yankee Clipper had once been married before . . . to another beautiful, blonde Hollywood actress named Dorothy Arnold, whom he married in 1939.

After Marilyn Monroe's first date with Joe Di Maggio she was asked how she liked him. The actress complained, "He struck out!" Di Maggio, however, was used to getting more than one chance at the batter's box and kept asking her out until she finally gave him another swing. Apparently he hit a home run his second time up because they soon got married.

According to Lefty Gómez, Joe Di Maggio used to be an avid reader of Superman comic books but was always afraid to buy them at newsstands for fear of being recognized.

When the Yankee slugger ended his hitting streak at 56 consecutive games in 1941, setting a major league record, it cost him $10,000 because the Heinz 57 people were ready to make a deal with him for $10,000 if he reached 57 straight games.

Dionne Quintuplets

The world-famous quintuplets appeared in two movies: *Reunion* and *The Country Doctor,* both of which were released in 1936.

Dirksen, Everett

The late Illinois senator was not given a middle name at birth but 11 months later his father, pleased that Republican William McKinley had just been elected president, gave baby Everett the middle name of McKinley.

Dirksen, sometimes referred to as the "Wizard of Ooze," used to say that "the oilcan is mightier than the sword."

Disney, Walt

According to Walter Wagner in *You Must Remember This*, Disney once confessed, "I love Mickey Mouse more than any woman I've ever known."

Movie director Alfred Hitchcock made an interesting observation about the famous animator: "Disney, of course, has the best casting. If he doesn't like an actor he just tears him up."

Disney once killed an owl. He was trying to capture it but the owl fought back and, in a panic, Disney stomped it to death. It was the only time he ever killed an animal.

Disney won more Oscars than any other person in the movie industry—he won 17 Oscars from 1931 to 1969 (some posthumously).

Disraeli, Benjamin

Disraeli, a distinguished statesman and novelist, was known to have a bad case of body odor. It is believed that he suffered from ozenia which is a disease characterized by a fetid nasal discharge.

The family name was originally spelled D'Israeli. His father was from the Jewish colony of Cento in Ferrara, Italy.

Disraeli, best remembered as a statesman, began his career at age 23 as a novelist when he wrote the roman à clef *Vivien Grey.*

Because Jews (as defined by religion) were excluded from parliament until 1858, Disraeli's career might have taken another turn had not his father baptized his children as Christians in 1817 after a feud with his Sephardic synagogue.

Dominguin, Luis Miguel

Spanish bullfighter Luis Miguel Gonzalez Lucas took his new last name from his father who, also a bullfighter, was the first "Dominguin."

Donahue, Troy

Troy Donahue appeared in the movie *The Godfather II* as a character named Merle Johnson which is Troy's real name.

Donleavy, J. P.

The American-born (Brooklyn) Irish writer studied bacteriology at Trinity College, Dublin, with the goal of becoming a doctor.

The writer is called Michael by his family and friends. Michael is his confirmation name.

Donleavy, once admitting that he did not read much as a child, said that his major reading material was "The Katzenjammer Kids" comic strip.

Dors, Diana

The buxom British blonde bombshell's real name is Diana "Daisy" Fluck but she changed her name for obvious reasons.

At 16 years of age Miss Dors appeared in the 1948 British movie *Oliver Twist.*

Dostoevski, Fyodor

The Russian writer made his stage debut in a benefit performance of *The Inspector General* on April 14, 1860. As Shpyokin, the postmaster, Dostoevski was "a subtle comedian, capable of evoking purely Gogolian laughter" according to P.I. Weinberg, the director.

Doubleday, Abner

Doubleday is often but erroneously credited with being the founder of baseball. No evidence whatsoever exists to justify this conclusion. Doubleday, a West Point graduate (1842) was a major general in the Civil War and fought with distinction at the Battle of Gettysburg.

Doubleday, Frank Nelson

Rudyard Kipling gave the publisher the nickname of "Effendi" which was Arabic for "chief" and also resembled his initials F.N.D. The name stuck and even his friends started calling him Effendi.

Douglas, Michael

The actor ("The Streets of San Francisco") and producer (*One Flew Over the Cuckoo's Nest, China Syndrome*) became a gas station attendant in Westport, Connecticut, after dropping out of college, and once won the Mobil Man of the Month award.

Douglas, Mike

Talk show host Mike Douglas did the singing voice of Prince Charming in Walt Disney's movie *Cinderella* but never received onscreen credit for it.

Mike is an excellent golf player. In 1974 he played a match with Jack Nicklaus in the Jackie Gleason tournament in Florida and carded a 73, while Nicklaus shot a 71. According to a photographer on the course, Nicklaus told his caddy, "This guy's a damn pro!"

Mike's real name is Michael Delaney Dowd, Jr.

Johnny Carson is generally regarded as the talk show king, but actually Mike Douglas has been on the air one year longer than Carson. Douglas's show was first aired in 1961. As of September 1980, Mike has taped over 4,750 shows.

Douglass, Frederick

Born Frederick Augustus Washington Bailey, he changed his name to Frederick Douglass when he left Maryland to go to New Bedford, Massachusetts. A friend and admirer of Sir Walter Scott's *Lady of the Lake* suggested the name Douglass to him.

Douglass was the first black nominated for U.S. president—at the convention in Chicago in June 1888. On the fourth ballot he received only one complimentary vote. On the eighth ballot the convention nominated Benjamin Harrison who went on to become the 23rd president.

Dowling, Eddie

The actor-playwright-director-producer was born Joseph Nelson Goucher. At 10 years old, he ran away from home and adopted the name Eddie Dowling, the "Dowling" being his mother's maiden name and the "Eddie" being for no particular reason. He changed his name mostly because, as the son of a French-Canadian father, he was called "canuck" and wanted to avoid that kind of epithet.

Downs, Hugh

Because Hugh Downs is color blind, he has numbered tags sewn into his clothes so he can wear the right combination of colors.

Doyle, A. Conan

A. Conan Doyle originally was going to name his fictional detective Sherrinford Holmes (Holmes being from author and physician Oliver Wendell Holmes) but, deciding that the name sounded awkward, settled on the name Sherlock.

The creator of Sherlock Holmes was a medical doctor who opened a practice in ophthalmology at 2 Devonshire Place in London but failed to attract a single patient. After starting the Holmes stories, however, he didn't need any patients.

Drake, Alfred

The popular stage actor (*Kiss Me Kate*), born Alfredo Capurro, has appeared in only one movie, *Tars and Spars* in 1944.

Dreyfuss, Richard

Dreyfuss had a walk-on part in *The Graduate*. He muttered a few lines to Dustin Hoffman while he was shaving.

Dubinsky, David

The labor leader's last name was originally Dobnievski but he decided to simplify the name.

Duchin, Eddie

The pianist and bandleader, a graduate of the Massachusetts College of Pharmacy, was going to be a pharmacist but when he started making more money playing the piano on weekends than he made in the drugstore during the week he decided to devote all his time to the piano.

Duchin, Peter

After Peter Duchin was graduated from Hotchkiss and Yale but before he became the popular orchestra leader and socialite, he was a U.S. Army enlisted man (sp/4) who played the glockenspiel in the post band at the Panama Canal Zone base.

Duchamp, Marcel

The abstract painter (*Nude Descending a Staircase*) is the brother of another famous painter, Jacques Villon, who changed his name from Gaston Duchamp.

Duke, Vernon

Composer Vernon Duke wrote both classical and popular music, using his real name, Vladimir Dukelsky, for serious music and the name Vernon Duke for his popular music. As Vladimir Dukelsky he composed the ballet *Zephyr et Flore*, several symphonies, and numerous concertos and sonatas for piano, violin, and cello. As Vernon Duke, he wrote popular songs like "April in Paris," "I Can't Get Started With You," and also wrote the music for the Broadway show *Cabin in the Sky*. He was given the name Vernon Duke by George Gershwin, one of his friends and idols.

Dullea, Keir

Dullea has seen the movie *2001: A Space Odyssey* 17 times, not to see his own performance but to admire Stanley Kubrick's direction.

Dumas, Alexandre

The author of *The Three Musketeers* and *The Count of Monte Cristo* was born Alexandre Davy de la Pailleterie. His grandmother was Marie Cessette Dumas, a black Haitian woman, and his grandfather was Antoine Alexandre Davy, marquis de la Pailleterie, an aristocrat. When political differences arose between his grandfather and Napoleon, he left his family and the country, at which time they adopted the surname of the grandmother.

Dumont, Margaret

The movie comedienne, featured in many Marx Brothers' movies, was bald and wore wigs (which Harpo Marx took delight in hiding!).

Miss Dumont was born Daisy Baker in Atlanta, Georgia and grew up in the house of her godfather Joel Chandler Harris, the creator of Uncle Remus and Br'er Rabbit.

Duran, Roberto

The young Panamanian boxing champion loves to pound on the bongos in his leisure time. In fact, he owns $20,000 worth of bongo drums!

Durant, Will and Ariel

Ariel's real name is Ida Kaufman. Will originally called her Puck but renamed her Ariel because "she was as strong and brave as a boy and as swift and mischievous as an elf"—like the character in Shakespeare's play *The Tempest*.

The historians were married when Ariel was 14 years old and Will was 27 years old. The day of their marriage Ariel took roller skates with her and, after the ceremony, tried to teach Will how to skate. (She was unsuccessful!)

Durant became a vegetarian and took daily enemas after being influenced by Dr. John Harvey Kellogg, the Battle Creek, Michigan health faddist and cereal pioneer. Durant says that the Kellogg regimen cured him of arthritis and has helped him stay healthy (he's 94 years old!).

Dylan, Bob

Dylan was once expelled from a college English class for using four-letter words to describe his professor.

Bob Dylan was brought to the attention of Columbia Records in 1961 when he was hired to play the harmonica accompaniment for a friend who was then cutting a record for Columbia. Dylan impressed the Columbia executives so much that he was signed up to record for them.

The first song Dylan ever wrote was a ballad to French sex kitten Brigitte Bardot.

At Hibbing High School in Minnesota, Dylan wore his hair in the same way rock singer Little Richard wore his—the rock singer was Dylan's idol.

Dylan's real name is Robert Allen Zimmerman. He took the name Dylan, according to Anthony Scaduto, because: "I needed a name in a hurry and I picked that one. It just came to me as I was standing in The Scholar (a coffeehouse in Minneapolis). He asked me how he should bill me and the name just came to me. Wasn't Dylan Thomas at all, it just came to me. I knew about Dylan Thomas, of course, but I didn't deliberately pick his name." (Note: The folksinger's middle name, Allen, is similar in sound and structure to the name Dylan.)

Dvorak, Ann

Born Ann McKim, the popular leading lady of the 1930's was the daughter of stage actress Anna Lehr and silent movie director Sam McKim. At first she used the stage name Anna Lehr but later settled on the name Dvorak, which was her mother's maiden name.

E

Earp, Wyatt

Wyatt Berry Stapp Earp moonlighted as a faro dealer at the Long Branch Saloon to make some extra money.

Earp's wife was Jewish. The former Josephine Marcus met Earp in Tombstone, Arizona where she was one of the few Jewish dancehall girls.

Eastwood, Clint

The spaghetti-western hero's first two movies were *The Revenge of the Creature* and *Francis Joins the Navy*.

Eban, Abba

Abba Eban's name at birth was Abba Solomon. After Eban's father died, the family moved from South Africa to London where Abba's mother became a secretary for a Zionist organization. In England Abba used the first name Aubrey which was the closest English name to his original name, and was therefore known as Aubrey Solomon. When his mother married

Dr. Isaac Eban, a London radiologist, Aubrey took the last name of his stepfather and became Aubrey S. Eban. Finally, when Israel became an independent state, Eban followed the Israeli custom and changed his first name back to Abba, thus becoming Abba Eban.

Ebsen, Buddy

Christian Rudolf "Buddy" Ebsen was originally the Tin Woodsman in the movie *The Wizard of Oz* but when his lungs collapsed from inhaling the aluminum dust makeup that was sprayed on him, he was replaced by Jack Haley (and a safer kind of makeup!).

Eddy, Mary Baker

Mary Baker Eddy was the only woman ever to have started a religion.

When Mary Baker Eddy died at age 90, she left an estate of $3 million.

Eddy, Nelson

Nelson Eddy is best remembered for his movie appearances with Jeanette MacDonald, obscuring the fact that he was an opera singer who made his debut at the Metropolitan Opera at the age of 23.

Eddy was a descendant of the eighth president of the United States, Martin van Buren.

Eddy was a copywriter for the N.W. Ayer advertising agency but was fired when the agency realized that he was more interested in singing than in writing copy for advertisements.

When the Statue of Liberty was built, Edison wanted to give the statue a voice by inserting a large phonograph in the mouth with the expectation that the voice could be heard throughout the New York harbor.

Although he shunned cigarettes, he smoked 20 cigars a day and also chewed tobacco whenever he could.

Edison established the world's first movie studio at Menlo Park, New Jersey and it was there that *The Great Train Robbery* was filmed.

He was called Al or Alva by his family and "Popsy Wopsy" by his first wife.

Edison had occasional failures, especially early in his life. When he was 15 years old he was experimenting with a battery and blew up a telegraph station. One year later, he derailed a train when he forgot to set a danger signal.

Most people are unaware that Edison was highly motivated by money. He once said, "Anything that won't sell, I don't want to invent."

Highly curious and sometimes careless, the inventor almost killed a friend once by pumping gas into his lungs to see if he would float.

A dyslexic, Edison received only three months of formal schooling in his lifetime. His mother withdrew him from the first grade after his teacher accused him of being "addled" and a daydreamer.

Before his death Edison had been granted 1,098 different patents from the United States Patent

Office, a record unsurpassed by any other inventor. The estimated value of his inventions at the time of his death was an incredible $25,683,544,343!

Edwards, Blake

Blake Edwards became addicted to drugs during World War II after receiving morphine injections to ease the pain of a broken back and neck. Edwards kicked the habit, though, after experimenting with marijuana and mescaline, and has become one of the most successful writer-producer-directors in Hollywood today.

His real name is William Blake McEdwards.

Eisenhower, Dwight D.

The U.S. general and 34th president was born David Dwight Eisenhower but changed his given names around just before attending West Point because he was always called Dwight by his parents.

Because of his fair complexion, Ike was also nicknamed Swede as a youth.

At Abilene High School in Kansas, Ike's classmates predicted that he would become a professor of history at Yale.

Eisenhower originally wanted to go to Annapolis but he was too old to enroll (he was 20 years old at the time) so he accepted a senatorial appointment to the United States Military Academy which had different age requirements.

At West Point Ike badly injured his knee trying to tackle Jim Thorpe.

An avid golfer, Eisenhower made a hole-in-one at the Seven Lake Country Club in Palm Springs, California, on February 6, 1968. (He was 77 at the time!) One of his foursome was Freeman Gosden from the old "Amos 'n' Andy" radio show.

Ike was the oldest President at the time he left office. He was 70 years and 98 days old at the time.

Ike was once demoted from Sergeant to Private at West Point for "wild dancing." (His partner was not Mamie!)

Ike had a pilot's license and was the only president to have one.

Einstein, Albert

Einstein's amazing brain is preserved in a mason jar in a laboratory in Wichita, Kansas. Before his death Einstein requested that his brain be studied and Dr. Thomas Harvey, a former chief pathologist at Princeton University, intends to fulfill the genius's request.

As a college professor, Einstein went to class without wearing socks.

Abba Eban offered Einstein the chance to be president of Israel in 1952 but the physicist declined on the grounds that he didn't think he could work well with other people.

Einstein once used a $1500 check (from the Rockefeller Foundation!) for a bookmark and then misplaced the book.

Einstein once said, "If I had it to do all over again I would be a plumber."

Although Einstein couldn't swim he loved to go out sailing for hours, refusing to take life belts or preservers with him.

The Internal Revenue Service should take note. Einstein once remarked that "the hardest thing in the world is to understand the income tax."

Eliot, George

Novelist George Eliot originally wrote under her real name (Mary Anne Evans), occasionally changing the spelling of her first name. After falling in love with George Henry Lewes, a journalist and critic, who encouraged her to concentrate on fiction writing, Mary Anne decided to take a pen name to preserve her identity and to secure "all the advantages without the disagreeables of reputation." She chose the name George Eliot because, in her words, "George was Mr. Lewes's Christian name, and Eliot was a good mouth-filling, easily pronounced word."

George Eliot's head was so large that it fascinated phrenologists!

Eliot, T. S.

The writer was a British citizen but he was born in St. Louis, Missouri, of parents originally from Boston, Massachusetts.

Elizabeth I, Queen of England

After surviving a case of smallpox, the queen became completely bald at the age of 29.

Queen Elizabeth I received as a gift the first silk stockings ever made.

Ellington, Duke

Jazz musician and bandleader Edward Kennedy Ellington was given the nickname Duke by a grammar school friend, Edgar McEntree, who was socially ambitious enough to want his best friend, a man of royal deportment, to have the title "Duke."

Ellsburg, Daniel

Daniel Ellsberg ("Pentagon Papers") went to Harvard College on a four-year scholarship awarded to him by the Pepsi-Cola Company.

Emerson, Ralph Waldo

The phrase "Hitch your wagon to a star" first appeared in Emerson's moral essay "Civilization." The context was as follows: ". . . 'It was a great instruction,' said a saint in Cromwell's war, 'that the best courages are but beams of the Almighty.' Hitch your wagon to a star. Let us not fag in paltry works which serve out pot and bag alone. Let us not lie and steal. . . Work rather for those interests which the divinities honor and promote,—justice, love, freedom, knowledge, utility."

Erhard, Werner

Warner Erhard, the founder of est, was born John Paul Rosenberg but allegedly changed his name to avoid discovery by his wife and family whom he had deserted. Being an ardent follower of the German philosopher Nietzsche, Rosenberg sought out a good, German-sounding name and found many such names in an *Esquire* article entitled, "The Men Who Made the New Germany." Two of the men featured in the article were Ludwig *Erhard*, the Minister of Economics, and *Werner* Heisenberg (not Werner von Braun, as some claim), originator of the "Uncertainty Principle." It is from these two men that Rosenberg took his new name Werner Erhard.

"Est" originally stood for "electronic social transformation" and was a term coined by L. Clark Stevens, author of *est: The Steersman Handbook*, a book which was brought to Erhard's attention before he founded his own est —Erhard Seminar Training.

Erhard's parents were originally Jewish but joined the Episcopal Church. He was brought up as an Episcopalian—not Jewish, as some people think.

In the mid-1950s, Erhard used the alias Jack Frost, when he worked as a car salesman (among other sales jobs) in Philadelphia.

Erikson, Erik

Erikson, the noted psychoanalyst and author of *Childhood and Society*, attributed his special interest in identity and childhood development to the discovery that Dr. Theodor Homberger the man who raised him, was his stepfather and not his natural father. Erikson's mother explained to him that she separated from his real father before his birth and several years later married Dr. Homberger who legally adopted young Erik.

Ervin, Sam Jr.

The North Carolina senator was a World War I hero in France. He was wounded twice and was twice cited for gallantry. His war decorations included the Silver Star, the Distinguished Service Cross, the United Daughters of the Confederacy's Cross of Military Service, a Purple Heart with one oak leaf cluster and the French Fouragere. After the war he received some Yankee learning at Harvard Law School and then returned to North Carolina to become "just a poor country lawyer."

Erving, Julius

According to Julius Erving, here is how he got his nickname "Dr. J.": "I had a friend, Leon Saunders, who had a habit of . . . lecturing people so I called him the professor. After that, he started calling me 'The Doctor.' It had something to do with the saying 'He has more moves than Carter has pills.' Somehow medicine got connected with it and Leon came up with 'The Doctor'." When he later became a professional basketball player, the nickname was shortened to "Dr. J."

Evans, Robert

The suave, smooth-talking movie producer and former garment company (Evan-Picone) executive used to be an actor on radio programs like

"Henry Aldrich" and "Archie Andrews" in the late 1940s.

The former production chief at Paramount studios was born Robert Shapera, the son of a New York dentist.

Evert, Chris

The diamond necklace (on which the name "Babe" appeared) that she used to wear was given to her by actor Burt Reynolds, a former boyfriend.

Ewbank, Weeb

The great football coach, born Wilbur Charles Ewbank, was given his nickname Weeb by a younger brother who could not pronounce the first name Wilbur.

Ewell, Tom

Born Yewell Tompkins in Owensboro, Kentucky, Ewell started to pursue a law career and attended the University of Wisconsin Law School but left with classmate Dominic Amici (later Don Ameche) in 1931 to become a stage actor. His stage name is a shortened version of his real name reversed (i.e., *Tom*kins *Y*ewell).

F

Fabray, Nanette

Nanette Fabray is one of few women in Holly-wood to undergo plastic surgery to make her nose *larger*.

Miss Fabray was not an "Our Gang" comedies regular as is often said and written. She was an extra and appeared in few of the movies.

Her last name was originally spelled Fabares but television host Ed Sullivan, who could not pronounce it, simplified it to Fabray.

Fairbanks, Douglas

The dashing actor's real name was Douglas Elton Thomas Ulman. His father, Charles Ulman, a mining speculator, was his mother's third husband. Ulman was also a Shakespearean scholar and was said to have stimulated Doug's interest in the theater. After divorcing Ulman for desertion, Doug's mother, Ella, reassumed the surname of her first husband, John Fairbanks, a New Orleans plantation owner. The two Ulman sons also adopted the name and Douglas Ulman became Douglas Fairbanks.

The athletic, swashbuckling actor inspired writer Jerry Siegel and artist Joe Shuster to create the comic strip character Superman. It was especially Fairbanks's portrayal of Robin Hood that gave the team the idea. (Clark Kent was based on the bespectacled Joe Shuster who now is legally blind.)

Falk, Peter

Falk was often discouraged from pursuing a movie career because of his glass right eye (which he received after his real eye was removed because of a malignant tumor—at age three) and in fact Harry Cohn, head of Columbia Pictures, once rejected Falk for a part because of it.

Falk has an M.A. in Public Administration from Syracuse University and was once an efficiency expert with the Connecticut State Budget Bureau.

Farouk, King

The overweight king was not Egyptian by blood but was predominantly Albanian.

In one of his automobiles the Egyptian king, a gadget freak, installed a horn that imitated the sound of a dog being run over.

Farmer, Fannie

Fannie Farmer became an invalid when she had a stroke while in high school. When she recovered sufficiently her mother sent her to the Boston Cooking School where she became proficient and went on to become a famous cook.

Farr, Jamie

Born Jameel Farah, the actor is the only member of the "M*A*S*H" television series cast who actually served in Korea. (It was not during the Korean War.)

Farr's first movie was *Blackboard Jungle* in which he played the role of Santini.

Farrell, Eileen

Metropolitan Opera singer Eileen Farrell auditioned for the "Major Bowes's Original Amateur Hour" radio program in 1940 but was told by Major Bowes that her voice was not good enough for her to get on the show.

Farrow, Mia

Mia Farrow's godparents are director George Cukor and the late columnist Louella Parsons.

Mia's full name is Maria de Lourdes Villiers Farrow.

She was on the cover of the first *People* magazine back on March 4, 1974. At the time, the movie *The Great Gatsby*, in which she appeared, was getting the full "hype" ("... the year's next big movie ...").

Faulkner, William

The author's last name was originally spelled Falkner (no "u") but he changed the spelling when he published *The Marble Faun* in 1924.

Fawcett, Farrah

The television actress was born with a tumor obstructing her digestive tract and had to be operated on when she was only 28 days old.

Faye, Alice

Born Alice Leppert, she adopted the name Faye as a stage name because Frank Faye was a big star when she was a chorus girl and she felt that the name would bring her good luck—which it did.

Feiffer, Jules

At five years of age Feiffer won a contest sponsored by John Wanamaker's department store in New York City for his drawing of Tom Mix arresting some outlaws.

Feldshuh, Tovah

The Broadway actress (*Yentl, Sarava*) was legally named Terry Feldshuh but adopted the name Tovah (meaning "good" in Hebrew—the name she was given at her synagogue) when she was 17 years old.

Feller, Bob

At only 17 years old, Bob Feller struck out 17 batters in one game in his rookie year with the Cleveland Indians.

Fernandel

The French comedian's real name is Fernand Joseph Desire Contandin. He originally used his father's stage name, Marc Sined, but in 1922 he appeared in Nice, France for the first time as "Fernandel." It was a name given to him by his girlfriend's mother who always referred to him as "Fernand d'elle" or "her Fernand."

Ferrari, Enzo

The Italian auto maker's name comes from the Italian word *ferro*, meaning "iron." He came from the city of Modena, famous for its metal workers and his father, in fact, owned an iron shop there.

Ferrer, Jose

The actor-director studied architecture for five years at Princeton University where he also organized a 14-piece band called Jose Ferrer and His Pied Pipers.

Ferrer, Mel

Mel Ferrer was born Melchior Gaston Ferrer, son of a New York socialite and physician Dr. Jose Ferrer. He is not related to the actor Jose Ferrer. Mel's family was from Cuba and Jose's came from Puerto Rico.

Like Jose Ferrer, Mel also attended Princeton University but Mel dropped out in his sophomore year to become an actor and writer.

In the early 1940s Ferrer's career was interrupted when he was found to have polio. While recuperating in Mexico, Mel wrote a children's book entitled *Tito's Hats*.

173

Ferrigno, Lou

The muscle man star of television's popular series "The Incredible Hulk" is hard of hearing due to an ear infection he developed at age three. The ailment caused a slight slur in his speech but it has not affected his current acting performance—he has no speaking lines.

Fiedler, Arthur

Arthur Fiedler used to refer to Beethoven's Fifth Symphony as a "fifth of Beethoven."

Fiedler was a bachelor for 50 years before marrying Ellen Bottomley, a Boston socialite. He was also conductor of the Boston Pops Orchestra for 50 years.

His recording of "Jalousie" was the first symphony orchestra record to sell over a million copies.

The conductor once did an ad for Black and White Scotch, although he didn't drink scotch—he was a sherry drinker.

Before he died, he had survived four heart attacks and major brain surgery.

Fiedler's last name is the German word for "fiddler" and that is how the family acquired the name. He came from generations of musicians, especially violinists and, in fact, his father, Emanuel Fiedler, played in the first violin section of the Boston Symphony Orchestra when he first came to the United States in 1885.

Field, Dr. Frank

The NBC television weather reporter is an optometrist by training, as is his son Storm Field, a weatherman on WABC-TV in New York.

Fielding, Temple

Temple Fielding, the namesake of Fielding Guides, is a descendant of Sir Isaac Newton and Henry Fielding, the 18th-century author of *Tom Jones* (the Fielding guide to sex and gluttony!).

Fields, Sally

Her stepfather is Jock Mahoney, the actor who played Tarzan in the late 1950s and early 1960s. In fact, Jock was the model for the Brian Keith role in Burt Reynolds's movie *Hooper*.

Her license plates read BR S GRL—for *B*urt *R*eynolds's' *girl* but apparently not for long!

Fields, W. C.

The line, "On the whole, I'd rather be in Philadelphia," does not appear on W. C. Fields's gravestone. In fact, his gravestone at Forest Lawn cemetery does not have any epitaph at all.

On a radio program sponsored by Lucky Strikes, W. C. Fields occasionally mentioned that he had a son named Chester—which was Fields's way of mischievously plugging a rival cigarette brand—Chesterfields.

If the comedian were still alive he would be pleased to know that a Carl La Fong and an

Egbert Souse (no accent *grave*) appear in the 1979–80 Manhattan telephone directory.

Fields's wife, Harriet Hughes, complained that he always ate with a bottle balanced on his head!

Born William Claude Dukenfield, the comedian shortened his last name to Field but theater managers invariably added an "s" so he decided to adopt the name Fields.

His son W. C. Fields, Jr. avoided show business and became a corporate lawyer.

Fields loved to read in the w.c. ("water closet") where he kept all of his books.

Most of W. C. Fields's estate was left to establish the "W. C. Fields College for Orphaned White Boys and Girls Where No Religion of Any Sort Is To Be Preached" but his wife and son contested the will, won the contest, and the college was never founded.

Fillmore, Millard

The 13th president of the U.S. was offered an honorary law degree from Oxford University in England but he refused the honor saying, "I had not the advantage of a classical education and no man should, in my judgment, accept a degree he cannot read." (Fillmore did not go to college, although he taught school for several years. He was admitted to the bar in 1823.)

Fisher, Bobby

The chess expert never graduated from high school.

Fisher, Eddie

Eddie's first name is Edwin, not Edward, as most people assume. His full name is Edwin Jack Fisher.

Under the strain of having seven performances a day in 1953, Eddie Fisher became addicted to "vitamin injections," later found to be methamphetamines (or "speed"), given to him by a "Dr. Feelgood."

The singer also had a weakness for gambling and once lost $125,000 in one night at a casino.

Fiske, John

The popular 19th-century American lecturer and historian was born Edmund Fisk Green but legally changed his name to John Fisk, after a great-grandfather, later adding "e" to the last name.

Fiske, Minnie Maddern

Born Marie Augusta Davey, the actress made her stage debut at age three, using her mother's maiden name Maddern. She became a Fiske when she married playwright Harrison Grey Fiske.

Fitzgerald, Barry

At 41 years old, William Joseph Shields (Fitzgerald's real name) retired from his civil service job and joined Dublin's Abbey Players, taking the stage name Barry Fitzgerald. One year later, he made his film debut in *Juno and the Paycock* (1930).

Fitzgerald, Ella

Ella Fitzgerald wrote the song "A-Tisket, A-Tasket" with bandleader Chick Webb, who discovered her.

Fitzgerald, F. Scott

Fitzgerald never did graduate from Princeton, as some people think, but he was always a loyal alumnus. In fact, he was reading the Princeton alumni magazine when he died.

Although he was in love with Sheilah Graham, Fitzgerald always misspelled her name as Shielah.

As an advertising copywriter after his discharge from the U.S. Army, Fitzgerald wrote the following headline for a midwestern laundry: "We keep you clean in Muscatine."

His wife Zelda was breastfed until she was four years old.

Fitzgerald's alcoholism and craving for sugar and candy was caused by hyperinsulism.

Fitzgerald, Geraldine

James Joyce's sister worked in the law firm of Miss Fitzgerald's father and in his famous book *Ulysses*. Joyce even mentioned the law firm, D. & T. Fitzgerald, by name.

Flack, Roberta

Roberta Flack not only has soul—she has smarts too. She graduated from high school at age 15 and won a scholarship to Howard University where she majored in music and graduated at age 18.

Flaubert, Gustave

The French writer (*Madame Bovary*) was a dyslexic.

Fleming, Ian

Fleming's first book *Casino Royale* sold only 7,000 copies in 1954 when it was first published.

Flood, Daniel J.

The former Pennsylvania congressman's unusual mustache is a carryover from his days as an aspiring actor when he grew the mustache for the role of a plantation owner.

The day Flood went to the Paramount Studios in Hollywood for a screen test was the day Rudolph Valentino was laid to rest. (Paramount liked Flood's profile but questioned his acting ability.)

Flynn, Errol

Flynn, before some of his amorous escapades, used to rub cocaine on his genitals because it heightened his enjoyment of sex.

In one of Flynn's first American movie appearances he didn't even have a "walk-on" part. He played a corpse resting in peace on a marble slab in *The Case of the Curious Bride* (1934).

Flynn was not born in England or Ireland. He was born in Tasmania—which may have accounted for his devilishness.

In his autobiography *My Wicked Wicked Ways*, the notorious womanizer admitted that he once had the unusual job of biting off sheep's testicles at a sheep ranch in Australia. Apparently, he was told, this was the "most sanitary way to deball a sheep." Flynn nonchalantly commented further, "The sheep never let out a bleep. You bit. You spat out something like a couple of olives and passed it on."

On screen Errol Flynn was suave, composed, and confident but off screen he had a "deep inferiority complex," according to David Niven, and even bit his nails.

Actor Robert Donat was originally supposed to play Captain Blood but because of a contract dispute with Donat, Warner Brothers decided to take a chance on newcomer Errol Flynn.

Fonda, Henry

Henry Fonda has appeared in approximately 82 movies in the past 45 years and has been nominated for an Academy Award only once—for his role as Tom Joad in *The Grapes of Wrath* in 1940. That year his close friend James Stewart won for his performance in *The Philadelphia Story*.

Fonda's maternal grandfather was named Henry Jaynes. Henry has a sister named Jayne, his middle name is Jaynes, and his actress daughter's name is Jane (no "y").

Fonda, Jane

When Jane Fonda's mother, Frances Seymour Brokaw, committed suicide in 1950 Jane was told that she died of a heart attack. She found out the truth one year later in a movie gossip magazine article.

Jane's revolutionary tendencies are hereditary. She is a descendant (on her mother's side) of Samuel Adams, a leader of the American Revolution.

Her daughter by Roger Vadim was named Vanessa after actress Vanessa Redgrave, whom she greatly admires.

Fonda, Peter

At age ten and a half, Peter Fonda shot himself in the stomach after finding out that his mother committed suicide.

Fontaine, Joan

Joan's first stage name was Joan Burfield (from the Burfield Street in Hollywood) and appeared in *No More Ladies* (1935) under that name. In her next 12 movies she appeared as either Joan Burfield or Joan St. John. After consulting with a fortune teller, she finally settled on the name Fontaine, which was the surname of her stepfather George M. Fontaine.

Fonteyn, Dame Margot

The English-born ballerina's real name is Margaret Hookman but she adopted her new name for stage purposes. "Margot" is a variation of "Margaret" and "Fonteyn" is an embellishment of her mother's maiden name Fontes.

Ford, Gerald R. Jr.

Ex-president Ford's name at birth was Leslie Lynch King, Jr. Jerry's mother divorced her first husband Leslie Lynch King, a wool dealer, in 1915 and married Gerald Rudolff Ford, a paint salesman, one year later. The future president adopted the name of his new father but later changed the spelling of the middle name to Rudolph, perhaps inspired by the reindeer of that name.

Ford was once a male model and in fact helped start the Conover modeling agency with Harry Conover in New York City. *Look* magazine once did a feature article in which Jerry and his girlfriend, Phyllis Brown, appeared in 21 pictures of "a fashionable couple." He also appeared on the cover of *Cosmopolitan* magazine.

Ford is a 33-degree mason.

Ford, Glenn

The veteran actor is also a veteran of the Vietnam War. He served three months there in 1967 as a briefing officer with the rank of lieutenant colonel.

Born Gwyllyn Samuel Newton Ford in Quebec, Canada, the actor is a descendant of Martin Van Buren, the eighth U.S. president, and is also the nephew of a former prime minister of Canada, Sir John MacDonald.

Ford, Henry

Henry Ford's original ambition was to find a way to produce watches so that they would sell for a dollar a piece but he was sidetracked when his father convinced him to work on the family farm.

After Ford was called an ignoramus by the *Chicago Tribune*, he sued them for a million dollars in damages but was awarded only six cents.

Henry Ford knew how to mass-produce cars but not friends. He once incurred the wrath of the tobacco industry by saying, "Study the history of almost any criminal and you will find an inveterate cigarette smoker."

Ford, Henry II

The former auto executive left Yale College in June 1940 without a degree because it was discovered that his senior thesis was "ghost-written."

Ford, John

The great movie director (*The Grapes of Wrath, How Green Was My Valley*) was born Sean O'Feeny (or O'Fearna) but changed his name to John Ford when he went to Hollywood where his brother Francis had already changed his name to Ford.

Forster, E. M.

The British writer was a homosexual and in fact his novel *Maurice*, written in 1913–1914 but published posthumously, is the story of a young man's discovery of his homosexuality.

Foster, Stephen Collins

Foster was born on July 4, 1826, the same day that John Adams and Thomas Jefferson died. The great American songwriter, whose ambition was to become the "best Ethiopian songwriter," wrote many songs about the South but actually visited the South only once—he went to New Orleans in 1852, the year after he wrote "Swanee River." Originally from Pennsylvania, by the time he settled in New York City, he was an alcoholic living on turnips and apples. He died penniless, lying in a Bowery gutter.

Foxx, Redd

The comedian's real name is John Elroy Sanford. He took the name Fred Sanford in his television series *Sanford and Son* as a tribute to his brother, Fred, who died five years before the series started. (His father's name was Fred, too.)

The names Lamont and Trimel from *Sanford and Son* were also tributes to two of Redd's childhood friends, Lamont Ousley and Steve Trimel, who ran away from home with him in 1939.

Among some black people, a person with light skin and red hair is often called "Red." In Harlem poolhalls, Sanford became known as "Chicago Red" because of his coloring and because he came to New York by way of Chicago. He took his new last name from baseball player Jimmy Foxx whom he admired as a youth.

One of Redd's pool partners in Harlem was "Detroit Red" or Malcolm Little, later known as Malcolm X.

Francis, Arlene

Born Arlene Francis Kazanjian, the actress and radio talk show hostess made her film debut in the 1932 movie *Murders in the Rue Morgue* as a prostitute victimized by Bela Lugosi.

Francis, Connie

Connie Francis's first appearance on television was as an 11-year-old accordion player Concetta Franconero (her real name) on George Scheck's "Startime," a children's variety show. The first time she used the name Connie Francis was on Arthur Godfrey's "Talent Scouts" show on which she won first place.

At age 15 Connie won the New Jersey state typing championship.

Francis, Kay

The movie actress (*Charley's Aunt, The White Angel*) was born Katherine Gibbs but had nothing to do with the secretarial school of that name.

Franklin, Aretha

The blues singer has a son named Kecalf—which is an acronym based on the initials of the boy's father, Ken E. Cunningham, her former road manager, and her initials. The name is pronounced "Kelf."

Franklin, Benjamin

For the United States national emblem, Franklin first wanted a turkey instead of an eagle.

The only schooling Franklin ever received was from age 8 to age 10.

Ben Franklin was the first Postmaster General of the United States.

Franklin is credited with inventing the first rocking chair.

Frazier, Joe

When the heavyweight boxer's father lost his left arm in an accident, Joe in effect became his left arm. His father would hold a bolt with his right hand and Joe would turn the screwdriver.

Freed, Alan

The disc jockey who ushered in the rock 'n' roll era majored in mechanical engineering at Ohio State University, class of 1942.

Freud, Sigmund

Freud was not an alcoholic or opium addict but he did have one habit—he smoked about 20 cigarettes a day.

Freud, who once asked the question "What does a woman want?" was even more perplexed by

American women. During and after his visit to the United States, American women were often the subjects of his erotic dreams and appeared as prostitutes.

Frost, Robert

Frost was so strongly identified with New England that most people don't know that he was born in San Francisco, California and lived in California until he was 11 years old.

Frost's family life was not exactly tranquil—he committed his daughter Irma to an insane asylum and his son committed suicide by shooting himself.

The poet had an interesting way of explaining how banks work: "A bank is a place where they lend you an umbrella in fair weather and ask for it back again when it begins to rain."

According to some biographers, Frost was a chronic liar. He always pretended to be poor when in fact he inherited a sizable amount of money from his grandfather. He also inherited a farm but contrary to his rustic image, he hated farming.

Frost's given names Robert Lee were bestowed upon him because his father, a newspaper editor, was sympathetic to the South during the Civil War.

Robert Frost won the Pulitzer Prize for poetry four times: in 1943 for *A Witness Tree,* in 1924 for *New Hampshire: A Poem with Notes and*

Grace Notes, in 1931 for *Collected Poems*, and in 1937 for *A Further Range*.

Fulbright, J. William

The Fulbright scholarships for study abroad received their name from this Arkansas senator not because he started an endowed trust with his own money, but because he introduced the senate legislation to launch the student exchange program.

Fuller, Buckminster

At last look, Fuller had the longest entry in *Who's Who*—139 lines or 116 more lines than Richard M. Nixon's entry.

Fuller's paternal great-aunt, Margaret Fuller, was a well-known trancendentalist and friend of Ralph Waldo Emerson.

After leaving Harvard College, Fuller briefly attended the United States Naval Academy in 1917.

Funt, Allen

Allen Funt thought up the idea for "Candid Camera" when he was in the U.S. Army Signal Corps. His job was to record servicemen's voices for their parents back home. In these taping sessions he noticed that the men became tongue-tied when they knew their voices were being recorded so Funt started to record them ten minutes early and found that they were not only natural in those first ten minutes but they also said very funny things. When Funt was discharged from the service, he packaged the idea into a radio program ("Candid Microphone") in 1947 on the ABC radio network. When television became popular he translated the idea into the new medium—as "Candid Camera."

Allen Funt graduated from New Utrecht High School in Brooklyn at age 15 and from Cornell, where he majored in art, at age 20.

G

Gabin, Jean

The French actor's family name was Moncorge but his father Joseph Moncorge performed under the stage name Jean Gabin, a name which the son later adopted.

Gable, Clark

Clark Gable may have been one of Hollywood's greatest lovers on screen but off screen was another matter. Carole Lombard, his third wife, once confessed, "My God, you know how I love Pa (Gable), but I can't say he's a helluva good lay." Mary Astor, in her famous diary ratings of her lovers, also gave Gable less-than-star billings.

In addition to his 65 talking pictures, Gable also appeared in at least six silent movies.

Gable's ears were not his only physical defect. He didn't have any teeth and had to wear dentures, much to the dismay of his leading ladies. Grace Kelly, after shooting *Mogambo* with Gable, said, "His false teeth were just too much."

During the filming of *Gone With the Wind* Vivien Leigh complained about his denture odor and threatened to stop shooting love scenes with him unless he washed out his mouth.

Compulsive about cleanliness, Gable used to take several showers a day and even shaved under his arms.

When Gable tried out for the lead in *Little Caesar* (!) he was turned down by Warner Brothers production head Darryl F. Zanuck who complained, "His ears are too big. He looks like an ape."

Galsworthy, John

The author of *The Forsyte Saga* was a law school graduate but never practised law.

Gam, Rita

Actress Rita Gam used her real name much to the chagrin of Louella Parsons, who once said about Rita, "How I wish she'd change her name."

Actress Grace Kelly was a bridesmaid at Rita Gam's wedding and Rita returned the favor a few years later when Grace married Prince Rainier of Monaco.

Gambling, John A.

John Gambling's early morning radio program on WOR radio in New York City is not only the longest running (fifty-four years) radio show in the history of radio, but it also has the largest audience—even larger than Johnny Carson's television audience in the New York area.

The program was started by his energetic father, John B. Gambling, who used to lead his listeners through calisthenic exercises to start off the day.

Gandhi, Mahatma

Gandhi's calmness and serenity may have been partially induced by his taking rauwolfia serpentine, a tranquilizer.

The Hindu leader was a lawyer by profession.

Garbo, Greta

Garbo's real name is Greta Louisa Gustafsson but Swedish film director Mauritz Stiller renamed her Garbo just before casting her in *The Story of Costa Berling*. (He also considered the name Gabor for her!) When she arrived in Hollywood the American studio executives wanted to change her name again because the name Garbo sounded "too close to garbage."

Gardner, Ed

Known for his role as Archie on the radio program "Duffy's Tavern," Gardner was born Edward Francis Poggenberg.

Gardner, Erle Stanley

Gardner, a lawyer by profession (he practised for five years) and creator of "Perry Mason," is thought to be the world's fastest writer—he used to churn out 10,000 words a day and worked on as many as seven books at a time.

In his 80 Perry Mason novels Gardner is said to have made only one legal error that has ever been detected.

Gardner, John

Author John Gardner (*On Moral Fiction*) wrote fiction for over 15 years before any of his works were accepted for publication.

Garfield, James A.

An avid student of classical literature, James Garfield graduated first in his class at Williams College (Mass.) and subsequently taught Latin and Greek at Hiram College in Ohio.

Garfield, the 20th U.S. president, was the last president to be born in a log cabin.

During the Civil War Garfield received several bullet wounds.

Garfield's mother lived at the White House.

Garfield was not only left-handed, he was ambidexterous. He could write Greek with one hand and Latin with the other at the same time.

Garfield, John

Born Julius Garfinkle, the aspiring actor changed his name to Jules Garfield when he joined the Group Theatre Acting Company in New York City. Later in Hollywood, they renamed him John Garfield and introduced him in the movie *Four Daughters*. Some studio executives still didn't like his last name and wanted to change it again until some astute observer pointed out that if a U.S. president had the name it couldn't be that bad.

Garfunkel, Art

Art Garfunkel met his future singing partner Paul Simon in a grammar school (Forest Hills, N.Y.) production of *Alice in Wonderland*. Paul was the White Rabbit and Art was the Cheshire Cat.

Simon and Garfunkel made their first recording under the name "Tom & Jerry." Their first big record, "Hey! Schoolgirl," sold 100,000 copies in 1957 and won them an appearance on Dick Clark's "American Bandstand" television program.

Garfunkel majored in architecture at Columbia University after reading Ayn Rand's *The Fountainhead*.

Garland, Judy

Judy Garland had a song written about her by composer David Raksin. It was titled "Judy" but it became better known when Otto Preminger used the melody as the theme for his great movie *Laura*.

Regarding her homosexual following, Judy said, "When I die they'll fly the flag at half-mast on Fire Island. I can see them now, standing at the meat rack, singing 'Somewhere Over the Rainbow.'"

According to Anne Edwards in her biography of Judy Garland, Judy died on the "john": "She was in a sitting position, her head collapsed onto her breast, like a small brown sparrow with a broken neck."

(See Jessel, George for origin of name Judy Garland.)

Garner, James

James Garner's last name was originally Baumgarner but he changed it because it was misspelled too often.

Garner is one of the best celebrity golfers. He has a 4 handicap! His brother Jack, another athlete, was once a professional baseball player with the Pittsburgh Pirates.

Garroway, Dave

The radio and television announcer (and original host of NBC's "The Today Show") finished 23rd in a class of 24 at NBC's announcing school.

Garson, Greer

Greer Garson won an Oscar in 1942 for her role in the movie *Mrs. Miniver* but almost turned down the part because she did not want to play the mother of a grown son (neither did Norma Shearer who did turn down the role). Louis B. Mayer persuaded her to take the part and if her outrageously long acceptance speech at the awards ceremony was any indication, Miss Garson was very thankful that she had appeared in the movie.

Garson's first name, Greer, was her mother's maiden name and was a contraction of the Scotch name MacGregor.

Garvey, Steve

Steve Garvey worked for the Dodgers long before 1970. Growing up in Tampa, Florida, Garvey was a batboy for the team during spring training. His father, a bus driver, drove the Dodger bus.

Garvey is one of few living people who has a school named after him. His junior high school in Lindsay, California dropped Abraham Lincoln's name and substituted Garvey's name.

His wife Cyndy graduated Phi Beta Kappa from Michigan State University.

Gatling, Richard Jordan

The inventor of the rapid fire machine gun bearing his name was a graduate of the Ohio Medical College (1850), although he never practiced medicine.

Gavin, Gen. James M.

Born James Ryan, "Slim Jim" was orphaned as an infant when his parents died and adopted by Mr. and Mrs. Maurice Gavin.

Gayle, Crystal

Born Brenda Gail Webb, the younger sister of country and western singer Loretta Lynn became Crystal Gayle at Loretta's suggestion. The name Crystal was inspired by the Krystal hamburger chain popular in the South.

Gaynor, Janet

After appearing in several Hal Roach two-reelers, actress Laura Gainer changed her name to Janet Gaynor and made her feature debut in *The Johnstown Flood*.

Gazzara, Ben

Baptized Biago Anthony Gazzara, the actor was raised in an Italian section of New York City and learned to speak Italian before he learned English.

Gehrig, Lou

Lou Gehrig was once hired by a breakfast cereal company to promote a cereal named "Huskies" but when the radio interviewer asked Lou what he attributed his strength and stamina to, he quickly answered, "Wheaties."

At one time Gehrig was considered as a replacement for Johnny Weismuller in the *Tarzan* movies but the deal fell through. Gehrig did appear in the western movie *Rawhide* in 1937 which was universally panned by the critics.

Geller, Uri

As a paratrooper in Israel's army, the psychic was wounded in the Six Day War in 1967.

Uri Geller was a male model in Israel in the late 1960's.

Genet

When *New Yorker* magazine founder Harold Ross hired Janet Flanner to write a Paris letter column he gave her the pleasant-sounding pseudonym Genet. Ross didn't know that in French "genet" meant a female donkey and was also the name of a post-French Revolution journalist of questionable reputation.

George I

George I, the King of England from 1714 to 1727, spoke to his prime minister Robert Walpole in Latin because he could not speak English very well (he was reared in Germany) and Walpole could not speak French or German. Latin was the only language the two men had in common.

George, Phyllis

In the 1970 Miss America Pageant entrant Phyllis George spent several minutes talking about her pet crab and singing dog.

Gerry, Elbridge

The Massachusetts politician not only gave us the word "gerrymander" but he also participated in the first filibuster in the House of Representatives. On June 11, 1790 he and William Loughton Smith of South Carolina made unusually long speeches on the House floor on the topic of changing the seat of government.

Gershwin, George

Born Jacob Gershvin, son of Russian immigrant Moishe Gershovitz, the composer adopted the name George Gershwin early in his career, after trying names like Wynn and Gerchwin.

Gershwin and lyricist Irving Caesar wrote "Swanee" in 15 minutes.

Gerulaitis, Vitas

Gerulaitis's father was Lithuania's top tennis player in the late 1930s and was a member of its Davis Cup team.

Giannini, Giancarlo

Giannini used to dub American movies into Italian. Through the years he was the voice of Jack Nicholson (*The Passenger*) and Al Pacino (*Dog Day Afternoon*).

In the Franco Zeffirelli stage production of *Romeo and Juliet* Giannini unzipped his fly onstage, shocking the critics and surprising the audience.

He does not have a high regard for his profession: "It's not a profession for a real man. I find myself on top of a woman making love, and I am really on top of a chair. The actress has gone home and the cameraman is shooting me making love to a chair. It's an insane profession."

Gibson, Charles Dana

The American artist and illustrator, famous for his "Gibson Girl" renderings, also inspired the alcoholic drink called a Gibson. At the New York Players Club one day, he ordered a martini but the bartender didn't have any olives so Gibson drank it with a pearl onion as a substitute.

Gielgud, John

The British actor's last name is not Scottish as some people believe but Lithuanian. He is of Polish extraction—his paternal grandfather fought with the Polish cavalry, but left Poland in 1831, following an insurrection. Gielgud's grandmother was a well-known Polish actress, Mme. Aszberger, of that period.

In 1922 Gielgud studied acting under Claude Rains (*The Invisible Man*) at the Royal Academy of Dramatic Art in London.

Gilbert, W. S.

When Gilbert was two years old he was kidnapped from his parents in Naples, Italy. Later after he teamed up with Arthur Sullivan they featured kidnappings in two of their operettas—"The Gondoliers" and "The Pirates of Penzance."

Although the team wrote 14 operettas together, they were not particularly fond of each other and collaborated through correspondence.

Gingold, Hermione

Hermione made her stage debut at age 11 in *Pinkie and the Fairies,* using the stage name Rosina Philipps.

Giovanni, Nikki

Commenting on her Italian surname, poet Nikki Giovanni (Yolande Cornelia Giovanni, Jr.) said, "It just means that *our* slavemasters were Italian instead of English or French."

Giscard d'Estaing, Valery

The French political leader's family name was originally just plain old Giscard but shortly before Valery's birth in 1926, his father added "d'Estaing" to the name, acknowledging the village of Estaing, where the family owned land.

Gleason, Jackie

"The Great One" has a theory that all hangovers are caused by stale ice or sometimes by potato chips, but never by booze.

There is a Ralph Kramden listed in the 1979–80 Manhattan telephone directory.

Goddard, Paulette

Born Marion Levy, the actress took the name Goddard after an uncle who influenced his friend Flo Ziegfeld to give Goddard her first stage job.

Paulette Goddard was David O. Selznick's first choice for the role of Scarlett O'Hara in *Gone With the Wind* until a women's group protested on the grounds that she was having an affair with (i.e., not yet married to) Charlie Chaplin.

201

Goethe, Johann Wolfgang von

Goethe took 60 years to write his magnum opus, *Faust*. He started it at age 23 and finished it at age 83, a few months before he died.

Goldberg, Rube

Rube Goldberg, a University of California engineering graduate (1904), worked as a sewer and water main engineer for the city of San Francisco before he became a cartoonist famous for his zany complex inventions.

Golden, Harry L.

The writer's family name was originally Goldhirsch but Ellis Island immigration officials changed the name to Goldhurst. After Harry served a federal prison term for using the mails to defraud in the 1930s, he decided to start a new life and, among other things, shortened his name to Harry Golden.

Goldsmith, Oliver

Author Oliver Goldsmith (*The Vicar of Wakefield*) gave us the phrase "Ask me no questions, and I'll tell you no lies." It appears in Act III, Scene 1 of *She Stoops to Conquer* and is uttered by the character Tony Lumpkin. The actual words are "Ask me no question, and I'll tell you no fibs."

Goldwater, Barry

Senator Goldwater was born on New Year's Day in 1909.

The conservative spokesman and student of American Indian culture has Navajo tattoos on his left hand.

Goldwater's paternal grandfather, "Big Mike" Goldwasser, Anglicized the family name when he emigrated from Poland (via Paris and London) to the United States in 1852.

Goldwyn, Samuel

The only book that Samuel Goldwyn was ever known to read in its entirety was *The Wizard of Oz* and even that took him weeks to read. He owned the movie rights to the book but refused to produce it because it was a "fairy story" and sold the rights to Louis B. Mayer of MGM.

Born Samuel Goldfisch (later Goldfish) in Poland, he emigrated to the United States and became a successful glove salesman in Gloversville, New York. With his glove earnings, he joined forces with Broadway producers Arch and Edgar Selwyn to form the Goldwyn Pictures Corporation, a movie production company. Sam soon became known as Sam Goldwyn and liked the name so much he legally adopted it. When Judge Learned Hand granted Sam legal permission to use the name Goldwyn, he declared that "a self-made man may prefer a self-made name."

Gordon, Max

Born Michael "Max" Salpeter, the Broadway producer took the name Gordon because his older brother, a burlesque comedian, had already adopted the name.

Gordon, Ruth

Ruth Gordon Jones made her Broadway stage debut in 1915—at the age of 19. She appeared as one of the Lost Boys in James M. Barrie's *Peter Pan.* Her performance prompted *New York Times* critic Alexander Woolcott to write, "Ruth Gordon was ever so gay as Nibs."

Ruth Gordon is tiny! She's five feet tall and weighs only 103 pounds.

Gordy, Berry Jr.

As a Ford Motor Company assembly line worker, Berry Gordy, Jr. made up songs in his head to relieve the monotony of the job. Some of the songs were recorded by local singers but Gordy, disappointed with the arrangements, felt that he could do better and formed his own record company. After hits like Jackie Wilson's "Lonely Teardrops" and "That's Why," Gordy started Motown Records and a whole new sound. (Smokey Robinson and the Miracles's recording of "Bad Girl" was the first record issued by Motown—in 1959 on the Tamla label.)

Goren, Charles

The expert bridge player and author received a law degree from McGill University, Montreal, in 1922. He practised law until 1936 when he published *Winning Bridge Made Easy.*

Gorky, Maxim

The Russian novelist and playwright was born Alexei Maximovich Peshkov. His parents died when he was very young and he was brought up by his maternal grandparents. His grandfather, a dyer who went bankrupt and was mentally unbalanced, treated young Peshkov cruelly and gave him a bitter outlook on life. When Maxim became a journalist and critic, he decided to take the pseudonym "Gorky" which means "bitter" in Russian.

Gorme, Eydie

Singer Edith Gorme was advised early in her career to change her name. Her mother objected to the idea on the grounds that if she became a success under a new name, "How would the neighbors know?" The young singer decided to bill herself as Edie Gorme but after being called "Eddie" she changed the spelling of her first name to "Eydie."

Gould, Chester

Chester Gould's cartoon strip *Dick Tracy* was originally called *Plainclothes Tracy*. It was based on the police attempts to deal with Al Capone and other gangsters (Capone was "Big Boy"). Captain Joseph Medill Patterson, co-publisher of the *Chicago Tribune*, persuaded Gould to change the strip's name and character to Dick Tracy, "Dick" being underworld slang for detective.

Gould, Elliot

Born Elliot Goldstein, he was given the stage name Gould by his mother just before his first television appearance because she thought it "sounded better" than Goldstein.

Gould, Morton

When the composer was only six years old he published his first composition, appropriately titled *Just Six*.

Goulet, Robert

The singer had cosmetic surgery to remove one-half-inch from each of his eyelids. He said they were sagging so much he had trouble seeing in the morning.

In his last years Elvis Presley occasionally shot bullets at his television screens, including one time when fellow Las Vegas entertainer Robert Goulet came on screen.

Grade, Sir Lew

The British movie and television producer, son of a tailor's assistant, was born Lewis Winograd-sky in Tolmak, Russia.

Graham, Rev. Billy

When Billy Graham was 18 years old he sold Fuller brushes door-to-door to earn spending money.

Graham studied the Bible extensively at various Bible schools but his undergraduate degree from Wheaton (Ill.) College was in Anthropology.

The Reverend was once a radio disc jockey on a musical program called "Songs of the Night."

His organization, Billy Graham Evangelistic Association, has a budget of more than $40 million a year. Among other things, they send out 100 million pieces of mail a year and process 2.5 million pieces of incoming mail, 77 percent of which contains donations of $8 on the average.

Graham, Martha

On her mother's side, the dance company founder is a direct descendant of Captain Miles Standish.

Graham, Sheilah

The writer was born Lily Sheil but after her marriage to Major John Graham Gillam, she started using the name Sheilah Graham, a combination of her last name altered and her husband's middle name.

In the company of a British millionaire, Miss Graham once lost control of her bladder and urinated (very discreetly of course) on the back seat of a Rolls Royce. Although she thought the chap didn't notice anything, the next time she was in his presence he was quick to point out the location of the "powder" room.

Graham, Virginia

When Virginia Komiss (her real name) was only 10 years old she wrote a play *My Other Face* about a good and a bad fairy. The play was actually produced and she received a full page of publicity for it in the *Chicago Tribune*.

Miss Graham graduated Phi Beta Kappa at age 18 from the University of Chicago.

As a cub reporter for the *Chicago Tribune*, Virginia Graham's first byline was for the St. Valentine's Day Massacre which occurred several blocks away from her school (she was still in high school at the time). She heard the shots, rushed to the scene, and was the first to call in the report to the *Tribune*.

Granger, Stewart

The suave British actor (*King Solomon's Mines*, *Beau Brummel*) was born with the name James Stewart, a name already being used by the American actor James Stewart, so he changed his name to Stewart Granger.

Hedda Hopper once claimed that Granger was a homosexual and had an affair with Michael Wilding. For the record, Granger has been married three times (to three very attractive women!) and has four children.

Grant, Cary

In the movie *His Girl Friday* Cary Grant makes a reference to the execution of a man named Archie Leach—significant only because that is Cary Grant's real name.

For the movie version of *My Fair Lady*, Jack Warner, head of Warner Brothers, wanted Cary Grant to play the role of Henry Higgins for box-office appeal. Grant wisely refused the part, telling Warner that only a fool would try to follow Rex Harrison.

Many people remember Mae West's line "C'mon up and see me some time" in *She Done Him*

Wrong but few people know that she uttered those words to the suave Hollywood newcomer, Cary Grant.

Grant, Lee

The Academy Award-winning actress's real name is Lyova Haskell Rosenthal. The real origin of her stage name is not known but, according to her, it had nothing to do with Civil War generals Lee and Grant.

Grant, Ulysses S.

The 18th U.S. president was born Hiram Ulysses Grant but later transposed his given names. On his appointment to West Point, Representative Thomas Lyon Hamer listed his name as Ulysses Simpson Grant, apparently assuming that his middle name was his mother's maiden name (a common practice) Simpson. Grant decided to keep the name that way.

Grant was the first and last president of the U.S. to get arrested while in his term of office. He was nabbed for driving a team of horses at excessive speed through the streets of Washington, D.C.

Grant's wife, Julia Boggs Dent Grant, had strabismus or "crossed-eyes."

Grant smoked about 20 cigars a day. (He was an occasional cigar smoker until the newspapers published a photograph of him smoking a cigar. Thousands of people started sending him cigars, most of which he gave away, but he kept enough to give him a large cigar habit.)

His best-selling memoirs, published by Mark Twain, made an estimated $500,000 in royalties.

Grant never saw the book in print or enjoyed the money—he died four days after the manuscript was submitted.

Grant had the reputation of drinking too much whiskey but he redeemed himself on his deathbed on July 23, 1885. His last utterance was, "Water!"

Grauer, Ben

Benjamin Franklin Grauer, radio and television commentator, sold $1,000,000 worth of Liberty Bonds when he was only nine years old.

Before his radio and television career, Grauer was a child actor. At age seven he created the role of Georgie Bassett in the 1918 Broadway production of *Penrod* in which Helen Hayes appeared as an ingenue.

Greco, Jose

Jose is one of the greatest Spanish dancers of all time—which is an accomplishment for a boy born in Montorio, Italy and raised in Brooklyn. He is the son of an Italian father and Spanish mother, actually, and he once said that he likes to speak Italian when he makes love and Spanish when he talks business.

Greenberg, Hank

The homerun slugger of the 1930s and 1940s had flat feet.

He married Caral G. Gimbel, the daughter of department store owner Bernard F. Gimbel.

Greene, Lorne

The Canadian actor's last name was originally just plain Green. He added the extra "e" to give it an extra touch of distinctiveness.

Lorne Greene's first movie appearance was in *The Silver Chalice* in which actor Paul Newman also appeared for the first time.

Greene, Shecky

During World War II Shecky was stationed on the aircraft carrier *Bon Homme Richard* where one of his shipmates was a whacky but funny marine named Jonathan Winters.

Greenstreet, Sidney

Greenstreet's screen appearance as Casper Gutman in *The Maltese Falcon* (1943) was his movie debut! He was a veteran British stage actor but he had never appeared in a movie until director John Huston, making his directorial debut, selected the 61-year-old actor to play opposite Humphrey Bogart.

Grey, Joel

Johnny Carson once asked Joel, "How come your name is Grey and your father's name is Katz?" Grey quickly responded, "My father changed his name!" Actually Joel Katz was the one who changed his name, first to Joel Kaye and then to Joel Grey.

In addition to fixing his name, Joel also fixed his nose. Watch the Warner Bros. musical *About Face* and you'll see the old Joel Grey.

Joel Grey's father, an old Borscht circuit comedian, starred in the musical revue *Hello, Solly!* on Broadway in 1967.

Grey, Zane

Grey's name at birth was Pearl Zane Gray (with an "a"). His ancestors, the Zanes, originated in Denmark, migrated to England, and eventually settled in Wheeling, West Virginia, and in an area which became Zanesville, Ohio. Young Gray always went by his first name, Pearl, but after graduating from the University of Pennsylvania School of Dentistry, he opened up a dental practice in New York City. He put up a sign "Dr. P. Zane Grey, D.D.S." which he thought sounded and looked more professional. (He not only submerged his first name, Pearl, but also changed the spelling of his last name.) He practised dentistry from 1898 to 1904 but eventually published 54 novels, including *Riders of the Purple Sage.*

Griffin, John Howard

After serving in World War II, Griffin went blind but ten years later regained his sight and then wrote his best-seller *Black Like Me,* not about being blind but about being black.

Griffith, Andy

The folksy actor was left back in the fourth grade, a humiliation that inspired him to become the class clown and paved the way for his future success as both a comic and serious actor.

After graduating from the University of North Carolina (1949), Griffith taught high school music for three years.

Griffith, D. W.

The pioneer movie director (*The Birth of a Nation, Intolerance*) acted in stock companies for several years under the name Lawrence Griffith.

Grimm Brothers

Brothers Jacob Ludwig Karl and Wilhelm Karl Grimm became famous for their collection of fairy tales but they were also well-regarded philologists. Jacob formulated Grimm's Law, a law in linguistics concerning consonant changes from Indo-European languages into Germanic languages, and they both worked on a German dictionary which they started in 1854 and was finished only recently (1971), many years after their deaths, by dedicated lexicographers.

Grodin, Charles

Grodin was valedictorian of his class at Peabody High School, Pittsburgh, Pennsylvania.

The actor's first movie role was the obstetrician in *Rosemary's Baby*.

Grofé, Ferde

The composer of *Grand Canyon Suite* was born Ferdinand Rudolphe von Grofé in New York City.

Grossinger, Jennie

Jennie Grossinger's famous resort in the Catskill Mountains was started because of a family misfortune. In 1914 Jennie's father, a garment worker in New York City, was ill and advised by a doctor to move out to the country. The Grossingers bought an old farmhouse near Ferndale, New York and started to raise crops. When their crops failed to provide them with enough money to pay their bills, they decided to accept boarders during the summer to raise some money. The resort became so popular that they stopped farming and ran the resort fulltime.

Guccione, Bob

The publisher of *Penthouse* magazine is not new to the magazine business. His first job was selling the *Saturday Evening Post* door-to-door in New Jersey.

Not always a millionaire publisher, Guccione once was a struggling artist who, needing money, read palms in the south of France (not a bad place to struggle) for $2 a reading.

Guevara, Che

Guevara was of Spanish and Irish descent but his paternal grandmother, a United States citizen, was born in California.

Che Guevara achieved fame as a guerilla and leftist leader in the Cuban revolution but by training he was a medical doctor. He was a graduate of the University of Buenos Aires medical school (1953).

Guillotin, Joseph Ignace

The machine that decapitated so many people during the French Revolution was named after a doctor, Dr. Joseph Guillotin, but he didn't invent the machine. He advocated its use because it was a more humane way of executing people—it was swift and painless. Another doctor, Dr. Antoine Louis, was the actual inventor of the guillotine. (Note: Initially the machine was called a *Louisette* or *La Petite Louison.*)

Guthrie, Tyrone

The noted British director and playwright was related to movie actor Tyrone Power. Guthrie's mother, Norah Power, was a granddaughter of the popular 19th-century Irish comedian Tyrone Power, who was the great-grandfather of the American screen idol.

Guthrie, Woody

Woodrow Wilson Guthrie was born in Okemah, Oklahoma the year (1912) Woodrow Wilson was elected president of the United States.

H

Haber, Joyce

Actress Julie Andrews has little fondness for the gossip columnist: "Joyce Haber needs open heart surgery and they should go in through her feet."

Hackett, Joan

The half-Italian, half-Irish actress is a second generation inveterate hat-wearer. Her mother worked in a factory and wore a cap even when she returned home. Miss Hackett now owns about 85 hats.

Hackman, Gene

While in the Marines, the movie actor (*The French Connection*) was demoted three times for minor infractions.

Hackett, Buddy

Buddy Hackett's real name is Leonard Hacker and he made the following remark about his name change: ". . . my agent, Abby Greshler, changed my name at the time I auditioned for the part of Henry Aldrich and lost out to Ezra Stone. I don't know why he changed it. It was a perfectly good name and my father was a good upholsterer."

The comedian says that his father invented the convertible sofa but "never made a dime off it."

Hadley, Reed

The movie and television actor's real name was Reed *Herring* but not wanting his name to be a "red herring" he changed his unusual surname to Hadley.

Hayes, Rutherford B.

He and his wife were teetotalers and served non-alcoholic drinks, including lemonade, in the White House, thus prompting the nickname of "Lemonade Lucy" for his wife.

Haldeman, Bob

As an advertising executive with the J. Walter Thompson agency in Los Angeles, the former presidential aide's accounts were Disneyland, Sani-flush and Black Flag insecticides, among others.

Haley, Alex

When Alex Haley, author of *Roots*, published his interview with jazz trumpet player Miles Davis in *Playboy* magazine (September, 1962) he started one of the best read (vs. *ogled* at) features of the magazine.

Haley graduated from high school at age 15!

Caught up in the Hollywood swirl of things, Haley's license plates read KINTE, an acknowledgement of his *Roots* protagonist.

Halley, Edmund

Halley, the British astronomer, not only was the first person to predict the return cycle of the comet now bearing his name but he also invented the diving bell used in underwater explorations.

Halston

The fashion designer was born Roy Halston Frowick but he uses his middle name (also his mother's maiden name) as his professional name.

Halston calls all of his clients "Sweetie-cake."

Hall, Gus

Born Arvo Kusta Halberg, the U.S. Communist Party official's new name is an Americanization of Kus(ta) Hal(berg) but he also used the names John Howell and John Hollberg before settling on Gus Hall.

Hall, Jon

Actor Jon Hall's real name is Charles Hall Locher but he made several movies under the name Charles Locher or Lloyd Crane before settling on the name Jon Hall. Hall, once the star of television's *Ramar of the Jungle,* is the nephew of Norman Hall, co-author of *Mutiny on the*

Bounty, Men Against the Sea, and *Pitcairn Island.*

Hall, Monty

Monty's real name is Monte (with an "e") Halparin. After having a successful radio program in Winnepeg, Canada, Monte decided to try to make it in Toronto. There he was offered a job by Jack Part, the manager of Toronto radio station CHUM, but was also asked to use a shorter name. Monte suggested cutting his name in half to "Hall" which Part liked, but only in part, because the following day's newspaper listed Monte as Monty (with a "y") Hall.

Monty was a pre-med student in college and was among the top ten Winnepeg students trying to get into medical school but was turned down because of alleged ethnic quotas. He even took several years postgraduate work but was still rejected. Medicine's loss was daytime television's gain.

Hamill, Dorothy

The popular iceskater has an ulcer.

Hamilton, Alexander

The American statesman was born on the island of Nevis in the British West Indies and was an illegitimate child.

He founded the *New York Post* newspaper in 1801 and used it to advance his Federalist beliefs.

Hamilton was only 32 years old when George Washington appointed him Secretary of the Treasury, making him the youngest cabinet member in the history of the United States.

Hamilton, George

The movie actor's nose was sculptured by a skilled plastic surgeon. (*Flesh and Fantasy*)

Hamilton, Margaret

While filming the movie *The Wizard of Oz*, Miss Hamilton—the Wicked Witch—was accidentally set on fire and was laid up for six weeks. The special effects in the movie were especially hazardous and, in fact, a broomstick exploded on her stand-in, Betty Danko, who was permanently scarred.

Prior to scaring generations of children in her role as the Wicked Witch in the movie *The Wizard of Oz*, Miss Hamilton was a nursery school and kindergarten teacher.

Margaret once acknowledged that most of her movie roles were as "a cantankerous cook or the acidulous aunt with a corset of steel and a heart of gold."

Hamlisch, Marvin

At age seven Hamlisch was one of the youngest students ever admitted to the Juilliard School of Music in New York City.

Marvin's first hit song was "Sunshine, Lollipops, and Rainbows" which he wrote for Leslie Gore in 1965 at age 16, *nineteen* years before Marvin won two Academy Awards for his work on *The Sting* and *The Way We Were*.

As a boy, he was nicknamed "Fingers" because he was always practicing the piano.

Hammer, Armand

The international businessman and millionaire art collector is a 1921 graduate of Columbia's College of Physicians and Surgeons and was probably the first medical student to earn a million dollars while attending medical school. After World War I, he encouraged his father, a physician who also had a wholesale drug business, to buy up medical supplies at then depressed prices and sold them when the prices rose again.

Hammerstein, Oscar II

As his name implies, there was another Oscar Hammerstein and he also had a claim to fame. Oscar II's father invented the first practical cigar-rolling machine and received a patent for it on February 27, 1883. This invention led to the production of the perennial staple for cigar smokers—the "five-cent cigar."

Hammett, Dashiell

The man who created Sam Spade, private detective, spent eight years as a Pinkerton agency detective and Hammett's real first name was Samuel.

Hampshire, Susan

The British actress (TV's "The Forsyte Saga") attended the Hampshire School in London—a school which was founded by her mother.

Hampton, Lionel

Raised by his grandparents, Lionel Hampton developed his talent for beating out a song by drumming on his grandmother's *pots* and *pans*.

Hancock, John

Hancock not only had the largest signature on the Declaration of Independence, he was also the first person to sign it.

Handel, George Frederick

In 1751 the German-born composer wrote *The Messiah* in only 24 days because he had financial difficulties and needed the money.

Harding, Warren G.

It is often said that President Harding, the 29th president of the United States, coined the word "normalcy" in his call for a "return to normalcy" but according to the Oxford Dictionary the word has been in the language since the mid-nineteenth century.

Harding was the first newspaper publisher to become a U.S. president.

Harding was an outstanding president if only because he had extremely large feet—he wore size 14 shoes.

Harding occasionally suffered nervous breakdowns and once was institutionalized for several weeks.

Harding was the only president who was the son of a doctor—Dr. George Tryon Harding.

Harlow, Jean

Jean Harlow's real name was Harlean Carpentier. The "platinum blonde" received her unusual first name from her mother, Jean Harlow Carpentier, who devised the name by combining her given name with her maiden name. At age 21, when she went to work as a Hollywood extra, she adopted her mother's maiden name, Jean Harlow, as a stage name and shortly thereafter started appearing in Laurel and Hardy comedies.

Harlow never wore a bra and rarely wore panties. In fact, she once remarked, "The men like me because I don't wear a brassiere. Women like me because I don't look like a girl who would steal a husband. At least not for long."

About Harlow's performance in her last movie, *Saratoga*, critic Graham Greene commented, "There is no sign that her acting would ever have progressed beyond the scope of the restless shoulders and the protuberant breasts; her technique was the gangster's technique—she toted a breast like a man totes a gun."

Harper, Valerie

Despite her convincing portrayal as Rhoda Morganstern on the popular television series "Rhoda," Valerie is not Jewish nor is she from the Bronx. She was born in Suffern, New York and also lived in California, Massachusetts, Michigan, New Jersey, and Oregon—and she is of mixed heritage, including English, French Canadian, Irish, Scottish, Spanish, and Welsh blood.

Valerie was once a hatcheck girl at the posh French restaurant Lutece in New York City.

Harriman, Averill

The ex-governor of New York was elected to the Croquet Hall of Fame, along with Moss Hart, George S. Kaufman, Harpo Marx, Darryl Zanuck, and Alexander Woolcott.

Harris, Richard

As a teenager the movie actor (*Camelot*) and singer contracted tuberculosis and was incapacitated for two and a half years.

Harris, Barbara

Barbara's best-known appearance was probably in the Broadway musical *The Apple Tree* but her first professional appearance was as a cherubic baby in a Betty Crocker ad.

Harrison, Rex

In his first professional stage appearance Rex was supposed to say "Fetch a doctor . . . baby" but he was a bit nervous and said, "Fetch . . . a baby doctor."

Rex played the male lead in the 1946 film *Anna and the King of Siam* and was later also asked to star in the Rodgers and Hammerstein musical play version *The King and I* but turned down the offer in order to appear in T.S. Eliot's *The Cocktail Party*.

Early in his career Rex was told to leave the acting profession because it was already too crowded and only people with exceptional talent could succeed.

Rex lost most of the sight in his left eye when he had a bad case of measles as a child and he is now considered blind in that eye.

Harrison, William Henry

Harrison, a medical school dropout (University of Pennsylvania), was the only U.S. president to study medicine.

Harrison was the oldest president ever inaugurated. He was 68 years and 23 days old when he was sworn in.

Harrison's inaugural speech was the longest of any president—8,443 words. He gave this long speech in extremely cold weather without wearing an overcoat came down with pneumonia, and soon died.

He was the only president whose grandson (Benjamin) became president.

The only book he ever wrote was *Discourse on the Aborigines of the Valley of Ohio*, published in 1839.

William Henry Harrison served only 30 days in office and was the first U.S. president to die in office.

Harrison's father, Benjamin (not to be confused with his grandson of the same name) was one of the signers of the Declaration of Independence.

Harvey, Laurence

Movie actor Laurence Harvey (*Room at the Top*, *The Manchurian Candidate*) was born Larushka Mischa Skikne in Joniskis, Lithuania.

Harvey, Paul

The colorful newscaster wears a toupee whenever he appears on television.

His annual income is at least $2 million—which is more than Walter Cronkite, David Brinkley, and Barbara Walters make combined.

Born Paul Aurandt, he adopted the name Harvey because it was easier to spell and pronounce.

Haver, June

Actress June Haver's name is not the fabrication of a press agent or movie studio. She was born June Stovenour but after her father died, her mother married Bert Haver whose surname June adopted.

Havoc, June

Christened June Hovick, "Baby June" married at the pubescent age of 13 and became a mother three years later.

Hawks, Howard

Hawks's preference for gangster, war, and cowboy movies belied his Ivy League background. He was a graduate of Phillips Exeter Academy in New Hampshire and of Cornell University where he majored in mechanical engineering.

At age 18 Hawks won a U.S. junior tennis championship and also raced cars professionally.

The film *Double Dynamite* with Jane Russell, Groucho Marx, and Frank Sinatra was so named because director Hawks thought it was a "clever way of alluding to Jane Russell's boobs," according to Groucho's son Arthur, and had nothing to do with the movie.

Hawthorne, Nathaniel

Hawthorne's family name was Hathorne but Nathaniel added the "w" while he was a student at Bowdoin College in Maine.

At Bowdoin, Hawthorne's classmates included poet Henry Wadsworth Longfellow and future U.S. president Franklin Pierce.

Hawthorne played cards for money at college and was almost expelled for gambling. It is also interesting to note that another Bowdoin cardsharp who played cards with Hawthorne was Pitt Fessenden who later became Lincoln's Secretary of the Treasury.

Hayakawa, Sessue

The Japanese actor's (*The Bridge on the River Kwai*) first name was originally Kintaro (his nickname was "Kimbo") but was changed to Sessue when he joined the Japanese Theatre company in Los Angeles in 1913.

After rupturing an eardrum and being disqualified from pursuing a career in the Japanese navy, 18-year-old Hayakawa tried to commit hara-kiri by stabbing himself 30 times but miraculously recovered.

Hayakawa gave his three story mansion in Hollywood to several Jewish friends who converted it into a synagogue. (It was later demolished to make room for a freeway.)

Hayakawa, S. I.

The California senator receives about $20,000 a year in royalties from his popular semantics book *Language in Thought and Action* which he published in 1941.

Hayden, Sterling

The veteran charactor actor (*The Asphalt Jungle, Dr. Strangelove, The Godfather*) was born John Hamilton on March 26, 1916, in Montclair, New Jersey.

Hayes, Helen

In 1905 at age five Helen made her first professional stage appearance as Prince Charles in a Washington, D.C. production of *The Royal Family*.

Helen's real name is Helen Hayes Brown—the name Hayes being her mother's maiden name.

Hayes, Peter Lind

Born Joseph Conrad Lind, his name was changed to Peter Lind Hayes at 10 years old when he appeared with his actress mother at the Palace Theatre in New York City.

Hayes, Rutherford B.

In the Civil War, Hayes, as a Union officer, was wounded four times and was erroneously reported dead at the battle of Cedar Creek, Virginia, on October 19, 1864.

Hayes was born posthumously.

Hayden, Carl

The late Arizona senator holds the record for the longest time served in Congress—56 years.

Hayward, Susan

As a young actress in Hollywood, Miss Hayward improved her speech by watching Ronald Colman movies every night, memorizing his lines, and trying to imitate his diction and speech patterns. She claimed that she saw *Prisoner of Zenda* 100 times.

Her real name was Edythe Marrener, and she was born in the Flatbush section of Brooklyn, New York.

She was the mother of twin sons named Timothy and Gregory.

Hayworth, Rita

Actress Rita Hayworth appeared in her early movies under her real name, Margarita Cansino, but could only get roles as Mexican girls and Indian princesses so she bleached her dark hair, underwent electrolysis to raise her low forehead hairline, took acting and dancing lessons, and changed her name to Rita Hayworth for "marquee appeal." "Hayworth" was her mother's maiden name (with an added "y") and "Rita" was short for Margarita. It is interesting to note that when Warner Brothers later signed her up to replace Ann Sheridan in, of all movies, *The Strawberry Blonde* in 1941, she became a big box office attraction.

According to a recent biography, Hayworth is of Sephardic Jewish ancestry.

Head, Edith

The perennial Hollywood costume designer has an M.A. in languages from Stanford University and was originally going to be a teacher but a moonlighting job as a sketch artist at Paramount studios launched a new career for her.

Hearst, William Randolph

Hearst was born a twin but the other baby died at birth, leaving him an only child to be lavishly spoiled by his mother.

Hefner, Hugh

At age 22, the future publisher and sexual libertarian was still a virgin!

Hefner originally named his new girlie magazine *Stag Party* but was forced to change the name when the publishers of *Stag*, an already existing magazine, threatened to sue him. The name *Playboy* was suggested by Hefner's friend, Eldon Sellers, whose mother had once owned a car by that name.

The first issue of *Playboy* was published in October of 1953 but was not dated because Hefner wanted to leave it on the newsstands for another month if it didn't sell well the first month. Another oddity about the first issue—Hefner's name does not appear once in the magazine.

Because Hef drinks so many Pepsi-Colas (two or three dozen a day!) most people think he is a teetotaler. On the contrary, he is a bourbon man and on occasion can toss down quite a few.

Hefner never smoked a pipe until he hosted his TV show "Playboy's Penthouse." He originally used the pipe only as a prop to keep his hands occupied but he eventually really started to smoke it.

The son of strict Methodist parents, Hefner was not allowed to attend movies on Sunday.

Heinz, Henry J.

When Henry J. Heinz started his food company in 1876, he offered more than 57 types of food products but he used the trademark "Heinz 57 Varieties" because he liked the number 57 especially the 7 which he thought had special powers and influence.

Heller, Joseph

The author of *Catch 22* wrote several scripts for the television series "McHale's Navy" and still receives residual payments for one of them.

Hemingway, Ernest

Hemingway used to lament the fact that *Ferdinand the Bull,* a children's book, outsold his *Death in the Afternoon* by ten times.

On a visit to China, Hemingway once ate monkey brains right out of the monkey's skull.

Hemingway believed that too much sexual intercourse was not conducive to good writing.

Not one for formalities, Hemingway once said that "wearing underwear is as formal as I ever hope to get."

Hemingway's mother was a classical music lover and always wanted Ernest to become a cellist.

After being wounded during World War I while in an ambulance unit in the Italian Army, Hemingway had his knee operated on and was given an artificial kneecap made of aluminum.

On a per word basis, Hemingway became the highest paid professional writer ever when he sold a 2,000 word article on bullfighting to *Sports Illustrated* in 1960 for $30,000—or $15.00 a word.

Hemingway, Mariel

The young movie actress (*Manhattan*) and granddaughter of Ernest Hemingway was named Mariel after the bay in Cuba where her parents vacationed in the 1950s.

Henderson, Skitch

The bearded bandleader, born with the distinguished name Lyle Russell Cedric Henderson, had this to say about his nickname, Skitch, in an interview with *Saturday Night* (July 1953), a Canadian magazine: "I don't know how that name started or when, but somewhere along the line I was tagged with it, and it has stuck. I've kept it because I think it fits me and it has a certain amount of distinctive publicity value. When I first signed up as a conductor with the NBC Symphony Orchestra, I debated whether to change it because it might be too undignified. But I decided to keep it. It's pretty well accepted and it's easy to spell."

Henie, Sonja

Ice skater Dorothy Hamill with her hair product endorsements may be cashing in on her talent and appeal but she has a long way to go before she catches up with Sonja Henie's record. Miss Henie leveraged her skating ability into eleven movies, scores of ice shows, and amassed a fortune estimated to have been $47,500,000.

Henry, O.

Utter the name Cisco Kid to trivia buffs and they'll mention Warner Baxter, Gilbert Roland, Cesar Romero, and Duncan Renaldo but they'll never mention that the character was created in 1907 by O. Henry in the story "The Caballero's Way" which appeared in his book *Heart of the West*.

In 1894, O. Henry (then named William Sydney Porter) and a friend started publishing a new, humorous weekly called *The Rolling Stone*. Its platform said: "The politics of *The Rolling Stone* is Independent with an inclination toward Presbyterianism, and the theory that the world is supported on the back of a mud turtle . . ."

O. Henry hated to write but he always had to in order to pay his bills.

Hepburn, Audrey

The Belgian-born movie actress, whose full last name is Hepburn-Ruston, is the daughter of a Dutch Baroness and a granddaughter of a former Governor of Surinam (Dutch Guiana).

During World War II, one of Audrey's uncles and a cousin were executed in Nazi prison camps. During the filming of the movie *Sabrina* Humphrey Bogart, when asked about Miss Hepburn's acting ability, said that she was "awright . . . if you don't mind a dozen takes."

Hepburn, Katharine

At age 12, Katharine and her brother Thomas saw a production of *A Connecticut Yankee in King Arthur's Court* and were impressed by a scene in which an actor did a trick with a noose around his neck. The next day she discovered her brother's lifeless body hanging in their attic. The facts were never ascertained but the death was assumed to be accidental.

Although Miss Hepburn has a reputation for not indulging in common vices, it is interesting to note that she was once expelled from Bryn Mawr College for smoking a cigarette.

When Hepburn married Ludlow Ogden Smith, a Philadelphia socialite, in 1928 she insisted that he change his last name to Ludlow so she would not have to be called Kate Smith.

Hepburn does not attend the Academy Awards ceremony because she is always afraid she will lose.

In a *McCall's Magazine* interview recently, the actress confessed, "Acting really isn't a very high-class way to make a living, is it? Nobody ever won a Nobel Prize for acting."

The consummate actress and proper New Englander once dived fully clothed into the Beverly Hills Hotel pool, after a few sets of tennis.

There is a scene in the movie *The Desk Set* in which Miss Hepburn is carrying a bouquet of white flowers as she leaves her office but by the time she reaches the curb the flowers are pink, an apparent lapse in continuity.

Herman, Jerry

The successful Broadway musical songwriter (*Hello Dolly, Mame*) originally studied interior decorating at Parsons School of Design in New York City but after selling a song he wrote for fun, he transferred to the University of Miami where he was a drama major.

Hersey, John

The Pulitzer Prize-winning writer (*A Bell for Adano*, 1945) was born in Tientsin, China, where his father worked for the Y.M.C.A. When John came to the United States, at ten years of age, he spoke Chinese better than he spoke English. He was then schooled at Hotchkiss preparatory school and also at Yale College where he polished up his English.

Hershey, Barbara

The movie actress's father was editor of the *Racing Form*, the daily newspaper that provides information on horseracing activity.

Barbara adopted the last name Seagull after being in the movie *Last Summer* in which she played a girl who nurses a wounded seagull. The seagull eventually died and Barbara "felt her spirit enter my body." (Her real name is Barbara Henzstein.)

When her son Free was born, she and husband David Carradine, a veteran of 500 LSD trips, were going to eat the afterbirth but at the last minute decided to bury it near an apricot tree.

Herter, Christian

President Eisenhower's Secretary of State, after graduation from Harvard College in 1911, studied architecture at Columbia University in New York City.

Heston, Charlton

In the late 1940s Charlton was a nude model for the Art Student Center League in New York and was paid $1.25 an hour for his services.

Heston admitted that he is addicted to peanut butter—and lamented the fact that you can't get good peanut butter in Europe unless you have a connection.

Heston's uncommon first name is his mother's family name and in fact he had a great-uncle named Percy Charlton who was also an actor.

Heyward, DuBose

The co-author (with his wife Dorothy) of the play *Porgy* contracted infantile paralysis at age 17 and was an invalid for three years. (Note: In the play Porgy is a crippled beggar.)

Hickok, "Wild Bill"

In poker, a hand with a pair of aces and a pair of eights is called "The dead man's hand" because it was the hand James Butler "Wild Bill" Hickok was holding when he was shot to death by Jack McCall in Deadwood, South Dakota, on August 2, 1876.

The famous U.S. marshal was once nicknamed "Duck Bill" because he had a protruding lip and a long nose, somewhat resembling a duck.

Hildegarde

Singer Hildegarde Loretta Sell got her first name from a character in a novel that her mother was reading during her pregnancy. She discarded her last name at the suggestion of Gus Edwards who signed her to appear in his revue *Stars on Parade*.

Hill, George Roy

The director of highly popular movies like *Butch Cassidy and the Sundance Kid* and *The Sting* studied music at Yale and was a member of the world-famous Wiffenpoofs singing group.

Hirschfeld, Al

Caricaturist Al Hirschfeld started hiding the name Nina in his drawings in the fall of 1945 to celebrate the birth of his daughter Nina. The first drawing to contain her name was for the musical *Are You With It?* (the name appeared on a circus poster entitled "Nina The Wonder Child").

If Hirschfeld ever puts more than one "Nina" in a drawing he will write the exact number of them after his signature. (Hint: Curtains, folds of costumes, hairdos, and wrinkles are obvious places to look for "Nina's.")

Hirohito, Emperor of Japan

In accordance with Japanese custom, Hirohito as heir to the Imperial Throne was separated from his parents when he was only three months old and was placed in the care of foster parents.

The name Hirohito translates into English as "broad-minded benevolence."

Hirt, Al

At age six Al got his first trumpet from his policeman father who bought it in a pawn shop. Later his father accidentally bent the mouthpiece while trying to fix it and left it with an air leak. Al continued to play the instrument but it did require extra breath to compensate for the leak. Using this extra power gave Hirt the ability to play extraordinarily well and helped create his unique style.

The names of Hirt's eight children are engraved on his trumpet.

Hitchcock, Alfred

Most people know that Hitchcock liked to make an appearance in every movie he makes but does anyone remember seeing him in the movie *Lifeboat*, which featured only eight actors stranded on a lifeboat? If you look closely, when one of the actors picks up a newspaper you'll notice a weight-reducing ad on the page and in the ad are photographs of Hitchcock—"before and after."

Hitchcock's movie *Blackmail* (1931) was the first talkie ever made in Britain.

He and his wife Alma were married for 53 years, probably setting a movie industry record.

Hitler, Adolf

Contrary to popular belief, Hitler's name was never Schicklgruber. His grandmother was an unwed mother named Maria Anna Schicklgruber whose son Alois took the last name of the man she eventually married—Hitler. Alois then married and his son Adolf Hitler was a product of this marriage.

The name on Hitler's birth certificate in Braunau was listed as Adolfus Hitler.

Hitler was a Catholic and early in his youth he wanted to become a priest. He even used to drape an apron over his shoulders in a priestly fashion and deliver "sermons" from a kitchen chair.

As *The People's Almanac* pointed out, Hitler owned 8,960 acres of land in Colorado. He knew a good ski resort when he saw one!

Hitler was never a paperhanger or house painter but was in fact an architectural artist of reasonable skill, notwithstanding the fact that he was not admitted to the Academy of Fine Arts in Vienna.

Hitler was an avid opera fan and he especially loved the operas of Richard Wagner. In fact, he could whistle every note of *Die Meistersinger*, which is a five-hour opera. Also, he wrote an opera once but despite some good themes, it was considered second-rate Wagner.

His favorite movie was *King Kong* and his favorite song was "Who's Afraid of the Big Bad Wolf."

His speeches were always written in large type because the Führer was too vain to wear eyeglasses.

Ho, Donald

The Hawaiian-born crooner has a "chop suey" (his words) background—he is of Portuguese, Dutch, English, German, and Hawaiian heritage. At prep school Ho's nickname was "Quack" because of his duck-like walk.

Hobson, Laura Z.

Whatever happend to Laura Hobson, the author of *Gentlemen's Agreement* which first appeared in 1947? She's alive and doing well in New York. She rides 1,000 miles a year on her bicycle in Central Park and recently published her tenth book, *Over and Above*.

The "Z" in her name was for Zametkin which was her real last name. The author of *Gentleman's Agreement* became Hobson when she married Thayer Hobson.

Ho Chi Minh

Ho Chi Minh was originally named Nguyen Van Thanh but changed his name in the early 1940's to Ho Chi Minh (meaning "Most Enlightened One") for political reasons. Prior to that, he also used other aliases like Nguyen A. Quoc, Nguyen Sinh Chin, Song Man Tcho, Nguyen O. Phap, and Ly Thuy.

In 1914 Ho Chi Minh served as an apprentice to the world-famous chef Escoffier at the Carlton Hotel in London.

Hoffer, Eric

The self-educated dockworker-turned-philosopher and writer went blind when he was seven years old, after an accident, but miraculously recovered his sight eight years later.

Hoffman, Dustin

Dustin Hoffman's first movie was not *The Graduate* (1967), as most people think, but *Madigan's Millions* (1966), a low-budget, Italian-made movie in which Cesar Romero starred.

Most sources say that Dustin's mother was such an avid movie fan that she named her son after Dustin Farnum, the silent screen cowboy star, but at least one good source says that she gave him the name because it was a nice, distinctive name and that it had nothing to do with Dustin Farnum.

Hoffman originally wanted to be a concert pianist and in fact he studied music at both the Los Angeles Conservatory of Music and Santa Monica City College, before transferring to the Pasadena Playhouse.

Hogan, Ben

One of the great golfers of all time, Hogan started to play the game *left-handed* as a young boy but didn't play very well so he switched to the other side to improve his game. Although Hogan did not win any major tournaments until he was 28 years old, he subsequently won four U.S. Open tournaments (1948–50–51–53), three of them after a near-fatal automobile accident in 1949.

(Another story has it that Hogan switched from left-hand golfing to right-hand golfing because he could not afford special clubs for left-handed people.)

Holden, William

The veteran motion picture actor was born William Franklin Beedle but assumed the stage name William Holden when he won a small part in the movie *Million Dollar Legs* in 1939. Paramount Pictures executives complained that the name Beedle sounded like an insect and changed his name.

Hollander, Xaviera

The "Happy Hooker" has a good business sense. She once remarked, "If my business was legitimate, I would deduct a substantial percentage for depreciation of my body."

Holliday, Doc

Wyatt Earp's friend was a dentist.

Holliday, Judy

Judy Holliday's real name was Judith Tuvim but when she became an actress she adopted the name Holliday because her real name, Tuvim, is the Hebrew word for "holiday."

Holly, Buddy

The short-lived rock 'n' roll singer's last name was spelled Holley but a record company misspelled it and he decided to keep it that way.

There is a Buddy Holly listed in the 1979–80 Manhattan telephone directory.

Holtzman, Elizabeth

Congresswoman Holtzman has a *twin brother* who is a neurosurgeon at Columbia Presbyterian Hospital in New York. In fact, when they were at Abraham Lincoln High School (Brooklyn, N.Y.) together she and brother Robert ran for vice-president and president of their class on the campaign slogan "Win with the Twins!" They won.

Hoover, Herbert

Herbert Hoover, a mining engineer graduate of Stanford University, published a book entitled *Principles of Mining* in 1909. He also won 89 honorary degrees in his lifetime.

Hoover's wife, Lou Henry, was the first woman graduate in geology in the United States, when she received her A.B. from Stanford University in 1898.

Although Hoover was a devout Quaker, he and his wife were married by a Catholic priest because no other minister was available.

Hoover's wife, Lou, called him "Bert"—which makes sense because he was "her Bert Hoover."

When Hoover left the presidency there were fewer federal employees at the White House than when he first took office.

He was a member of Stanford University's first graduating class (1895).

He was the first president born west of the Mississippi River (West Branch, Iowa).

He and Thomas Alva Edison were named as the two greatest engineers in United States history by Columbia University School of Engineering and Applied Science in a 1964 survey.

Hoover, J. Edgar

Hoover, who was not exactly known as a lady's man, was photographed kissing only one girl in his lifetime—child actress Shirley Temple.

At Central High School in Washington, D.C. where he was class valedictorian (1913), Hoover's nickname was "Speed."

Hope, Bob

Comedian Bob Hope likes to kid about other famous people's wealth but by consensus Hope is extremely rich himself. *Fortune* magazine says that Hope is worth $250–$300 million and is one of the fifty richest men in America and *Time* magazine wrote that he is worth $500 million. He amassed his fortune primarily by investing in land, especially in the late 1930's when it was only $30 an acre.

At school in Cleveland, Ohio, Hope was called Les (his full name was Leslie Townes Hope) but after his classmates started calling him "Hopeless" he changed his first name to just plain Bob.

Bob was born in England (Eltham, Kent) and did not come to the United States until he was four years old.

The comedian is serious when it comes to marriage. He and his wife Delores have been married for 47 years.

Hope hates jewelry and never wears a watch, claiming to have a built-in clock.

He gets free cars from Chrysler (seven of them) and gets free gas from Texaco, both of whom have been sponsors of his shows.

Hoppe, Willie

Hoppe was a billiard player not a pool player, although he occasionally participated in exhibition matches in pool.

Hopper, Hedda

Hedda once said that her real name, Elda Furry, "sounded like a small blonde animal with soft skin that people like to stroke" and being stroked made her hair rise on her head, so she used alternate names like Ella Furry, Elda Millar, and Elda Curry, as the latter appeared in the Broadway musical comedy *The Pied Piper*. At that time she met actor De Wolfe Hopper whom she later married and thus became Elda Hopper. "Wolfie," as he was called, previously had been married to women with the first names of Ella, Ida, Edna, and Nella! Elda, noting the similarity of her name to her predecessors, decided to change her first name, and she and a numerologist came up with the name Hedda.

Her son William Hopper played the part of Paul Drake on the "Perry Mason" television series from 1957 to 1966.

Horne, Marilyn

The opera singer sang Dorothy Dandridge's songs in the movie *Carmen Jones*.

Horowitz, Vladimir

The pianist is the son-in-law of Arturo Toscanini.

Houdini, Harry

Houdini, born Ehrich Weiss, became interested in magic at an early age but after he read *Memoirs of Robert-Houdin* (Jean Eugene Robert-Houdin was France's greatest magician.) he became obsessed with the idea of being a magician. It was Jacob Hyman, Ehrich's friend and co-worker, who suggested that he add an "i" to "Houdin" and adopt the name Houdini. The name "Harry" came from Ehrich's nicknames "Ehrie" and "Erie" although some sources say that he used the name Harry because Harry Kellar was the most popular American magician at that time.

Like Rudolph Valentino in the same year, Houdini died of peritonitis in 1926. It was caused by a punch Houdini received in the stomach by an admirer who was testing Houdini's ability to tolerate body blows.

Houk, Ralph

As a major league baseball player, Houk appeared in only 91 games and had a .272 batting average.

In World War II, a sniper shot at Houk but the bullet went through his helmet, narrowly missing his head.

Housman, John

The esteemed producer made his onscreen debut at age 71 in *The Paper Chase* and won the Academy Award for Best Supporting Actor.

Howard, Ron

While still in high school, Ron Howard (TV's "Happy Days") won a national Kodak film contest for a movie shot with a Super 8 movie camera.

Howe, James Wong

The late cinematographer's real name was Wong Tung Jim, but one of his grade school teachers felt compelled to Anglicize the name and came up with James Howe. Later, as a successful cameraman, he reinserted the name Wong and became known as James Wong Howe.

Howe, Julia Ward

Author of the poem "The Battle Hymn of the Republic," Julia Ward Howe was the first woman ever elected (1908) to the American Academy of Arts and Letters.

Hudson, Rock

Actor Rock Hudson's name at birth was Roy Scherer, Jr. When his father lost his job during the Depression he left home and abandoned the family. His mother married a second time to Wallace Fitzgerald whose surname Roy legally adopted. He became Rock Hudson when agent Henry Wilson who, noticing the actor's impressive physique, conjured up two large and powerful images—the *Rock* of Gibraltar and the *Hudson* River.

After graduating from high school, Hudson joined the Navy and was stationed as an airplane mechanic in the Philippine Islands. After a bomber went out of control and crashed into another plane, however, Hudson was blamed for the incident and subsequently transferred to a laundry detail.

Rumors abound about Rock's offscreen preferences, but for the record, he was married to Phyllis Gates, his agent's secretary, from 1955 to 1958.

Hughes, Howard

Although Hughes could obviously afford to buy gold Rolls Royces, he preferred black Chevrolets and had a whole fleet of them. Curiously enough, however, when he had a date he would borrow a Lincoln or Cadillac from local car dealers on the pretext of being a potential fleet buyer.

Hughes often traveled with a coffin-like box which some people assumed contained special electronic gear but a Hughes aircraft employee once opened it and discovered that it contained hundreds of comic books, which Howard liked to read before going to sleep every night.

For a while, Hughes had a fear of flushing his urine down a toilet so he began to keep it in jars which he stored in his Bel Air chateau. He also sent urine and feces specimens to UCLA Medical school for a daily analysis.

Hughes not only attended Rice Institute in Houston, Texas, for a year and dropped out but he also married Ella Rice, whose family founded the school, and also "dropped out" of the relationship, divorcing her four years later.

Hughes had two favorite topics of conversation, according to his business associate Noah Dietrich: business and women's breasts!

In his pre-recluse days, the Hollywood Howard Hughes invented the uplift brassiere for Jane Russell for a movie (*The Outlaw*) he was producing.

As a young man, Hughes was an excellent golfer. He was a scratch player but gave up the game when he was told that he would probably not be able to beat Bobby Jones in the national amateur tournament.

He never permitted doctors to take X-rays of him.

Humphrey, Happy

The mammoth wrestler, born William J. Cobb, once weighed 802 pounds in the peak of his wrestling career but by July of 1965 he reduced his weight to only 232 pounds.

Humphrey, Hubert

Ex-vice president Humphrey was originally not a Minnesotan but a *South Dakotan*. He was born in Wallace, S. D. and raised in Doland, S. D., and did not leave that state until he left to attend the University of Minnesota during the Depression.

At Doland High School, where Humphrey was class valedictorian, captain of the debating team, and three letter athlete, his nickname was "Pinky" because his skin was pink and fair and sunburned easily.

Hunt, E. Howard

The Watergate conspirator (who spent 33 months in prison) has written 54 books, most of which are spy thrillers.

Hunt, H. L.

The eccentric multimillionaire used to crawl around his mansion on his hands and knees several minutes a day. Calling it "creeping" he started doing it after recovering from an auto accident. He said that it was as good an exercise as swimming.

Hunt always traveled coach or tourist class on commercial airlines, so when the family purchased a private jet plane it was suggested that it have a coach section for H. L.

The Hunt family house in Dallas, opposite White Rock Lake, is a replica of George Washington's Mount Vernon except that it is five times larger and supposedly features pay phones for visitors who have to make phone calls.

H. L. Hunt used to park his car several blocks from his Dallas office in order to save a fifty-cent parking charge.

Hunter, Alberta

The great blues singer's mother was a maid in a Memphis brothel.

Hunter, Catfish

Baseball pitcher Catfish Hunter has shotgun pellets in his right foot from a hunting accident that happened in his senior year of high school. He and his brother were hunting during a Thanksgiving vacation when his brother's shotgun misfired, hitting Hunter's right foot. Surgeons removed most of the pellets, but had to amputate one toe.

Hunter liked to catch catfish as a young boy but he did not get the nickname "Catfish" in his youth. Charlie Finley gave him the name when Hunter joined the Oakland Athletics.

Hunter, Evan

Born Salvatore Lombino, he changed his name to Evan Hunter shortly after graduating Phi Beta Kappa from New York City's *Hunter* College in 1950—four years before his best selling novel *The Blackboard Jungle* was published.

Hunter has also used the pen names Richard Marsten and Hunter Collins.

Hunter, Jeffrey

Born Henry H. McKinnies, the movie actor's best role was as Jesus in *The King of Kings* (1961) which is noteworthy only because he died at approximately the same age at which Jesus Christ died.

Hunter, Kim

The stage and movie actress (*Streetcar Named Desire*) was born Janet Cole, but when producer David O. Selznick gave her a contract with Vanguard Films, he changed her name, saying to her, "Janet Cole could be anyone, but Kim Hunter had individuality and would go far as an actress."

Hunter, Ross

When actor Martin Fuss went to Hollywood in 1944, the casting director for Columbia Pictures, Max Arnow, recommended that he change his name to Ross Hunter. Martin, not being fussy, accepted the new name. After acting for eight years he became a producer of many successful movies, including *Imitation of Life* (1959) and *Airport* (1969).

Hunter, Tab

Tab Hunter appeared in his first movie (*The Lawless*) using his real name Art Gelien but shortly thereafter his agent decided that a handsome actor needed a handsome name. As the story goes, the agent said, "We gotta tab him something!" Knowing that Gelien liked to hunt and ride horses, he *tab*bed him *Hunter*.

Huntley, Chet

Television newscaster Chet Huntley was a descendant, on his father's side of the family, of U.S. Presidents John Adams and John Quincy Adams.

Huston, John

In 1948, both John and his father won Academy Awards for their work in *The Treasure of Sierra Madre*—John as Best Director and Walter as Best Supporting Actor. It is the only time a father and son combination has achieved this honor.

Huston, Walter

The character actor's family name was originally spelled Houghston.

In his son John's first directorial effort *The Maltese Falcon*, Walter played Captain Jacoby but he is easy to miss because he appears on the screen for about a half a second.

I

Iaccoca, Lee

The auto executive's full name is Lido Anthony Iaccoca. He acquired the unusual first name because his parents had fond memories of their honeymoon at Venice's Lido.

Indiana, Robert

Most known for having painted the word "LOVE" with the red "LO" on top of "VE" and on a blue and green background, artist Robert Clarke took the name of his home state, Indiana, rather than "endure the pangs of his actual identity."

Inge, William

Playwright William Inge was originally an actor and later a drama critic for the *St. Louis Star-Times* but after seeing a Chicago production of Tennessee Williams's play *The Glass Menagerie*, he was inspired to write a play. His first play, *Farther Off From Heaven*, was not exceptional but his first Broadway play, *Come Back*,

Little Sheba, was very popular and gave him a new career.

Inge was a distant relative of 19th-century stage actor Edwin Booth and presidential assassin John Wilkes Booth.

Inouye, Daniel

The senator from Hawaii originally wanted to be a doctor but after he lost his right arm in World War II he decided to study law.

Ionesco, Eugene

When Ionesco's first play, *Bald Soprano*, was produced he was 38 years old, a relatively old age for a playwright to make a debut.

Irving, Washington

The 19th-century writer coined the term "the almighty dollar." It appeared in "The Creole Village" sketch in his *Wolfert's Roost and Other Papers* (". . . the almighty dollar, that great object of universal devotion throughout our land, seems to have no genuine devotees in these peculiar villages . . .")

Ivan the Terrible

Although the Russian ruler enjoyed throwing dogs off towers, roasted his live pet cats, killed his oldest son, Ivan, and executed thousands of people, he became devoutly religious in his fifties, was a true hermit, and died as the monk Jonah.

J

Jackson, Andrew

Jackson had tuberculosis while he was president but it never interfered with his ability to perform his duties.

He was the first president on whom an assassination attempt was made. The assassin was a psychotic house painter, Richard Lawrence, whose two pistols misfired, leaving Jackson unscathed.

Jackson, like Rutherford B. Hayes, was born posthumously on March 15, 1767. His father died several days before the future president was born.

Jackson called the presidency "dignified slavery."

Before entering politics, Jackson was reputed to have been in 100 duels and in fact once killed a man in 1806 for insulting his wife.

When Jackson married Rachel Donelson he was the first president to marry a divorcee.

Jackson was also the first president to ride a train while president, when he went from Ellicotts Mills to Baltimore on the Baltimore and Ohio railroad on June 6, 1833.

At age 14, while a prisoner of the British in 1781, Jackson refused to shine an officer's boots and was hit by a sabre blow which not only scarred him for life but also gave him a lifetime dislike for Great Britain and the British.

Jackson, Henry "Scoop"

The Democratic senator from the state of Washington was 48 years old when he first got married.

Jackson, Jesse

The civil rights leader was an illegitimate child and knowledge of that fact inspired him to make something of himself.

Jackson, Reggie

The Yankee slugger has never hit over .300 in his major league career! His highest average was .297 was in 1979.

Jackson, Stonewall

The West Point graduate (1842) was given the nickname Stonewall by General Barnard E. Bee during the Civil War for his strong and steady resistance at the first battle of Bull Run.

Jagger, Mick

Jagger attended the prestigious London School of Economics on a government grant but left after two years to devote all his time to singing in his rock group.

He got his name for The Rolling Stones from the song "The Rolling Stones Blues" which was written by one of his idols, Muddy Waters.

According to *People* magazine, Mick's first sex experience (at age 13) was "with boys at school," clarifying the statement, "I think that's true of almost every boy."

James, Harry

The popular bandleader's parents were circus performers and as a child Harry appeared with them, billed as "The Youngest Contortionist in the World."

James II, King of England

James II invented the earliest type of semaphore code in 1670 when he was Lord High Admiral in the British Navy.

James, Joni

Joni, whose record "Why Don't You Believe Me?" was a big hit in 1952, was born Joan Carmella Babbo in Chicago, Illinois.

Janis, Byron

The famous concert pianist was born Byron Yanks—Yanks being a shortened version of the original family name, Yankilevitch—and is married to Maria Cooper, daughter of the late movie actor Gary Cooper.

Jannings, Emil

Actor Emil Jannings was born in Brooklyn, New York, but had a gutteral accent and spoke broken English because as an infant he was taken to Germany, where he grew up speaking German.

Jannings was the first man to win an Academy Award for Best Actor but he was also the first actor to not be at the ceremonies to receive the award.

Although his mother was Jewish, Jannings made propaganda movies (*Ohm Krüger*, for one) for the Nazis.

Janssen, David

Actor David Janssen's real name was David Harold Meyer but when his mother, Bernice Dalton, a former Ziegfeld girl, divorced his father, she married Eugene Janssen and eight-year-old David adopted his stepfather's surname.

When he was six months old he won a nationally sponsored Sears "Prettiest Baby" contest.

As a teenager, Janssen appeared in the movie *Swamp Fire* (1946) in which he played Johnny Weismuller's younger brother. The film was also noteworthy because it was one of few "straight" (non-Tarzan, non-Jungle Jim) movies Weismuller made.

Jarvis, Howard

When the man of Proposition 13 fame was not "on the wagon" he started his days off with an eye-opening shot of vodka.

Javits, Jacob

The Republican senator's first wife was Marjorie Joan Ringling, whose father was Alfred T. Ringling, the circus owner. The marriage ended in divorce in 1936, after three years.

Jacob Javits is usually thought to be the first Jewish U.S. senator but he was actually preceded by David Levy Yulee who was elected as senator from Florida more than a hundred years ago.

Javits was the class president of the first graduating class of George Washington High School in New York City.

Jaworski, Leon

After receiving his law degree in 1925 the special Watergate prosecutor became the youngest person ever to pass the Texas bar.

Jefferson, Thomas

Although the third president of the United States was a champion of equal rights and civil liberties, he once owned as many as 130 slaves. With one of them, Sally Hemings, he was romantically linked and was believed to have fathered several of her children.

Jefferson was a oenophile and spent over $10,000 on wine for his personal consumption during his eight years as president. Perhaps related to his love for wine, Jefferson also was constantly plagued with migraine headaches.

Among his nicknames were "Long Tom"—for being six feet two and a half inches tall and "Red Fox"—for his red hair.

The cause of Jefferson's death on July 4, 1826, was attributed to excessive diarrhea.

The third president of the United States invented the dumbwaiter.

It took Jefferson only 18 days to write the Declaration of Independence.

Jefferson had a brother and sister who were twins. Randolph and Ann Scott Jefferson were both born on October 1, 1755.

Jenner, Bruce

The Olympic decathlon gold medal winner is a descendant of Edward Jenner, the British doctor who discovered the smallpox vaccine.

Jessel, George

Georgie claims to have invented the Bloody Mary cocktail! In 1927 he was living it up in Palm Beach and had an occasion to cure a hangover. The bartender offered Georgie a glass of vodka, which at that time was an obscure, unheard of liquor. Jessel didn't like the smell of the vodka so he asked for some Worcestershire sauce, tomato juice (he knew that Constance Talmadge used to clear her head with a tomato juice concoction) and lemon to kill the taste and smell of the vodka. When Mary Brown Warburton, a Philadelphia socialite, decided to taste the new drink, she spilled it all over her white evening gown, calling herself "Bloody Mary" and that became the name of the "curative" morning-after-the-night-before drink.

At Jessel's suggestion, Frances Gumm, "The Little Girl with the Big Voice," changed her name to Judy Garland in the early 1930s while they were both playing at the Oriental Theatre in Chicago.

Jessel was once stabbed by Lupe Velez, the volatile Mexican actress. She learned that he was out with a beautiful blonde the night before and became upset enough to stab him in the hand with a steak knife. His hand was not severed but the relationship was.

Jimmy the Greek

Born Demetrios George Synodinos, the oddsmaker Americanized his name to James G. Snyder which, in his Runyonesque profession, evolved into Jimmy the Greek.

Both Jimmy the Greek and Dean Martin were born in Steubenville, Ohio in 1917 and, in fact, were and are good friends.

Joel, Billy

In the early 1970s Joel played the piano at a Los Angeles bar called "The Executive

Lounge," using the name William Martin, his given names.

At Hicksville High School on Long Island, singer Billy Joel ("Just the Way You Are") was not given a diploma because he played hookey so often.

Joffrey, Robert

The Joffrey Ballet Company founder's real name is Abdullah Jaffa Bey Khan. He is the son of an Afghanistani father and Italian mother.

John, Elton

As a child, Elton John was fat! "I was fat, about 200 pounds and I had a terrible inferiority complex. That's why I'm so outrageous onstage, I think, and why I wear ridiculous clothes. I'm catching up for all the games I missed as a child."

Elton's real name is Reginald Kenneth Dwight which he thought "sounded like a cement mixer" so he took his first name from saxophonist *Elton* Dean and last name from singer *John* Baldry. "Changing the name helped a lot. I'm still the same person as Reg Dwight, but Elton John gave me a feeling of confidence." He added the middle name Hercules to give him strength and to encourage him to succeed.

About being a bisexual, the rock singer explained, "There's nothing wrong with going to bed with somebody of your own sex. People should be very free with sex—they should draw the line at goats." The flamboyant singer's sexual orientation may have something to do with the fact that his father, an RAF squadron leader, did not like him and in fact wanted a girl instead of a boy.

In a *People* magazine interview, John confessed, "If I could really, really go back and do anything I wanted, I'd like to be the singles champion at Wimbledon."

Regarding John's bisexuality, a *People* magazine article reported that he is having sex at least three times a week and with women more than men.

After breaking up with a six-foot two-inch blonde (a woman) when he was 21 years old, Elton tried to commit suicide but it was, needless to say, unsuccessful. He said that it was a "Woody Allen-type suicide"—he turned on the gas and "left all the windows open."

John-Paul I, Pope

Pope John-Paul I, who died 33 days after being elected pope, did not have the shortest term of any pope. On March 24, 752 A.D. Pope Stephen II was elected and died two days later.

Johnson, Andrew

Of all the U.S. presidents, Johnson was the youngest when he got married—he was only 18 years and 127 days old on the day he married 16-year-old Eliza McCardle on May 5, 1827.

Johnson never went to school and, in fact, was taught to read and write by his young wife.

Although he was not a drinker, Johnson was drunk at his inauguration and rambled on about his humble origins (he was poorly educated).

Andrew Johnson, who narrowly missed getting impeached and removed from office, also had the dubious distinction of having the most vetoes overridden—15 of his total 28 vetoes were overridden by Congress.

Almost everybody knows that Harry S Truman owned a haberdashery shop but few people know that Andrew Johnson was a tailor before he entered politics and even continued to make his own clothes while he was president.

Johnson, Howard

As a youth, Johnson was advised by his father to carry sales data (he was a salesman for his father's company) and customer names in his head. Because Johnson developed his talent for keeping names and figures in his head, he didn't even have an office or secretary when the Howard Johnson restaurant chain sales were $100 million a year.

Johnson, Lyndon Baines

L.B.J. was the first president sworn in by a woman. Her name was Judge Sarah Tilghman Hughes and the swearing-in occurred on the presidential airplane *Air Force One* at Love Field in Dallas on November 22, 1963.

He was the first Democratic president to carry the state of Vermont.

Johnson's wife "Lady Bird" was named Claudia Alta Taylor at birth but the family cook thought that she looked "purty as a lady bird" and the nickname stuck. L.B.J. became so enthralled with the initials L.B.J. that he even named one of his dogs Little Beagle Johnson.

Although he was a Southerner, the late president was not a bourbon drinker. He drank scotch, specifically Cutty Sark scotch.

Some sources say that L.B.J. was the tallest (six foot three inch) president but actually he was the second tallest—Abraham Lincoln was slightly taller—six feet four inches.

Johnson, Philip

The highly-regarded architect (New York State Theater, Asia House, and numerous art galleries) decided to be an architect when he was about 36 years old. Prior to that he designed watches and women's clothes but felt he was "lousy" at it and switched to architecture.

Johnson, Samuel

The noted lexicographer would literally climb a tree to avoid guests he didn't like.

Johnson, Van

In the early 1940s actor Van Johnson was in an automobile accident on the way to a movie screening and smashed his head badly enough to require surgical insertion of a metal plate in his forehead.

In another accident, during a stage performance of *The Music Man* in 1963, Johnson lost the tip of a finger but was rushed to a nearby hospital in time to have it stitched back on.

Jolson, Al

The famous singer was born Asa Hesselson in St. Petersburg, Russia. Under Czar Alexander, every 14-year-old boy, except the eldest son in each family, had to serve in the army for 20 years. Jewish families sought to avoid military service for religious reasons and bribed local officials or changed their sons' names. And so Cantor Hirsch Hesselson changed the name of his son Asa to Yoelson. The family eventually emigrated to the United States where Asa became Al Yoelson, then Al Joelson, and finally Al Jolson when he and his brother Harry teamed up with Joe Palmer to form the vaudeville act *Jolson, Palmer & Jolson.*

Jones, Bobby

The winner of the Grand Slam in golf in 1930 was a lawyer.

Jones, Casey

Casey, whose real name was John Luther Jones, did not get his nickname from any connection with Kansas City but from his being born near Cayce (two syllables), Kentucky.

Jones, Grace

The sexy, feline disco queen is the daughter of a Pentecostal minister who preaches in Syracuse, New York.

Jones, Jack

The second-generation singer (his father was Allan Jones of the 1930s) eats earthworms and prefers them in a quiche. The crooner commented, "Birds sing well after eating worms, so why not?"

Jones, James

The late author got the title for his best-selling book *From Here to Eternity* from the Yale College Wiffenpoof Song (". . . doomed from here to eternity, God have mercy on such as we . . .")

Jones, Rev. Jim

The People Temple minister used mascara to darken his hair and eyelashes and to simulate chest hair.

He also claimed that he had the largest penis in the world.

Jones, John Paul

The Revolutionary War hero's real name was simply John Paul but when he was accused of killing a sailor in the West Indies he added the name Jones (after a friend) and sought refuge in the United States.

After the Revolutionary War, Jones became a rear admiral in the *Russian* Navy.

Jones, Tom

The singer's real name is Thomas Jones Woodward. In 1963 he billed himself as Tommy

Scott, the Twisting Vocalist, but was soon advised by his agent, Gordon Mills, to use the name Tom Jones in order to take advantage of the popular movie *Tom Jones*.

Jones, Shirley

Unlike a lot of actresses, Shirley Jones uses her real name but it is noteworthy that Miss Jones was named after child actress Shirley Temple and was born two years after Miss Temple made her film debut (1932) in *The Red-Haired Alibi*.

Jong, Erica

The former Erica Mann graduated Phi Beta Kappa from Barnard College in 1963.

She once sold mutual funds in Germany for Bernard Cornfeld's Investor's Overseas Service. (Her husband was stationed there with the U.S. Army.) She also taught at the University of Maryland's Extension Division evening courses.

Jonson, Ben

When Ben Jonson, the author of the play *Volpone*, asked his benefactor Charles I of England for a square foot in hallowed Westminster Abbey after he died, that is exactly what he got. He was buried in an upright position in order that he not take up more space than he bargained for.

Joplin, Janis

The late rock singer habitually sucked her thumb until she was eight years old.

Jordan, Hamilton

President Carter's chief of staff was born with bowed legs that were so bad he had to wear braces to bed for 11 years in order to correct the problem. He also has flat feet—which kept him out of the sevice.

Now a man of stature, Jordan had leaner days in his past. At the University of Georgia, he once lived at a local motel but was evicted when he hit the motel manager with a big, wet wad of toilet paper.

Jordan does not wear any underwear.

In his junior year at the University of Georgia, Jordan had a part-time job as a mosquito exterminator.

The presidential aide was exempt from the draft but he did serve a year in Vietnam as a volunteer relief worker.

Jorgensen, Christine

When transsexual George William Jorgensen, Jr. went to Denmark in May, 1950, for a sex change operation, he consulted Dr. Christian Hamberger, an eminent endocrinologist and hormone expert. Dr. Hamberger supervised Jorgensen's sex transformation and it was in deference to the doctor that she adopted a feminine version of his first name Christian.

Jourdan, Louis

The suave French actor is generally considered to be one of the best croquet players in the world and in the history of the game. He acquired the talent by practicing on the plush course on Samuel Goldwyn's Beverly Hills estate.

Born Louis Gendre, the handsome Frenchman started acting on the Paris stage in the late 1930s, using the name Pierre Jourdan but changed his first name back to Louis in 1941.

Joyce, James

Joyce was almost totally blind when he wrote his dream-filled book *Finnegan's Wake*.

K

Kahn, Sammy

The prolific songwriter wrote "Let It Snow" with Jule Styne on the hottest day of the year.

Kaltenborn, H. V.

The NBC radio newscaster (full name was Hans von Kaltenborn) was technically a baron. His father, Baron Rudolph von Kaltenborn, a Hessian Guards officer from a long line of nobility, came to the United States when Hesse was being absorbed from Prussia.

Kane, Carol

The actress used to have recurring nightmares about friends falling down flights of stairs or about being run over by cars, according to *People* magazine.

She has been a vegetarian since she was 14 years old.

Kanin, Garson

After dropping out of high school during the Depression, the future writer formed his own jazz band, "Garson Kay and His Red Peppers," in which he played saxophone.

Kant, Immanuel

The German philosopher (*Critique of Pure Reason*) was only five feet tall, had a concave chest and a deformed right shoulder, and died a virgin.

Karloff, Boris

When London-born William Henry Platt joined the Ray Brandon Players in Kamloops, Canada, he decided that Pratt was not a good stage name and selected the name "Karloff," which was a family name on his mother's side. The first name Boris just came to his head and seemed to go well with "Karloff."

Karloff was so successful and so stereotyped as a monster character after the movie *Frankenstein* that it was not until 1941, when he made his Broadway debut in *Arsenic and Old Lace* (as the villainous brother) that he played a non-monster, real person role.

Kaufman, George S.

Acknowledging Kaufman's influence on Groucho Marx's career, Groucho admitted, "Kaufman molded me. Kaufman gave me the walk and the talk."

Kaye, Danny

Kaye pilots his own plane and is even qualified to fly commercial airplanes.

In the dancing act of Dave Harvey and Kathleen Young at the opening performance of *The Three Terpsichoreans* in 1933, David Daniel Kominski accidentally fell and, in doing so, got a big ovation. They decided to write the "accident" into the act and Danny was given billing as Danny Kaye, a name he chose by keeping only the first letter of his real last name.

Kaye, Nora

The ballerina's real name is Nora Koreff. Early in her career she changed her name to Koreff-Kaye but then changed it to simply Kaye, reversing a trend for ballerinas to adopt Russian-sounding names, because "an American dancer ought to have an American name." Her father, incidentally, was Gregory Koreff, a former Moscow art theater actor.

Kazan, Elia

The movie director's (*Gentleman's Agreement, On the Waterfront*) Greek father wanted him to go into the family rug business.

Kazan, Lainie

The sexy singer thought her real name (Lainie Levine) made her sound like a Jewish stripper so she adopted her mother's maiden name Kazan.

Keach, Stacy

Stage (*Indians*) and movie (*Conduct Unbecoming*) actor Stacy Keach was born with a

275

hairlip but after four operations he was left with only a slight scar.

Keaton, Buster

When Joseph Frank Keaton was six months old, he fell down a staircase in a boardinghouse and, in doing so, got the nickname Buster. Harry Houdini, who toured the vaudeville circuit with Keaton's parents at the time, was staying at the same boardinghouse and was the first person at the scene of the accident. He picked up young Keaton and remarked to the baby's father, "That's some buster your baby took!" Keaton's father liked the name Buster and immediately started calling him Buster.

Keaton, Diane

Although one of her cats is named Buster Keaton, actress Diane Keaton is no relation to the comic genius. (Her real name is Diane Hall— Keaton is her mother's maiden name.)

She once did a deodorant commercial in which she jogged around the kitchen, held up a can of deodorant and exclaimed "This stuff is great!"

Keats, John

The Romantic poet was originally going to be a surgeon and in fact did spend over three years as an apprentice to the family surgeon in Edmonton, England, and then worked at Guy's and St. Thomas's hospitals in London for another three years, before devoting himself completely to poetry in 1817.

His epitaph reads, "Here lies one whose name was writ in water."

A poet to the end, Keats's final words upon dying were, "I feel the flowers growing over me."

Keeshan, Bob

Now known for his Captain Kangaroo television show, Keeshan was Clarabelle the Clown on the "Howdy Doody" show in the early 1950s but was fired because of a dispute with management over a talent agent.

Kefauver, Estes

Kefauver's first name was Carey.

Kefauver's coonskin cap trademark originated in 1947 when he decided to run for a senate seat against Edward H. Crump, the Democratic boss of Memphis. During the campaign, Crump ran a newspaper ad that called Kefauver a "pet coon." Having a sense of humor, Kefauver reacted by wearing a coonskin cap and declaring in a speech, "I may be a pet coon but I'll never be Mr. Crump's pet coon."

Keller, Helen

Most people assume that Helen was born blind and deaf but she did not become so until she was almost two years old.

Kelley, Clarence

The former FBI director was recently in a television commercial. It was for a product which photographs interiors of gems and is supposed to foil jewelry thieves.

Kelly, Alvin "Shipwreck"

The champion flagpole sitter spent a total of 20,613 hours on top of flagpoles, including 1,400 hours in rain or sleet, 210 hours in below-freezing temperatures, and 47 hours in snow. Kelly acquired his nickname "Shipwreck" after surviving five sea disasters.

Kelly, Emmett

The great clown was named Emmett by his Irish immigrant father in honor of Irish patriot Robert Emmett whom he greatly admired.

Kelly first started out as a cartoonist and in fact his world-famous portrayal as a hobo clown ("Weary Willie") was originally conceived by him as a cartoon character. When he could not get a job as a cartoonist with the newspaper syndicates, however, Kelly began working at church suppers and carnivals by giving "cartoon-talks" and eventually did the talks as a clown in white-face. During the Depression, when the only employment he could get was as a clown, he decided to become the tattered, pathetic hobo now familiar to people all over the world.

Kelly, Gene

The dancer-choreographer-director studied journalism at the University of Pittsburgh.

Kelly, Grace

Grace Kelly is the only movie star ever to appear on a postage stamp. When she married Prince Rainier III, the government of Monaco issued commemorative stamps honoring the royal couple.

She was not the first member of her "Main Line" family to be in the theater: one of her uncles was George Kelly, the Pulitzer Prize-winning playwright-author of *Craig's Wife* and another uncle was Walter C. Kelly, the famous "Virginia Judge" of vaudeville.

Kelvin, Lord

Lord Kelvin, formerly named William Thomson, was so precocious that he was only 10 years and four months old when he entered Glasgow University.

Keenan, George

After reading F. Scott Fitzgerald's *This Side of Paradise*, the future U.S. Foreign Service officer, decided to go to Princeton University.

Kennedy, John F.

According to Rip Horton, Jr., one of John F. Kennedy's schoolmates at Choate, Kennedy's first sex experience was in a Harlem brothel at a cost of three dollars. (It was a white woman, Horton clarified.)

Many people identify John F. Kennedy with Harvard and also assume that he went to law school. Actually Kennedy's first college choice was Princeton; and, after a brief stay at the London School of Economics, he did, in fact, attend Princeton but quickly dropped out for health reasons. Upon recuperating, Kennedy enrolled at Harvard College (his father's *alma mater* and college choice for all his sons). After graduating from Harvard, Kennedy then took courses at Stanford's Graduate School of Business before leaving to join the Navy in World War II. Kennedy never did attend any law school.

Kennedy was the first president to serve in the U.S. Navy and was the first president born in the twentieth century.

Although Kennedy was certainly "Ivy League" (Choate, Harvard) he disliked button-down collars and urged his staff not to wear them.

Kennedy was the only president to be born under the sign of Gemini.

Kennedy was the only president to win a Pulitzer Prize. As author of *Profiles in Courage* he was awarded the prize for biography in 1957.

Kerouac, Jack

Kerouac wrote a complete novel, *Mexico City Blues* while sitting on a toilet smoking marijuana in the apartment of writer William Burroughs (*Naked Lunch*).

The beat-generation writer's full name was Jean-Louis Lebris de Kerouac.

Kerouac went to Columbia University on a football scholarship but a leg injury ended his football career.

The original manuscript of *On the Road*, written in three weeks, was typed single-spaced with no margins on 250 feet of teletype paper.

Kesey, Ken

Ken Kesey, author of the novel *One Flew Over the Cuckoo's Nest*, was displeased by the movie version of his book because it was told from the viewpoint of McMurphy and not Chief Bromden, as in the original book.

Although the movie *One Flew Over the Cuckoo's Nest* grossed over $60 million, Kesey was paid only $28,000 for the movie rights.

Ketcham, Hank

Hank Ketcham's wife Alice gave him the idea for his successful cartoon strip *Dennis the Menace*. After a hard day with her four-and-one-half-year-old son, she complained to her husband, "Hank, our son Dennis is a menace." Hank, already a cartoonist, realized that a "Dennis the Menace" cartoon strip was a good idea and sold it to the Post-Hall syndicate in 1951.

Key, Francis Scott

As a prisoner on a British warship during an attack on Fort McHenry in Baltimore, Maryland, in 1814, Francis Scott Key wrote the words to what eventually became known as "The Star-Spangled Banner," but when it was first published it was entitled "The Defense of Fort McHenry." The music used with the anthem was from an old English drinking song "To Anacreon in Heaven."

Key was a lawyer by profession and served as district attorney in Washington, D.C. from 1833 to 1841.

Keynes, John Maynard

The British economist was a homosexual.

At Cambridge University in England Keynes's nickname was "Snout"—a disparaging reference to his elongated nose and thin face.

Kidd, Captain

Sentenced to death for piracy, Captain Kidd was hanged on May 23, 1701, at Wapping, England, but the rope broke. Still alive, he probably could have escaped but he was so drunk he did not and was quickly hanged again.

Son of a Calvinist minister, Kidd was a successful and legitimate sea captain for most of his life.

Kidd, Michael

The Broadway choreographer (*Guys and Dolls*, *Finian's Rainbow*) studied engineering in college but abandoned it because he found it too impersonal.

Kiley, Richard

Actor Richard Kiley (*The Man From La Mancha*) got started in show business in 1941 when he was paid $15 to say the word "Duz" in a radio commercial.

Killy, Jean-Claude

Champion skier Jean-Claude Killy is a descendant of an Irishman named *Kelly* who settled in Alsace, France after fighting as a mercenary in Napoleon's army.

It happens to the best skiers! In 1958 Jean-Claude broke his leg during a race and was out of competition for almost two years.

King, Alan

As a young boy, Irwin Alan Kniberg started a musical combo called "Earl Knight and his Musical Knights" (he played the drums!) and played at bar mitzvahs, weddings, and other social events in the Williamsburg area of Brooklyn. When he graduated to the Borscht Circuit in the Catskills, he started using the name King—which he got by removing "ber" from Kniberg and rearranging the letters.

King, B. B.

Born Riley B. King, the singer and guitarist became known as Riley King, The Blues Boy from Beale Street as a Memphis disc jockey, then the Beale Street Blues Boy, and finally B. B., short for Blues Boy.

King, Martin Luther Jr.

The civil rights leader was offered the movie role of a Georgia senator by director Otto Preminger, but he turned down the offer because he thought it would jeopardize his cause.

When King received the Nobel Peace Prize in 1964 for his nonviolent civil rights campaigns, he was the youngest person ever to win the Peace Prize—he was 35 years old.

King was baptized *Michael* Luther King, Jr. but six years later his father, Rev. Michael Luther King, Sr., who strongly admired reformation leader Martin Luther's thinking and moral courage, decided to rename himself and his son after the great theologian.

Kinsey, Alfred

The sex research pioneer really did know a lot about "the birds and the bees." He was an ornithologist and an entomologist. As a young boy he published a study on *bird* activity in the rain, and later at Harvard University he published a comprehensive study of gall *wasps*.

Kipling, Rudyard

Cecil Rhodes, the diamond millionaire, gets all the credit for establishing the Rhodes scholarships but actually Rudyard Kipling, then living in Capetown, South Africa, and Rhodes *both* spent seven years together planning the development of the scholarships. Kipling also helped develop the boy scout system with Sir Robert Baden-Powell and the scouts' "wolf cubs" were in fact named after the Mowgli in his children's stories.

Kirby George

Comedian and mimic George admitted that he was a heroin addict in the late 1950s, but he committed himself to the public health service hospital in Lexington, Kentucky and was rehabilitated. Unfortunately several years ago he was apprehended and jailed again for drug-related charges.

Kierkegaard, Sören

The Danish philosopher used some pseudonyms that sounded like names from Dickens's novels or W. C. Fields's movies: Victor Eremitus, Johnnes DeSilentio, Nicholas Notabene, Virgilius Haufniensis, Hilarius Bookbinder, Johannes Climacus, Frater Taciturnus, and Constantin Constantius.

Kissinger, Henry

The former presidential adviser and former "swinger" once commented that "power is the ultimate aphrodisiac."

Kitt, Eartha

Eartha Kitt was born in *North*, South Carolina and was given her unusual first name by her sharecropper father who, having his first good harvest in years, decided to thank Mother Earth by naming his daughter after her.

Klein, Robert

At age 14, Klein appeared on the "Ted Mack Amateur Hour" television show as one of the Teen Tones, a singing group that lost to a "one-armed piano player."

Knievel, Evel

Robert Craig Knievel said that he was given the nickname "Evil" in jail (for theft) when a man named Knoffle in the next cell and said, "Double the guard! We got 'Evil' Knievel in one cell and 'Awful' Knoffle in the next." The name stuck but he later changed the spelling to Evel to match the last four letters of Kni*evel*.

Knox, Henry

Before joining the Boston Grenadier Corps in 1772 Henry Knox owned a bookstore in Boston.

The Revolutionary War hero in his peak weighed 300 pounds. He and his wife (who was not exactly svelte) were known as "the largest couple in the city" when they resided in New York City after the war.

After swallowing a chickenbone, Knox died on October 25, 1806.

Kosciusko, Thaddeus

In 1794 the Revolutionary War hero and general was made dictator of Poland and led the country in battle against the invading Russians. (Unfortunately, the Russians annihilated the Polish army and Kosciusko was taken as a prisoner.)

After his death, Kosciusko left part of his estate to help found the Colored School of Newark, New Jersey, one of the first educational institutions for black students to be established in America.

Kosinski, Jerzy

The Polish writer (*Being There*) speaks and reads Polish, Russian, Ukrainian, Italian, Spanish, and Esperanto (which was developed by a Pole) but to help him with his English late at night he frequently dials "O" and asks the operators questions about grammar or definitions of words.

The author started writing under the name Joseph Novak.

Kramer, Jack

John Albert Kramer, one of America's tennis greats, calls himself and is known by the name "Jake."

Kristofferson, Kris

While Kris Kristofferson was in England on a Rhodes Scholarship, he was launched on a singing career by a London promoter who gave him the name Kris Carson.

Kris was a helicopter pilot in the U.S. Army while stationed in Germany.

Kroc, Ray

In the 1920s long before Ray Kroc became the head of the McDonald's (Hamburger) Corporation, he was musical director of radio station WGEN in Chicago. He arranged music, played the piano, and hired musicians and singers—and one of his discoveries was Sam and Henry, a song and patter team, who later became famous as Amos 'n' Andy.

Krupa, Gene

Krupa's mother enrolled him in piano lessons but he was so clumsy on the piano his father refused to pay for any more lessons. Krupa decided to take up the drums.

Kubrick, Stanley

As a 16-year-old high school student, Stanley Kubrick, an aspiring still photographer, sold his first photograph to *Look* magazine for $25. The photograph was of a morose newstand dealer surrounded by newspapers announcing the death of President Franklin D. Roosevelt.

Kuhn, Bowie

The Commissioner of Baseball is called "Commish" (accent on the second syllable) by his wife and children.

The six foot five baseball commissioner has the unusual first name because he is in fact a descendant of James Bowie, after whom the heavy sheath knife was named.

Kurtz, Swoosie

The up-and-coming actress's first name is really Swoosie. Her father, an Air Force pilot, flew a B-17 named Swoosie during the war and thought the name was good enough for his daughter. (A swoose, according to her, is half swan, half goose!)

Ky, Nguyen Cao

The former Prime Minister and Air Marshal of South Vietnam is now living in the U.S. and owns Ski's liquor store in Norwalk, California. He picked a liquor store over a McDonald's franchise or carwash because of the profit potential.

L

Lacy, Jerry

Better known as the actor who played Humphrey Bogart in the Broadway and movie versions of Woody Allen's *Play It Again Sam*, he appeared recently in a Visa credit card advertisement as a second prize winner ($500) in the Chase Visa Shopping Spree Sweepstakes.

Ladd, Alan

His son, Alan Ladd, Jr., made more money in 1978 than Alan made in his whole career. Alan Ladd, Jr., president of the Twentieth Century-Fox Film Corporation (whose *Star Wars* grossed more than $500 million), earned $1,944,384.92 in salary and incentive bonuses in 1978.

Ladd's mother committed suicide when he was 24 years old.

Ladd, Cheryl

Born Cheryl Stoppelmoor, the "Charlie's Angel's" first job in Hollywood was to do a singing voice-over for a Hanna-Barbera cartoon.

Lafayette, Marquis de

The French-born American hero was a major general in the U.S. Army at the age of 19.

For his part in the American Revolution, Lafayette was given American citizenship and was the first foreigner ever awarded this honor.

LaGuardia, Fiorello H.

Although the colorful New York City mayor (1933–1945) was born in New York, he attended high school in Prescott, Arizona (his father was an Army bandmaster) and spent eight years in Budapest, Hungary with his mother before returning to the United States in 1906.

Lahr, Bert

Comedian Bert Lahr, born Irving Lahrheim, used to meet with other show business aspirants on Forty-Second Street, according to his son John Lahr in *Notes on a Cowardly Lion:* "The meeting place was the Automat across the street from the Fitzgerald Building. There, deals were made, dreams plotted, acts revised. It was there that Pearlman decided to change his name to Jack Pearl, and Irving Lahrheim became Bert Lahr. 'We had no money,' recalls Pearl. 'We had nothing, just little kids trying to make a reputation in show business. Bert and I were both in kid acts. I went up to his house. I used to say to him, 'Cut off your name, I'll cut off mine.' Everybody said, 'Watch this kid, watch this Lahr.'"

Laine, Frankie

Singer Frankie Laine's real name is Frank Paul Lo Vecchio. After an audition for a job at WINS radio in New York, the singer adopted the last name "Lane" at the suggestion of the program director. Later, when he discovered that there was a female singer named Frances Lane, Frankie added the "i" to his last name to avoid any confusion.

Laird, Melvin

The ex-Secretary of Defense was elected a Wisconsin state senator at age 23 and was the youngest state senator in the United States. Laird had two things going for him though. He ran for the seat his father had before he died and having just been discharged from the service, he campaigned in uniform.

Lake, Arthur

The actor, best known for his role as Dagwood Bumstead in the *Blondie* series, was named Arthur Silverlake at birth but had his last name shortened by producer Carl Laemmle, Jr., just before Arthur's first movie. Lake's father and uncle, incidentally, had a circus aerialist act and were known as "The Flying Silverlakes."

Lake, Veronica

Born Constance Ockleman, she became Constance Keane when her mother married Anthony Keane, a staff artist with the *New York Herald Tribune*. The attractive actress went to Hollywood in the late 1930s as Connie Keane but producer Arthur Hornblow, Jr. decided to change her name to Veronica Lake—the Lake being for the "calm coolness" of a lake he saw in her navy blue eyes, and Veronica, he thought, was a good name for a woman with her classic features.

LaLanne, Jack

On the television show "You Asked for It" in 1952 LaLanne did 1,033 pushups in 23 minutes.

The license plates on his Stutz Black Hawk reads REDUCE, which summarizes the major goal of his health spas.

Lancaster, Burt

Although he was raised in the East Harlem section of New York City, Burton Stephen Lancaster traces his ancestry to the royal English House of Lancaster.

Lancaster left New York University (where he majored in physical education) after two years to team up with Nick Cravat, a childhood friend, to form the acrobat team "*Lang* and Cravat." They worked in vaudeville, carnivals, and many circuses, Kay Brothers and Ringling Brothers, among others.

Producer Mark Hellinger wanted to change Burt Lancaster's name to Stuart Chase but Lancaster managed to defend and keep his real name.

Landers, Ann

Columnists Ann Landers ("Ann Landers") and Abigail Van Buren ("Dear Abby") are twin sisters. Their real names are respectively Esther Pauline Friedman ("Eppie") and Pauline Esther Friedman ("Popo").

Landon, Michael

Landon was born as Eugene Maurice Orowitz in Forest Hills, Queens, son of Broadway actress Peggy O'Neill and publicist Eli Orowitz.

While at Collingswood High School in New Jersey, he set the high school record for the javelin by throwing it 211 feet 7 inches.

Landry, Tom

The pressure of a play-off game or Superbowl is water off a duck's back for Dallas Cowboy's coach Landry. As an Army Air Corps bomber copilot in World War II, he flew 30 missions over Germany and in France surviving a "deadstick" landing in which both wings of his B-17 bomber were sheared off.

Lanza, Mario

In Lanza's movie *For the First Time* a convict named Cocozza is mentioned. Cocozza was Lanza's real last name.

Lasky, Jesse

Before entering the movie business Lasky was a professional cornet player.

Lasser, Louise

Louise Lasser's father was S. Jay Lasser, the noted tax expert and author.

Lassie

The original dog movie star was actually a *male* collie named "Pal."

Laughton, Charles

Laughton's double in the movie *Henry VIII* was the wrestler Man Mountain Dean (Frank Simons Leavitt) who went on to appear in 30 other movies.

Laurel and Hardy

Stan Laurel's partnership with Oliver Hardy began by accident. Stan, an actor who was once Charlie Chaplin's understudy, started to write, produce, and direct Hal Roach's comedies. Hardy was about to appear in Roach's *Get 'Em Young* but when he burned his arm Roach asked Laurel to take Hardy's place. Roach liked Stan's performance so much that he put him in Hardy's next movie, *Sleeping Wives* (1926) and launched the greatest comedy team ever to appear on the movie screen.

Rivaling Mickey Rooney and Artie Shaw, Laurel was married *eight* times (to four women!) while partner Hardy was married only three times.

Laurel's real name was Arthur Stanley Jefferson and, contrary to his screen image, he was an intelligent, quick-witted, and assertive man.

Lauren, Ralph

The popular clothes designer, (born Ralph Lifshitz), famous for his Ivy League and new

"Cowboy Cool" look, has won six Coty awards, more than any other designer.

Laver, Rod

Rod Laver's "rocket" serve owed some of its speed to his 12-inch left forearm—the same size forearms that heavyweight boxing champion Rocky Marciano had.

Lavin, Linda

The actress's mother, Lucille Potter, was a singer with the Paul Whiteman Band.

Lawrence, Carol

The Broadway actress was born Carol Maria Laraia but after appearing on Chicago television programs in the early 1950s and having her last name mispronounced so often, she decided to change it to Lawrence.

Lawrence, Gertrude

British stage and movie actress Gertrud Alexandra Dagmar Lawrence Klasen was the daughter of a professional singer whose stage name was Arthur Lawrence. When she was ten years old, she adopted her father's stage last name, calling herself "Little Gertie Lawrence" and toured the English provinces with her father. She added the "e" to "Gertrud" later.

Lawrence, Steve

Young Sidney Liebowitz (Steve's real name) started in show business as a piano accompanist to his brother Bernie and played nightclubs and bars in the New York area. When Bernie was drafted into the service Sidney changed his name to Steve Lawrence, using the first names of his two nephews, and became a singer on his own.

Lazar, Swifty

The literary agent extraordinaire was given his nickname "Swifty" by Humphrey Bogart after Lazar made five deals in one day.

Lazar, a lawyer by training, was once an assistant district attorney.

Leachman, Cloris

Actress Cloris Leachman went to Northwestern School of Drama on an Edgar Bergen scholarship.

Leakey, Richard

The second-generation anthropologist (*Origins* and *Homo Habilis*) quit high school and never studied anthropology at a university. Anthropology was so much a part of his upbringing that he already knew more about anthropology than most university professors.

Leary, Timothy

Long before Professor Leary "turned on and tuned out" he attended the United States Military Academy at West Point, New York, where he studied for 18 months, after transferring from Holy Cross College.

LeCarré, John

The novelist's real name is David John Moore Cornwell. As a British foreign service officer writing novels on the side, Cornwell knew that he shouldn't use his real name so he took a pen name—from a London shopfront he once passed while riding a bus.

Lee, Canada

The stage actor's full real name was Leonard Lionel Cornelius Canegata. Early in his career he was a professional boxer known as Lee Canegata, but fight announcer Joe Humphries reversed and shortened the name to Canada Lee.

Lee, Gen. Robert E.

The noted Civil War general was the originator of the idea to offer a college course in journalism —at Washington University (now Washington and Lee) in 1896.

Lee, Gypsy Rose

The sexy "ecdysiast" (a term coined by H. L. Mencken for another famous stripper) learned the art of striptease from a woman known as Tessie the Tassel-Twirler.

Mike Todd called her "The Best Undressed Woman in America."

Lee, Peggy

One of her first singing jobs was on radio station WDAY in Fargo, North Dakota. The station manager liked her singing but didn't like her name, Norma Dolores Engstrom, so he changed it to Peggy Lee.

Lee, Pinky

Pinky's real name is Pinkus Leff but his agent suggested that he take the name Lee so that the three-person act in which Pinky appeared would be called "Port, Lee (two nautical terms!) and Dotty."

Leigh, Vivien

Vivien was born Vivien Mary Hartley in Darjeeling, India where her father, a British stockbroker, and mother used to spend six months every year. After marrying Herbert Leigh Holman, a London lawyer, she pursued a career in the theater and decided to adopt her husband's middle name as her stage name.

Lemmon, Jack

Jack Lemmon was born on an elevator at the Newton-Wellesley Hospital in Newton, Massachusetts on February 8, 1925.

Lemmon was elected "class poet" at Phillips Andover Academy, Class of 1943.

Jack once used the stage name Timothy Orange (vs. lemon, get it?) in a Harvard play because he was on academic probation and was not supposed to be acting.

For a chemistry class at Harvard, Lemmon wrote a paper entitled "Economic Consequences of C_2H_6OH Displacement by Olea Europa in a Mean Martini." It was a 14-page dissertation on how bartenders save money by putting olives in martinis, thereby displacing 8 percent of the more expensive alcohol. Lemmon received a passing mark but the professor questioned his "oblique sense of values."

Jack's full name is John Uhler Lemmon III.

At Harvard College, Lemmon was president of the Hasty Pudding Club, the dramatic society.

When Harry Cohn, head of Columbia Pictures, signed Lemmon to star with Judy Holliday in *It Should Happen to You* he wanted to change Jack's last name to Lennon but Jack pointed out that it sounded like Lenin, the Russian revolutionary, and added, "They'll say I'm a commie!"

Lennon, John

The ex-Beatle's full name is John *Winston* Lennon. He was born in Liverpool on October 9, 1940, during a Nazi air raid, and his patriotic mother decided to name him after Winston Churchill.

John takes credit for giving the Beatles their group name. He was an ardent fan of Buddy Holly and the Crickets and sought out names of other insects for the newly-formed rock 'n roll band to use. He settled on the insect beetle but changed the second "e" to an "a" to give it a musical twist ("beat"). The original five-man "beetle-browed" group was called "The Silver Beatles" back in 1960.

Leonardo da Vinci

The Florentine artist and scientist was the illegitimate child of Piero da Vinci and a woman named Caterina.

The real title of da Vinci's famous painting known as the *Mona Lisa* is *La Gioconda*.

Some sources indicate that da Vinci invented the scissors.

Lerner, Alan Jay

Lerner and Loewe not only had hit songs from *My Fair Lady* and *Camelot* in common, but they were both boxers at one time. Alan Lerner boxed at Harvard (and lost the sight of one eye) and Fritz Loewe boxed before he became a composer, once losing to Tony Canzoneri.

The successful lyricist has been less successful with his marriages. He has been married *seven* times!

Lerner wears white gloves while he is working to avoid getting ink on his hands.

Lerner attended both Choate preparatory school and Harvard College with John F. Kennedy.

Lester, Richard

The American-born movie director (*Help, A Hard Day's Night*) has a B.S. degree in clinical psychology from the University of Pennsylvania, and was graduated (Class of 1951) at age 19.

Levene, Sam

The veteran Broadway actor, born in Russia in 1905, was originally named Levine (with an "i") but he changed the spelling to give it a touch of distinction.

Levine, James

At age four, conductor James Levine had not yet learned the alphabet and he could barely count to ten, but he had been playing the piano for a year.

Levine's father, an executive of a dress manufacturing film using the label LeVine, was a band leader in the 1930s and used the professional name Larry Lee.

Lewis, Jerry

The movie director and comedian was born Joseph Levitch but he adopted his father's stage name "Lewis" (his father was Danny Lewis, a nightclub singer whose specialty was nostalgic songs) and changed his first name to Jerry. Why? He didn't think anyone with the name Levitch could get laughs. Also he didn't want to use the name Joey Lewis because there was already another comedian, Joe E. Lewis, with a similar name.

Jerry has some interesting idiosyncrasies: He never wears the same pair of socks more than once! While on stage, he never carries anything in his pockets except for photographs of his family. It's his good luck charm.

Don't cross Jerry. He once got in a feud with his agent and had the agent's picture printed on rolls of toilet paper which he encouraged his friends and relatives to use at every opportunity.

In the movie *My Friend Irma,* Jerry's hand was temporarily paralyzed from squeezing too many oranges in many takes of one scene but he finished the movie with his hand immobilized to avoid holding up production.

Eddie Cantor once claimed that he raised over a billion dollars for the March of Dimes and other causes but he was greatly overexaggerating. Jerry Lewis, however, when he reaches Cantor's age when he died (72 years) will have raised about *$1.2 billion* for Muscular Dystrophy at the rate he has been raising money!

Lewis recently admitted that he was addicted to the pain-killer drug Percodan for 13 years and was almost driven to committing suicide. He started taking the drug after chipping a piece of bone in his upper spinal column.

Lewis, Jerry Lee

Jerry first married at age 14 to a girl three years his senior. At age 22 he married his 13-year-old second cousin, Myra Gail Brown, his bass player's daughter.

Lewis's flamboyant style didn't always work in his favor. He was thrown out of Waxahachie Texas bible school for playing "My God is Real" boogie-woogie style.

Lewis's son Steve Allen Lewis was named after the television comic who first allowed him to play "A Whole Lot of Shakin' Goin' On" at a time when it was banned on the radio as being vulgar.

Earlier in his career, Lewis drank so heavily that he "needed a fifth of tequila just to sober up."

Lewis, Joe E.

The late comedian, born Joe Klewan, started his career as a singer, but after Chicago mobsters slashed his throat he could no longer sing and took up telling jokes and drinking.

Lewis, Sinclair

Nobel Prize-winning Sinclair Lewis once did ghost writing for writer Jack London!

H. G. Wells was Lewis's favorite novelist and in fact the writer named his son, Wells, in honor of the famous writer.

In the early 1920s while in London, Lewis rode through the crowded streets of Piccadilly, shouting "Beaver!" to every passerby with a beard! Lewis died in a nursing home in Rome, Italy.

Lewis, Ted

The vaudeville and Broadway singer, born Theodore Leopold Friedman, adopted the last name of Al Lewis, a musician with whom Ted was once teamed, so that his name would fit on a marquee.

Liberace

Liberace, whose full name is Wladziu Valentino Liberace, is the son of a Polish mother and Italian father—which is why he has such an unusual full name. Wladziu is Polish for Walter, the Valentino came from Rudolph Valentino, who was his mother's idol (Liberace's younger brother was christened Rudolph Valentino Liberace!) and Liberace is an Italian name. When Lee, as he is called by his friends, started playing the piano professionally, he decided to take a stage name. At the Wunderbar Night Club in Warsaw, Wisconsin, the name given to him was Walter Buster Keys but after six months he decided to use only his real last name, thinking that if his idol Paderewski could do it he could do it too.

Liberace's costume budget has been as much as $200,000 a year not including the cost of his jewelry.

Talk show host Johnny Carson did the first imitatation of Liberace on television. It was in 1951 on a local Los Angeles TV station. (At the time, Liberace was appearing on another L.A. station.)

After seeing Liberace in his gold lamé costumes in his Las Vegas act, Elvis Presley adopted the idea and appeared in a similar outfit in his next movie.

Lincoln, Abraham

Abraham Lincoln was not the only president born in a log cabin. Andrew Jackson, Zachary

Taylor, Millard Fillmore, Franklin Pierce, James Buchanan, and James Garfield also were born in log cabins.

A recent study by Illinois congressman Paul Findley indicated that "Honest Abe" was not all that honest. In filing his travel expenses, Lincoln put in for 3,252 miles round trip between Washington, D.C. and Springfield, Illinois but the mileage is actually 1,800 miles round trip, giving Lincoln some extra spending money.

Lincoln used to take off his shoes at any opportunity because he had large corns on his feet.

Lincoln was 6 feet 4 inches tall by age 14.

Lincoln was the first president born outside the original 13 states.

When he was assassinated, Lincoln was wearing a Brooks Brothers natural-shoulder frock coat, according to author Stephen Birmingham.

Honest Abe was once arrested for "ferrying without a license" but, serving in his own defense, was acquitted.

In 1849 Lincoln was awarded a patent for a system of "buoying vessels over shoals." He was the only president to be granted a patent.

Only one of Lincoln's sons lived beyond his teens, Robert Todd Lincoln, who later served as President Garfield's Secretary of War.

After Lincoln's assassination his wife Mary Todd Lincoln became mentally unstable and eventually was placed in an insane asylum for four months. Lincoln's mother, Nancy Hanks Lincoln, was an illegitimate child.

Robert Lincoln, the president's son, was cross-eyed.

In his prime, Lincoln could split 50 rails an hour for up to 12 hours.

It is ironic that Lincoln first uttered the truism, "The ballot is stronger than the bullet."

As postmaster of the New Salem, Indiana post office, Lincoln was paid an annual salary of $55.70.

Lincoln, Elmo

Lincoln, the first actor to play Tarzan in the movies, was born Otto Elmo Linkenhelter.

Lind, Jenny

The first private railroad car was not built for a railroad or steel magnate but for the "Swedish Nightingale," Jenny Lind who came to the United States for a singing tour in 1850.

Jenny Lind was an illegitimate child.

Lindbergh, Charles

Charles Lindbergh was not from St. Louis as some people think—except for Minnesotans who know that he was raised in Little Falls, Minnesota and people from Detroit, Michigan, who know that he was born there. His plane *The Spirit of St. Louis* was so named because St.

Louis businessmen gave Lindy the money to build the single-engine plane.

Lindbergh's father, a lawyer, was a Republican congressman representing Minnesota's Sixth District from 1907 to 1917.

Eight years after Lindbergh made the first nonstop solo airplane flight from New York to Paris, he helped Dr. Alexis Carrel develop the first artificial heart.

Linden, Hal

Early in his career Hal Linden ("Barney Miller") whose real name is Harold Lipshitz, was passing through New Jersey on a bus when he saw an immense storage tank on which the name of the town, Linden, was written in large letters. He liked the name and decided to adopt it as his stage surname.

Lindsay, John Vliet

The ex-mayor of New York City and former "Silk Stocking" district congressman had a twin brother, David A. Lindsay, also a lawyer, but few New Yorkers were ever aware of this fact until his twin died of cancer on December 23, 1977.

Lindsay, Vachel

The American poet's daughter, Susan, married (second marriage) Bertrand Russell's son.

Lindsay committed suicide by drinking a bottle of Lysol.

Linkletter, Art

In Moose Jaw, Saskatchewan, Art Linkletter was born Arthur Gordon Kelley but was abandoned at the age of one month and adopted by Fulton John and Mary Metzler Linkletter.

There is a special reason why Art Linkletter is active in the campaign against teenage drug abuse—in 1969 after taking LSD, his youngest daughter, Diane, committed suicide.

At San Diego State College, Art was captain of the championship basketball team, played in the AAU National Handball Championships, and also held the Southern California 50-yard back-stroke swimming title one year.

Linnaeus, Carolus

The Swedish botanist, born Carl von Linné was originally a medical doctor but at Uppsala University in Sweden he exchanged his chair of medicine for the chair of botany—his true love. He became interested in flowers at an early age and was even nicknamed "The Little Botanist" at age eight.

Linowitz, Sol

The former chairman of the Xerox Corporation once played violin in the Utica Symphony Orchestra and to this day still plays the instrument "moderately well for a youngster, sadly for a grownup."

Sol's three brothers changed the spelling of their surname to "Linowes" apparently to simplify it.

Lloyd, Harold

The silent screen comedian lost his right thumb and index finger while shooting a movie and subsequently had to wear gloves or special prosthetic fingers when he was being filmed or photographed.

Lockwood, Margaret

The British actress, who appeared in Alfred Hitchcock's *The Lady Vanishes* (1938), was born in Karachi, India where her father was a British civil servant.

Loeb, William

The archconservative newspaper publisher (*Manchester, New Hampshire Union Leader*) is the godson of President Theodore Roosevelt, for whom his father was private secretary.

Loewe, Frederick

The composer and Alan Jay Lerner collaborator, who wrote the song "The Rain in Spain" in ten minutes, wanted to name their musical about Professor Higgins and Eliza Doolittle *Fanfaroon.*

Logan, Josh

At Princeton, Class of '31, Logan was elected the "wittiest" in his class, "thinks he's the wittiest," "most original" and "thinks he's the most original." (The student "most likely to succeed" was

Leonard Firestone, son of the tire company executive.)

Logan's father slit his own throat while in a sanatarium. (Logan was three years old at the time.)

Director Josh Logan's mother, because of an intermarriage within the family, is also his cousin!

Lollobrigida, Gina

Like other Italian actresses, one of Gina's early jobs was posing for Italian comic strips (no pun intended) known as *fumetti* which use photographs instead of cartoon-drawn figures.

Lombard, Carole

Lombard made her first movie when she was 12 years old, using her real name Jane Alice Peters. Later, however, the Fox studio felt that her real name was too ordinary and asked her to change it. Her mother picked the first name Carol at the advice of a numerologist and the name Lombard was taken from a neighbor of that name. The extra "e" was added to "Carol" in 1930 when the name was misspelled in the advertising for her move *Safety in Numbers*. She kept the new spelling because she thought it would bring her good luck.

London, Jack

London was a dedicated socialist and even ran for the office of mayor in Oakland, California on the Socialist ticket in 1905 but lost, receiving less than 500 votes.

London, Julie

Singer and actress Julie London (born Julie Peck), daughter of a vaudeville song-and-dance duo, made her radio debut at the age of three when she sang "Falling in Love Again."

Long, Huey

Although the record has since been beaten, Senator Huey Pierce Long of Louisiana once set the senate filibuster record on June 12, 1935, by speaking for 15½ hours on the floor of the Senate. He started at 12:30 p.m. and finished at 4 a.m. the next day. When published in the *Congressional Record*, Long's speech occupied over one hundred pages. (see Wayne Morse and J. Strom Thurmond)

Longfellow, Henry Wadsworth

The American poet ("Hyperion," "Evangeline") was a professor of modern languages by profession and taught at Bowdoin, Harvard, and in Europe. In 1854, at 47 years old, he found teaching a burden and retired to devote all his time to writing poetry.

The phrase "Into each life some rain must fall" originated in the third stanza of his lyric poem "The Rainy Day." It is followed by the line, "Some days must be dark and dreary."

Loos, Anita

Miss Loos's brother, Dr. Clifford Loos, along with Dr. Cabot Lodge of Boston, developed the group insurance system now known as Blue Cross.

Lopez, Nancy

Although Miss Lopez is the daughter of Mexican-Americans and was raised in New Mexico, she does not speak any Spanish.

The golfer's CB handle is "Jive Cookie."

Loren, Sophia

Sophia's Oscar (*Two Women*) statuette is a fake. The original one was stolen by thieves so she replaced it with a replica.

The actress has a shrapnel wound on her head, inflicted during World War II.

Sophia's sister, Maria, married Romano Mussolini, son of the Italian dictator Benito Mussolini.

Every day Sophia wears something red for good luck.

Miss Loren claims to be a witch of sorts. She gets visions and premonitions that (occasionally) come true (a plain crash, a robbery, a fire).

Louis IX, King of France

Saint Louis, as he was later known, has the distinction of being the only king in France's history to be breastfed by his own mother.

Louis, Joe

Louis was world heavyweight boxing champion for 11 years 8 months (from June 22, 1937 to

March 1, 1949 when he announced his retirement), longer than anyone else in boxing history. In that period he defended his title 25 times.

The heavyweight boxing champ's full name is Joseph Louis Barrow. His name was shortened by John Roxborough, a successful Detroit bail bondsman who supported local black athletes. After he saw Joe fight at the Brewster Street Gym he was impressed enough by his boxing ability to become his promoter and mentor. Roxborough thought Joe's name was too long so he convinced Joe to shorten it.

Joe Louis was a cocaine addict but kicked the habit in 1969 (the year he correctly predicted that Muhammad Ali would lose to Joe Frazier.)

In his first fight, at age 16, he was floored 6 times in 3 rounds.

Louis XIII, King of France

The French king (1601–1643) was prematurely bald at age 23.

Louis XIV, King of France

Prince Louis Dieudonne, later Louis XIV, was born on September 5, 1638 with two teeth already in his royal mouth.

Louis XV, King of France

A mistress inspired the construction of the first elevator. Louis XV, who lived on the first floor of the Versailles Palace, needed a quick way to get to his mistress' (Mme. de Chateauroux) room on the second floor so he had a "Flying Chair" or rudimentary elevator built and installed in 1743.

Louise, Tina

The sexy stage and movie actress was born Tina Blacker, became Tina Meyer when her mother remarried, and then changed her name to Tina Louise on entering the theater because, in her words, "It's entirely my name. To me it means joy. Nobody in any family can be hurt if anything happens to this name because it is my name only."

Lovelace, Linda

Linda Lovelace's throat received incredible camera coverage in the movie *Deep Throat* but the upper part of her body did not get any exposure—to avoid showing the scars she has from an automobile accident in which she went through the windshield.

Loy, Myrna

When Myrna Williams was hired to dance a stage prologue to *The Thief of Bagdad* at Grauman's Chinese Theatre in Hollywood, she was told that her name sounded too prissy. At someone's suggestion, Myrna picked the name Loy which sounded mysteriously Oriental.

Lucas, George

The film director is estimated to have made $80 million from the gross of the movie *Star Wars* and its toy and record spin-offs.

Luce, Charles

The board chairman of Con Ed was kept out of World War II because one of his legs is shorter than the other—as a result of having polio as a child.

Luce, Clare Boothe

The congresswoman's family name was originally Booth but she added the "e" to avoid being associated with the family of Lincoln assassin, John Wilkes Booth.

Ludwig, Daniel K.

Few people have ever heard of this man but he is richer than any Rockefeller, Ford, Dupont, or Kennedy combined. A shipping and real estate magnate, he is worth about $3 billion.

Lugosi, Bela

Lugosi's real name was Bela Ferenc Dezsco Blasko. He was born in Lugos, Hungary (part of Transylvania!) from which he took his professional surname Lugosi.

After the immense success of the movie *Dracula*, Lugosi was asked to play the Frankenstein monster in the movie *Frankenstein* but turned down the role because it did not have any lines other than grunts and groans. Boris Karloff got the role as everyone knows but later grew tired of it and Lugosi played the Frankenstein monster in *Frankenstein Meets the Wolf Man* (1943).

It is hard for Americans to believe this but Bela Lugosi was once a leading man and a romantic lead at that on the Hungarian stage. Later, as an established star in Hollywood, he used to claim that he was the John Barrymore of Hungary.

Although Lugosi's screen roles often required that he drink the blood of his victims, in real life he became ill at the sight of his own blood and would often pass out.

Unfortunately, Bela was both an alcoholic and drug addict at various times in his life. He was always fond of Egri Bikaver, a Hungarian red wine, but eventually his drinking became enough of a problem for him to join Alcoholics Anonymous. He became addicted to drugs when he was prescribed morphine to assuage severe leg pains and often sought out the drug (or methadone) to obtain relief.

As he designated in his will, Lugosi was buried in his Dracula cape and tuxedo, which demonstrated that he was a true character actor to the hilt.

Lugosi invariably played monsters, villains, and sinister characters but one of his straight roles was in *Ninotchka* (1939) in which he played a Russian commissar, Razinin.

Lunt, Alfred and Lynn Fontanne

The distinguished stage actor and his wife were married for 55 years. When asked if Miss Fontanne ever contemplated divorce, she responded, "Murder yes, but divorce, no."

The couple rarely appeared in movies. Lunt was in six movies, of which one was a talkie and Fontanne was in only three movies. The only movie in which they both appeared was *Second Youth* (1924).

Lupescu, Magda

Born Elena Wolff, she received her new last name when her father decided to Latinize "Wolff" into "Lupescu," the Rumanian word for wolf. She was given the first name Magda by the press after her affair with Crown Prince Carol of Rumania was made known.

Lupino, Ida

Miss Lupino's father, Stanley Lupino, was a British actor.

Lynde, Paul

When Paul Lynde went to Northwestern University School of Drama in 1944, Charlton Heston, Patricia Neal, Jeffrey Hunter, and Ralph Meeker were some of his classmates.

In his senior year at Northwestern, Lynde was named "Best Actor of the Year."

At one point early in his career, he weighed 260 pounds but when he found that his choice of roles was being severely limited he went on a crash diet and lost about 80 pounds.

Lynn, Loretta

Born Loretta Webb, the country and western singer was given her first name by her mother after actress Loretta Young (whose real first name was Gretchen!) and when she married Oliver Vanetta Lynn, a one-time coal miner, she became Loretta Lynn.

Married when she was only 13 years old, she became a mother at age 14 and a grandmother at age 31!

Lyons, Leonard

The well-known newspaper columnist, whose real name was Leonard Sucher, was originally a lawyer. He was a graduate of St. John's Law School and actually practiced law from 1929 to 1934.

The columnist was given his new last name by the editor of the *Jewish Daily Forward,* where he worked early in his journalism career.

M

Mabley, "Moms"

Born Loretta Mary Aiken in Brevard, North
Carolina, the comedienne took the name Jackie
Mabley from her entertainer boyfriend Jack
Mabley. ("He took a lot off me. The least I
could do was take his name." (She later earned
the nickname "Moms" because of her motherly
attitude toward people.

MacArthur, Gen. Douglas

According to author William Manchester in
American Caesar, MacArthur, Franklin D.
Roosevelt, and Winston Churchill had a com-
mon ancestor.

In 1903 MacArthur graduated first in his class
of 93 at the United States Military Academy at
West Point, New York, and attained the highest
marks of anyone in the previous 25 years.

Macaulay, Thomas Babington

The British essayist, statesman, and historian
best known for his comprehensive *History of*

England, was admitted to the London bar but did not practice law because he preferred to contribute to literary reviews and to aid the antislavery cause.

MacDonald, Jeanette

Nelson Eddy once complained to Fredric March that he would never shoot another love scene with Jeanette MacDonald unless she stopped burping in his face.

MacGraw, Ali

The movie actress's first name at birth was *Alice.*

Ali MacGraw, a 1960 graduate of Wellesley College, is no fool but she was born on April Fool's Day in 1939.

MacLeish, Archibald

The poet and Pulitzer Prize-winning playwright (*J. B.*) was a Harvard Law School graduate (1919) and practiced law for three years.

MacLeod, Gavin

The star of the "Love Boat" television series was born Allan George William See in Mount Kisco, New York. When he made his Broadway debut in *A Hatful of Rain* with Shelley Winters, he changed his name to Gavin (a name he liked) MacLeod (a tribute to an acting instructor he had had at Ithaca College).

Madison, James

Madison, the fourth President of the United States, was a bachelor until age 43 when he married Dolley Todd, a widow.

Both of Madison's vice-presidents, George Clinton and Elbridge Gerry died while in office.

Madison's last words were, "I always talk better lying down." Perhaps only Dolley Madison knew the truth of those words.

James Madison was the smallest U.S. president. He was five four and weighed only 100 pounds.

Madison died on June 28, 1836 and was the last surviving signer of the U.S. Constitution.

Madison, Guy

The movie and television actor's real name is Robert Moseley but talent agent Henry Willson, noting Moseley's fondness for ice cream ("You never saw a *guy* who liked to eat so much ice cream!"), got the idea for his new name after seeing a Dolly Madison ice cream sign.

Magnani, Anna

The fiery Italian actress (*The Rose Tattoo*) was born in Alexandria, Egypt.

Magritte, René

When the Belgian surrealist painter was 14 years old, his mother committed suicide by drowning herself in the Sambre River.

Mahler, Gustave

Mahler may not have written the best symphony in the world but he did write the longest one. His symphony No. 3 in D Minor is 1 hour and 34 minutes long and its first movement alone is 45 minutes.

Born a Jew, Mahler later converted to Catholicism.

Mahan, Alfred Thayer

The rear admiral and naval historian (*The Influence of Sea Power upon History, 1660–1783*) was born at West Point, New York, where his father was a professor of military engineering at the United States Military Academy. The younger Mahan was a graduate of the United States Naval Academy at Annapolis, Maryland.

Mailer, Norman

Mailer did not major in linguistics or pugilistics at Harvard College, as some people think. He studied engineering.

At last count, Mailer had eight children by six women, including four wives.

When asked at his 35th reunion at Harvard what advice he would give to the class of 1978, Mailer tersely replied, "Study magic."

Mailer became a cook in the Army to get a promotion ("his stripes") and years later bragged that he taught his five wives how to cook.

After stabbing his second wife, Adele Morales, with a penknife Mailer spent 17 days in the psychiatric ward of Bellevue Hospital in New York City for observation.

Majors, Lee

On his television series Lee Majors may have bionic legs and a bionic right arm but in real life he has a glass nose—he has broken it five times!

Malcolm X

The Black Muslim leader's last words were, "Let's cool it brothers ..."

Malden, Karl

Karl Malden, whose real name is Mladen Sekulovich, said that he changed his name "to fit theater marquees" and he did have a point! His new surname, it should be noted, is a variation of his original given name.

Karl's unique nose got some of its character while he was a student at Emerson High School in Gary, Indiana. As a football player he broke his nose twice which, according to Karl, aided and abetted its bulbous appearance.

Speaking of broken noses, Marlon Brando owes his flattened nose to Karl, who broke it during a sparring session when they were appearing in the Broadway production of *A Streetcar Named Desire*.

Manchester, William

The writer (*Death of a President*, *American Caesar*) was wounded at Okinawa during

World War II, became temporarily blind and partially deaf, and was discharged as a 100 percent disability case.

He once paid a library fine of $505.69 for a book (*Six Plays of Clifford Odets*) overdue 29 years from the University of Massachusetts library.

Mancini, Henry

At Aliquippa High School, Aliquippa, Pennsylvania, Class of 1942, Mancini was "a true music lover, collects records, plays in the band, and has even composed several beautiful selections. He wishes to continue his study of music and to have an orchestra of his own some day."

Manilow, Barry

The singer was an advertising major at City College in New York City but after one year transferred to New York College of Music.

His pet beagle is named Bagel.

Manners, David

The Canadian-born movie actor (*Dracula, The Mummy*), born Rauff de Ryther Duan Acklom, was a descendant of William the Conqueror.

Mansfield, Mike

The ex-senator, U.S. Ambassador to Japan was born in Greenwich Village, New York City, where his father was a porter at the Van Rensselaer Hotel. But at age three he was sent to Montana to live with an aunt and uncle.

During World War I, Sen. Mansfield served in three branches of the armed services—the Army, Navy, and Marines. At age 14, he ran away from home and joined the Navy. Nineteen months later, his real age was discovered and he was immediately discharged. He then joined the Army but they found out his real age and also discharged him. Finally the determined youth joined the Marines.

Mantle, Mickey

Mantle's career total of 536 home runs was a significant achievement but his 710 strike-outs were even more significant.

The Yankee slugger was named after baseball great Mickey Cochrane.

Marat, Jean Paul

Before he became a leader of the French Revolution, Marat was a doctor. He studied medicine in Bordeaux and Paris, practiced in London for a while, got an honorary doctor of medicine degree from the University of St. Andrews in 1775 and spent many years in private practice before becoming a revolutionary journalist.

Marceau, Marcel

Marceau's father, a Jewish butcher from Strasbourg, died at Auschwitz during World War II.

The mime's real last name is Mangel.

In school silent mime Marceau won prizes for *recitation*, and was an excellent artist.

Marceau's wife, Anne, says that he never stops talking at home.

March, Fredric

Frederick McIntyre Bickel made his stage debut as Fred Bickel at Ford's Theatre in Baltimore, but after he won the lead in *The Melody Man* (1924) he changed his name to Fredric March at the suggestion of John Cromwell, the play's producer. The problem with Bickel was that it rhymed with pickle—which is why he decided to use a shortened version of his mother's maiden name, Marcher, instead.

Marconi, Guglielmo

The Italian physicist and inventor of radio telegraphy had a glass eye.

Marquand, J. P.

The novelist (*The Late George Apley*) was a chemistry major at Harvard, Class of 1915.

Marquand was once mistakenly identified as a check forger at the Abercrombie and Fitch department store.

Marsh, Jean

Jean Marsh's contribution to the popular television series "Upstairs Downstairs" was not just good acting—she conceived the idea (with ac-

tress friend Eileen Atkins) and wrote the original outline for the series.

Marshall, George C.

Marshall is the only U.S. general to have been
awarded the Nobel Prize (1953). He won the
award not for his military accomplishments,
obviously, but for his work in developing the
European Recovery Plan, later known as the
Marshall Plan.

Marshall, John

Two days after Chief Justice Marshall died
(July 6, 1835) the Liberty Bell in Philadelphia
cracked while tolling his death.

Marshall, Peter

The host of television's "Hollywood Squares"
quiz show was born Pierre la Cock. His son, a
major league baseball player, is Pete la Cock.

Marshall, Thurgood

Marshall was named Thoroughgood at birth but
the name was eventually shortened to Thur-
good. The Supreme Court justice (the first black
ever appointed to the Supreme Court) was
named after a paternal grandfather who went
by the names Thoroughgood and Thornygood
so he could draw two pensions when he retired.

Martin, Billy

The name on the baseball manager's original
birth certificate was erroneously listed as Alfred

Manuel Pesani but the surname of his natural father, a Hawaiian of Portuguese descent, was Martin. Billy's mother, Joan Salvini Pesani, not yet married to Billy's father, put her former husband's surname on the certificate. He received the name Billy because his grandmother, Raffaela Salvini, used to call him *bellis,* short for *bellisimo,* meaning "very beautiful" in Italian.

Martin, Dean

Dean Martin's real name is Dino Crocetti but as a singer in Walker's Cafe in Steubenville, Ohio, and then with Ernie McKay's band, he used the name Dino Martini. (He was probably trying to take advantage of tenor Nino Martini's popularity at that time.) One night bandleader Sammy Watkins heard Dino and signed him up for an engagement in Cleveland. At that time Dino gave up the name "Martini" and Americanized his name to Dean Martin.

Martin not only had his name changed but also had his nose changed. With a loan from comedian Lou Costello, arranged by agent Lou Perry, he had his nose fixed.

Because of a traumatic experience in which he was trapped in an elevator for several hours, Martin hates elevators and will try to avoid them even if it requires climbing many flights of stairs.

Dean Martin's reputation as a drunk was created after his split with Jerry Lewis. It was to give him an image around which an act could be developed, as Phil Harris and Joe E. Lewis had successfully done.

Dean has a fear of illness and death and conspicuously avoids hospitals and funerals.

According to the *Guinness Book of World Records,* Martin's $34,000,000 three-year contract with NBC is the largest TV contract ever signed.

Martin, Mary

Miss Martin was originally considered for the Eliza Doolittle role in the Broadway play *My Fair Lady* but after she heard the first five songs that Alan Jay Lerner and Frederick Loewe had written for it she told her husband that "those dear boys have lost their talent" and turned down the part.

Martin, Steve

The "Wild and Crazy Man" was a cheerleader in high school.

Marvin, Lee

As a Marine in World War II, Marvin was shot in the spine while fighting in the Pacific war zone. He was not only awarded a Purple Heart but also received and still receives a $40-a-month lifetime disability pension.

Marx, Groucho

Although Groucho was Jewish he never tasted a bagel until he was 81 years old. In certain ways, he was almost anti-Semitic. He didn't want comedienne Totie Fields to play his mother in the Broadway play *Minnie's Boys* ("I don't want that fat Jewish broad playing my mother!" —Shelley Winters, nee Schrift, ended up getting the role). He also knew that many of the Marx Brothers' fans thought they were Italian so he didn't want to lead them to believe otherwise.

Groucho didn't like public displays of affection and wouldn't talk to his daughter Melinda for a year because she kissed her husband on the lips in public.

Flowers and candlelight reminded Groucho of funeral parlors so he didn't like to see them in any dining room.

While in England, Groucho had lunch with writer Somerset Maugham, one of his fans, but was greatly disappointed when he found out that Maugham was a homosexual.

When author Margaret Mitchell found out that *Gone With the Wind* was going to be made into a movie, she did not want to get involved with the production of it but she did have one suggestion—as an avid fan of the Marx Brothers, she proposed that Groucho Marx be cast in the role of Rhett Butler.

Groucho's favorite book was *Charlotte's Web*, a children's book written by E. B. White. (It is a story about a spider named Charlotte and her friend Wilbur the Pig. Charlotte dies at the end but not before leaving lots of baby spiders to whom Wilbur remains loyal.)

In the movie *Animal Crackers* the reference to Capt. Jeffrey T. Spaulding, the African explorer was an in-joke alluding to a Hollywood dope pusher, known as Capt. Spaulding, according to Kenneth Anger in *Hollywood Babylon*.

Marx, Harpo

Harpo had eclectic tastes especially when it came to dinner guests. As Oscar Levant pointed out in *A Smattering of Ignorance*, "One could never be sure in accepting a dinner invitation to Harpo's whether one's companions would be H. G. Wells and Don Budge, or Somerset Maugham and Salvador Dali. Frequently the combinations were even more remarkable—Aldous Huxley and Maxie Rosenbloom."

Marx, Karl

The revolutionary philosopher once worked as a reporter for the *New York Tribune* in their London office.

Mason, James

Actor James Mason has a degree in architecture from Cambridge University in England but when he left school in 1931, according to him, "The great depression was still having its effect and there was little work around for a hopeful young architect" so he "drifted into acting."

Mason, Marsha

The Academy award-winning actress once did a television commercial in which she had to dance around a toilet bowl.

Masters, Edgar Lee

The American poet and novelist (*Spoon River Anthology*) was a lawyer and was a law partner of Clarence Darrow for a brief period in Chicago, Illinois.

Masterson, Bat

The legendary sheriff and U.S. Marshal became a sports writer toward the end of his career, writing for the *Morning Telegraph* in New York.

Mathis, Johnny

On "The Tonight Show," the popular singer admitted that he ate and liked monkey brains, which he had eaten in the Philippines. Mathis said that the brains tasted "metallic . . . like fresh blood." He also admitted eating dog meat.

Mathis's record album "Johnny's Greatest Hits" was on Billboard's best-seller chart from late 1958 to July, 1968, a total of 490 weeks.

At Roosevelt Junior High School in San Francisco, Mathis was the first black ever elected class president.

Matthau, Walter

Matthau's son, David, appeared in the movie *California Suite*. He was the bellhop at the Beverly Hills Hotel who came by when Walter was trying to drag the passed-out call girl into the hall.

Walter's mother, Rose, spells her last name Mat-
thow and she doesn't know why he changed
the spelling of his name to Matthau.

His wife Carol was married, twice, to writer
William Saroyan.

Maugham, Somerset

As a young doctor at a hospital in Lambeth, a
London slum, Somerset Maugham was moved
enough by his experiences to write a novel
about them. The book, *Liza of Lambeth,* was a
modest success but encouraged him enough to
pursue writing and abandon his career in medicine.

Mauldin, Bill

The two time Pulitzer Prize-winning cartoonist
costarred with Audie Murphy in the movie *The
Red Badge of Courage* in 1951.

Max, Peter

Pop artist Peter Max and his wife were so "into"
astrology that they named their children
Adam Cosmo and Libra Astro.

May, Elaine

Elaine May's surname at birth was Berlin (her
father was Jack Berlin, an actor in the Yiddish
theater) but it became May when as a teenager
she married Marvin May. Elaine's teenage
daughter Jeannie, however, has chosen to use
the surname Berlin.

...eran television actor used to appear as ...cGaren.

...James Kenneth McManus, the sports ...cer was given his new professional name ...when he started working there in 1950.

...st job at CBS-TV was on an early evening ...show which the producers wanted to ...e Real McKay." To match the program's ...hey made him change his last name ...cManus to McKay and he has used the ...ver since.

...William

...nt McKinley's wife, an invalid and epi-...had a seizure at his second inaugural

...ley always wore a red carnation in his

...od

...en was a movie actor before he became ...s for his poetry. He made his screen debut ...1957 beach and bikini movie *Rock, Pretty*

..., Ed

...ahon's big break came when he was the ...door neighbor of Dick Clark, the host of

May, Rollo

The noted psychologist and writer got his unusual first name from his mother, who named him after the "Little Rollo" character in Jacob Abbott's series of books. As a young boy, May hated the name but when he later found out that there was once a Norman leader named Rollo the Conqueror, he not only accepted the name but was proud of its distinctiveness.

Mayer, Louis B.

After the movie studio head was dead and buried, an anonymous observer commented, "The only reason so many people attended his funeral was that they wanted to make sure he was dead."

Mays, Willy

In his first major league game, Willy Mays went hitless in five times at bat and had only one hit (a homer, of course) in his first 26 times at bat.

Inflation, lawyers and agents have really changed the salaries in sports. In 1954 Willy batted .345, hit 41 home runs, batted in 110 runs, and won the Most Valuable Player Award in the National League, for which his reward was the salary of $17,500 the following year.

McCambridge, Mercedes

Mercedes McCambridge was born in Joliet, Illinois but she is as Irish as they come—she is the daughter of John Patrick McCambridge and

Marie Mahaffry McCambridge and was born on St. Patrick's Day, March 17, 1918.

McCarey, Leo

The Academy Award-winning director of the movie *Going My Way* (1944) started off his career as a lawyer. After graduating from the University of Southern California Law School he worked as a lawyer but losing his first trial and other discouraging setbacks made him quit the legal profession.

McCarthy, Charlie

Charlie was no dummy. Northwestern University, the alma mater of Edgar Bergen, awarded McCarthy the honorary degree of "Master of Innuendo and Snappy Comeback."

McClellan, General George B.

The Civil War Union general was governor of New Jersey from 1878 to 1881.

McCoy, Tim

Unlike many other western movie heros Tim McCoy was a real cowboy and an expert on American Indians. McCoy was raised in Wyoming, worked as a cowhand on the range, was a cavalryman in World War I, and knew Indian ceremonies and sign language well enough to be adopted into several tribes. McCoy entered the movie business when as state adjutant general of Wyoming he was asked by Famous Players-Lasky to hire and supervise five hundred Indians and act as translator on location.

Also unlike other : was not particula "I've never been s The horse doesn't you want to know tl

McCrary, Jinx (Falkenb

Jinx was born Euge Barcelona, Spain, v was a mining enginee

Her father nicknam thought it would brin

McCrary, Tex

Tex McCrary (full Crary) received a de Yale University in 193 back home in Texas c journalism.

McDaniel, Hattie

For her role as Scarlet the movie *Gone With tl* won the Oscar for Bes was the first time a Ne award.

McDonald, Ross

McDonald, whose real n got the last name for his from Miles Archer, the of Sam Spade in Dashiel *tese Falcon.*

McGavin, D

The vet Davin M

McKay, Jim

Born as announ by CBS

Jim's fir variety call "Tl name from N name e

McKinley,

Preside leptic, ball.

McKi lapel.

McKuen,

McKu famou in the *Baby.*

McMahon

McM next-

television's "American Bandstand" program, in Philadelphia. After Edward R. Murrow interviewed Clark at his apartment for Murrow's "Person to Person" show, Clark threw a party at which McMahon met Chuck Reeves, Clark's, producer. Reeves referred Ed to Al Stark, producer of the "Who Do You Trust" quiz program, who was looking for a new announcer. Ed tried out for the job, won it, and became a classic "second banana" to the up-and-coming Nebraskan, Johnny Carson, the host of "Who Do You Trust."

McPherson, Aimee Semple

In 1930, four years after her "kidnapping," the famous evangelist had a brief sexual relationship with comedian Milton Berle, whom she met at a charity show in Los Angeles.

McQueen, Butterfly

In a production of *A Midsummer Night's Dream*, Thelma McQueen danced in the "Butterfly Ballet" and did so well she became known as Butterfly McQueen thereafter.

McQueen, Steve

Steve did most of the motorcycle driving in *The Great Escape*, but he did not make the actual jump over the barbed wire fence which was a highlight of the movie. The jump was made by British scrambler motorcyclist Jeff Smith.

While in England to film *The War Lover* McQueen cut his lip badly in a Sussex car race but director Philip Leacock did not want to delay the production of the movie so he made Steve, who was playing a B-17 bomber pilot, wear an oxygen mask—an inconsistency which few film goers ever notice.

At age 13, McQueen was sent to reform school (Junior Boy's Republic at Chino, California) after being caught stealing hubcaps. He now visits the school a couple of times a year and has also set up an annual scholarship award that goes to the best student.

As a result of a skin diving accident, worsened by age, Steve is almost totally deaf in one ear and partially deaf in the other one. His inability to hear is often mistaken as aloofness and antipathy.

McWhirter, Ross

The co-compiler of the *Guinness Book of World Records* and twin brother of Norris McWhirter, was shot to death in London on November 27, 1975, after announcing a $100,000 reward he was offering for information leading to the arrest of an Irish Republican Army zealot whose bomb killed or injured 200 people.

Mead, Margaret

Miss Mead used to give so many lectures that she would sometimes forget who her audience was. She gave one lecture on the sex deviations among the Tchambuli tribe in New Guinea to a group of theologians. They apparently found the lecture interesting because no one interrupted Miss Mead.

340

Regarding women in the United States, Margaret Mead once said, "American women are good mothers, but they make lousy wives."

The eminent anthropologist, who in her youth wanted to be a portrait painter, majored in English at college (De Pauw University and Barnard College) and received an M.A. in psychology from Columbia University in 1924.

Meade, George G.

The West Point graduate (1835) and Civil War general was born in Cadiz, Spain of American parents.

Meadows, Audrey and Jayne

Before joining the road company of *High Button Shoes*, Audrey Cotter and her sister Jane took the stage name of Meadows which was a family name (their father was Rev. Francis James Meadows Cotter, an Episcopal missionary in China, where both Jayne and Audrey were born). Jane also added the "y" to her name to give it that "un-plain" look.

Meany, George

The AFL-CIO labor leader began his career as a plumber.

Meat Loaf

The corpulent rock star got his nickname (now his legal name) in the seventh grade from his classmates who acknowledged his unusual physique (five foot two inches, 240 pounds) and his real name (*Marvin Lee Aday*).

Medici, Lorenzo de

To "Lorenzo the Magnificent" we owe the lamentable institution of the income tax. He imposted the first income tax in 1451 (it was immediately called the "catastro") but it was so unpopular (as it still is) that when the family was overthrown in 1492, the tax was quickly repealed.

Mehta, Zubin

When the popular orchestra conductor moved to Los Angeles in 1974 he bought the Brentwood home of Steve McQueen for $400,000.

Meir, Golda

When Golda Mabowitz married sign painter Morris Meyerson in 1917, she became Golda Meyerson but many years later, she changed her name, as she related in her autobiography *My Life*: "In the summer of 1956, just as I was settling into my new office and getting used, among other things, to being called Mrs. Meir—the closest I could get to a Hebrew version of Meyerson, and still obey Ben-Gurion's order that I take a Hebrew name (Meir means 'illuminate' in Hebrew) ..."

Melba, Nellie

Born Helen ("Nellie") Porter Mitchell in Australia, the singer married Charles Nesbitt Frederick Armstrong and then went to Europe for vocal training under Mathilde Marchesi. Madame Marchesi felt that the name Nellie Armstrong was not a good name for an opera singer and suggested that Nellie find a more suitable name. Being from Melbourne, Nellie suggested the names Melbourne and Melbourna and then settled on the name Melba.

Both Peaches Melba and Melba toast were named after the famous soprano.

Melchior, Lauritz

The Danish *tenor* made his debut at the Royal Opera House in Copenhagen as a *baritone*, singing the role of Silvio in *Pagliacci*.

Melville, Herman

While Melville was writing *Moby Dick*, he was a neighbor and friend of Nathaniel Hawthorne, who was then writing *The House of Seven Gables*. In fact, *Moby Dick* contains the following dedication: "IN TOKEN OF MY ADMIRATION FOR HIS GENIUS THIS BOOK IS INSCRIBED TO NATHANIEL HAWTHORNE."

In June of 1839 on his first sea voyage, Herman Melville got seasick! However, he quickly adjusted to the new environment and loved it enough to write about it for the rest of his life.

Melville was a customs inspector in New York City for 19 years, from 1866 to 1885.

Mendelssohn, Felix

Mendelssohn was only 17 years old when he wrote the overture to *A Midsummer Night's Dream*.

Menjou, Adolph

Adolph Menjou, always suave and sophisticated, in between movies used to pick up his unemployment checks in a chauffeur-driven Rolls Royce.

Merman, Ethel

Her daughter, Ethel Jr., died of an overdose of tranquilizers, mixed with alcohol in 1967.

Born as Ethel Zimmermann, she took her stage name in 1930 when she was appearing with the popular singer Al Siegel at the Brooklyn Paramount. She thought her real name was too long and wanted to use her mother's maiden name (Gardner) or her grandmother's maiden name (Hunter) but her father vetoed both names. They compromised by letting the family name be halved from Zimmermann into "Merman."

Merrick, David

The successful Broadway producer, whose real name is David Margulies, allegedly changed his last name so that if he failed as a producer in the New York theater he could always return to his St. Louis law practice without any shame. The name change was unnecessary because Merrick quadrupled his money in one of his first Broadway ventures and has been successful ever since.

As an undergraduate at Washington University in St. Louis, Merrick won second prize in a playwriting contest which is significant only because his play was judged to be better than that of another aspiring playwright—Tennessee Williams.

Merrill, Dina

The socialite actress was christened Nedenia Hutton, named after her father Ned Hutton, and is a cousin of five-and-ten heiress Barbara Hutton.

Michelangelo

In the four years it took him to paint the Sistine Chapel he never washed himself.

Michelangelo was left-handed.

Michener, James

Michener was an orphan and does not know who his parents were. All he knows is that he was born in New York City and was soon adopted by Edwin and Mabel Michener, a Quaker couple from Doylestown, Pennsylvania. Regarding his heritage, he once remarked: "I could be Jewish, part Negro, probably not Oriental, but almost anything else. This had loomed large in my thoughts."

He published his first book at a relatively old age. He was 40 years old when *Tales of the South Pacific* was published.

In an early job as a textbook editor at MacMillan publishing in New York City, Michener selected a photograph of actor Errol Flynn to epitomize American manliness (Flynn was born in Tasmania!) in a high school American history textbook. The book was distributed to schools two weeks before the movie star was accused of statutory rape.

Michu

Billed by Ringling Brothers' Circus as the shortest man in the world, Michu is actually one inch taller than Kenny Baker, the man who played R2D2 in the movie *Star Wars*.

Midler, Bette

In 1965, long before Bette became nationally known, she appeared briefly in the movie *Hawaii* as a missionary's wife who was always seasick.

Bette's movie-fan mother named her after actress Bette Davis but insisted on the affected one-syllable pronunciation.

Bette was the president of her high school class ('63, Radford High School, Honolulu, Hawaii) despite her being "the only Jewish girl in a Samoan neighborhood."

In high school, Bette "sang like a toad," according to her speech teacher, but she was in the Honor Society.

Mies Van Der Rohe, Ludwig

The architect was born Ludwig Mies in Aachen, Germany but added Van Der Rohe, his mother's name, early in his career.

Mill, John Stuart

The noted Transcendentalist, economist, and philosopher, had an IQ estimated to be in the range of 190–200, one of the highest IQ's on record.

Milland, Ray

Ray Milland's real name is a mouthful—Reginald Alfred John Truscott-Jones. His last name became Mullane when his divorced mother married an engineer named Mullane, but he took the name Jack Milland while doing walk-ons in the English provincial theater. Later in Hollywood, he used the name Ray instead of Jack, but his friends still call him Jack.

Millay, Edna St. Vincent

After graduating from Vassar College Millay moved to Greenwich Village in New York City where she wrote verse and short stories for magazines, using the pseudonym Nancy Boyd.

Miller, Arthur

Playwright Arthur Miller took only six weeks to write his American classic *Death of a Salesman*.

Miller, Henry

Early in his writing career, Miller used to sell short stories to the magazines *Smart Set* and *Snappy Stories*—a fact remarkable only because they were stories that appeared in the magazines twenty years before. All Miller did was to change the names of the characters.

In a *People* magazine interview Miller said that he hated his mother because of "her Germanic sense of discipline" and fondness for cleanliness and order. She also didn't like his writing and harped, "Henry, why can't you write a book like *Gone With the Wind?*"

Miller insists that his dead mother laid out at the funeral parlor kept opening one eye every time he went close to the corpse.

The writer was not always a saint but his middle name was Valentine.

When poet Ezra Pound submitted Miller's book *Tropic of Cancer* to Obelisk Press, Pound exclaimed, "Here's a dirty book that's worth reading."

Miller, a sensualist *ab ovum*, reflecting on childbirth commented, "To enter life by way of the vagina is as good a way as any."

Miller, Jason

The actor (*The Exorcist*) and playwright (*That Championship Season*) married comedian Jackie Gleason's daughter in 1963. They were both acting students at Catholic University in Washington, D.C.

Milton, John

The British epic poet originated the phrase "all hell broke loose." It appears in Book IV of *Para-*

dise Lost ("But wherefore thou alone? wherefore with thee came not all hell broke loose?").

Mindszenty, Cardinal Jozsef

The Roman Catholic prelate was born Jozsef Pehm in Csehimindszent, Hungary. In his forties he adopted his new last name in defiance of a fascist movement for Hungarians to maintain German names. He dropped the name Pehm (his father was of German descent) and adopted part of the name of his native village.

Minelli, Liza

Liza Minelli was named after the Gershwin song "Liza" in honor of Ira Gershwin, a close friend of Vincent Minnelli and best man at his wedding to Judy Garland.

Liza's adventures as a child provided the inspiration for Kay Thompson's (her godmother) *Eloise* stories.

She once played hooky from Scarsdale High School in Westchester County, New York and flew to London and back on the same day!

Liza was once introduced on "The Jack Paar Show" as Dyju Langard, an Armenian singer and her real identity was not revealed until she finished her singing. (Dyju Langard is an anagram of the name Judy Garland.)

Liza made her movie debut in the last scene of the film *The Good Old Summertime* with Van Johnson.

Mitchell, Margaret

In her Atlanta neighborhood Margaret Mitchell was known as Peggy Marsh. She was married to John Marsh, her second husband.

She wrote the last chapter (the one in which Rhett Butler leaves Scarlet O'Hara) first.

Gone With the Wind was the only book she ever wrote.

At the 1939 Academy Award ceremonies, *Gone With the Wind* won in almost every category yet no mention of Margaret Mitchell was ever made.

Mitchell, William

The pioneer of U.S. military aviation was born in Nice, France where his American parents were on vacation. (His father, John Lendrum Mitchell, was a U.S. Senator from Wisconsin.)

When 18-year-old Mitchell entered the service in 1898, he received a commission and was the youngest second lieutenant in the U.S. Army.

After Mitchell's court martial trial in 1925, he wrote and lectured about the importance of aviation and made some amazing predictions, one of which was that the Japanese would attack the United States "some fine Sunday morning."

Mitchum, Robert

Robert Mitchum is still married to his first wife, whom he married in 1940—an unusual phenomenon for a movie actor, especially one with a "bad boy" image.

Mitchum got his first movie part in a Hopalong Cassidy western (*Hoppy Serves a Writ*, released in 1943). He replaced an actor who had just been killed when a horse threw him.

An excellent impersonator, Mitchum can imitate people like Charles Laughton, Ronald Colman, and, would you believe, Katharine Hepburn!

Mitchum has never been part of the Hollywood scene and once said that he had been to only one movie star's house, Kirk Douglas's, and that was only for ten minutes.

Mix, Tom

The movie cowboy's Rolls Royce had a radiator cap to which a pair of antlers were attached.

Tom Mix was born in *Mix* Run, Pennsylvania.

Molière

Born Jean Baptiste Poquelin, the French playwright changed his name shortly after joining a theater company of the Bejart family. Coming from a bourgeois family, he chose to use a pen name, Moliere, to avoid possible embarrassment to his family, given that theater work was not highly regarded.

Mondale, Walter F.

A frugal midwesterner, the U.S. vice-president buys his clothes right off the rack at *J.C. Penney's*.

His Norweigian surname was originally Mundal but his great-grandfather Americanized it to Mondale.

Monroe, James

In the Revolutionary War, Monroe received a shoulder wound at the battle of Trenton, N.J., on December 26, 1776.

Monsarrat, Nicholas

The best-selling novelist (*The Cruel Sea*) and Cambridge graduate served an apprenticeship in law but became a writer for *Yachting World* after failing the bar exam.

Montague, Ashley

The anthropologist's full name is Montague Francis Ashley Montagu.

Montague wrote the book entitled *The Natural Superiority of Women* which sounds like a natural best-seller in these times. Actually his anthropological thesis in the book is that "Being a good wife, a good mother, and a good homemaker is the most important occupation in the whole world."

Montalban, Ricardo

The "Fantasy Island" star is not the only person in his family to do commercials (Chrysler Cordoba). Montalban's older brother, Carlos, plays El Exigente in the Savarin coffee commercials.

Montalban was paralyzed for 12 hours during the filming of *Across the Wide Missouri* after a horse threw him. To this day his back is still stiff and painful.

A Roman Catholic and practitioner of the rhythm method of birth control, Montalban says that "10 days of abstinence awakens passion."

Montand, Yves

Yves Montand's real name is Ivo Montand Livi and he's Italian and Jewish, not French. He was born in Monsummano, Italy in 1921 but when he was two years old his family left Italy (Mussolini was gaining power) and moved to Marseilles, France.

Montessori, Maria

The Italian educator was a medical doctor by training and was the first woman in Italy to graduate from medical school (1894, the University of Rome).

Miss Montessori was an illegitimate child.

Montez, Lola

The notorious "Spanish" dancer and lover of King Louis I of Bavaria was born Marie Delores Eliza Rosanna Gilbert in Limerick, Ireland, in 1818.

Montezuma

The Aztec emperor had a few unusual habits. He never wore the same robe twice and in fact changed his robes four times a day. He also always dined by himself, surrounded by a screen of woven gold so no one could see him, not even his many wives and concubines. And after finishing each meal, he threw away the dishes, never using them twice.

Montoya, Carlos

The noted flamenco player, taught to play the guitar by his mother, is a full-blooded gypsy and once said that some people can master the techniques of playing a guitar but "only the gypsy can play with his heart."

Although Montoya was born in Spain, he is an American citizen. (When he took the citizenship test his English was so sketchy that he answered "No" to the question "Do you like the American form of government?" not fully understanding the question.)

Moon, Rev. Sun Myung

The founder and leader of the Unification Church has *11* children.

Moore, Archie

The former light-heavyweight boxing champion was born Archibald Lee Wright. After his parents were separated, he was raised by an aunt and uncle, Cleveland and Willie Pearl Moore, whose name he adopted because, in his words, "It was less questions to be called Moore."

Moore, Garry

The crew-cutted, panel show host and TV personality, once the highest paid performer on television, was born Thomas Garrison Morfit but was renamed Garry Moore in 1940 by a Pittsburgh woman in a contest sponsored by the radio station for whom Garry worked as an announcer.

Moore, Mary Tyler

Mary casts an image of being a midwestern girl from Muscatine, Iowa, or Minneapolis but she was actually born and raised in—where else?—Brooklyn, New York.

She was educated in parochial schools and at one time considered becoming a nun because she liked the idea of self-sacrifice and helping people.

When Mary was 17 years old, she appeared in a Hotpoint appliance commercial as Happy Hotpoint, a three-inch high pixie superimposed over Hotpoint appliances.

Mary was in the "Richard Diamond" television series with David Janssen, but you might not remember her. She played the role of Sam, the telephone switchboard operator, whose legs and hands appeared on camera and whose voice was heard but her face never shown.

She auditioned for the role of Danny Thomas's daughter in *Make Room for Daddy* but was turned down because Danny made the observation, "How could a guy with a nose like mine have a daughter with a nose like hers?" Danny's daughter, Marlo, won the role because she definitely had Danny's nose but once out of the series she underwent plastic surgery and emerged with a pretty nose not unlike Mary Tyler Moore's.

She didn't use her middle name "Tyler" until Danny Thomas was casting for "The Dick Van Dyke Show" and asked for the girl with the nice nose and three names. She tried out, got the part, and continued being Mary *Tyler* Moore.

Moore, Robin

Moore, the author of *The Green Berets* and *The French Connection*, inherited a large sum of money from his father, the co-founder of the Sheraton Hotel chain, but he lost all of it and for the last 21 years has had to write for a living.

The author writes nude from the waist up because according to him clothes cut off the oxygen supply to the brain.

Moore was christened Robert Lowell Moore, Jr.

Moravia, Alberto

The Italian writer (*The Woman of Rome*) was born Alberto Pincherle.

Moreno, Rita

Rita Moreno is not Chita Rivera, but it is easy to get the two actresses confused. Rita was born Rosita Dolores Alverio in Humacao, Puerto Rico. Chita was born Dolores Concita Figueroa del Rivero in Washington, D.C. Chita originated the role of Anita in the Broadway production of *West Side Story* (and was later replaced by Rita), but it was Rita who appeared in the movie version of the play and won an Academy award for her performance. Chita, an Aquarius, is only 13 months younger than Rita, a Sagittarius.

Morgan, Dennis

Dennis Morgan as Rick Blaine in the movie *Casablanca?* That's who was in the projected cast in the early stages of production. Losing out to Humphrey Bogart, Morgan appeared in the movie *Thank Your Lucky Stars* instead of *Casablanca.*

Born Stanley Morner, Morgan began his career as an opera singer.

Moriarity, Michael

The stage and movie actor's paternal grandfather, George Moriarity, played third base for the Detroit Tigers and later became manager of the team.

Morris, Jan

Born James Humphry Morris, the transexual British writer selected as a given name "the still adrogynous Jan, not because I wished always to straddle the sexes, but because I thought it would make the change of habit less abrupt for my relatives and friends (and perhaps, I thought, too, at the back of my mind, that if I failed to succeed in my new persona I could somehow retreat into the old)."

Morse, Wayne

On April 24 and 25th, 1953 the Oregon senator spoke for 22 hours and 26 minutes on the Tidelands Oil Bill, the longest uninterrupted filibuster on record.

Mostel, Zero

In recognition of the sum total of his grade school academic achievements, Samuel Joel Mostel's classmates nicknamed him "Zero."

Mountbatten, Earl Louis

Born Louis Battenberg, the British sea lord and his family changed the family name to Mountbatten in 1917.

Moynihan, Daniel Patrick

As the U.S. ambassador to India, Moynihan had the distinction of giving India the largest sum ever written by check—16,640,000,000 rupees.

Mozart, Wolfgang Amadeus

Mozart published his first compositions, four violin sonatas, at age six and one year later, at age seven, wrote his first symphony.

For reasons unknown, early in his career Mozart used to write obscene letters to his relatives.

Mozart wrote the overture to his opera *Don Giovanni* the night before its premiere performance.

Mudd, Roger

The CBS-TV anchorman is a descendant of Dr. Samuel Mudd, the Maryland doctor who gave medical assistance to John Wilkes Booth, the escaped assassin of President Abraham Lincoln.

Muhammad, Elijah

The Black Muslim leader's real name was Robert Poole but when he met "Allah" in the human form of W. D. Fard and Fard disappeared, Poole changed his name to Elijah Muhammad, announcing to the world that he was an apostle of Allah.

Muni, Paul

Muni's native tongue was Yiddish.

Munsel, Patrice

The spelling of the opera singer's last name was originally Munsil but she changed the spelling around 1943 when she signed up with impresario Sol Hurok, probably to avoid the name being mispronounced as rhyming with "tonsil."

Murray, Bill

Now a regular on the "Saturday Night Live" television program, Bill once attended medical school but dropped out to join the Second City comedy troupe.

His brother Brian Murray is a writer for the "Saturday Night Live" show.

Murrow, Edward R.

Murrow used to keep a bottle of scotch at his feet while broadcasting and usually took a swig before each broadcast.

The outstanding journalist and newscaster was born Egbert Roscoe Murrow but changed his first name to Edward in his sophomore year of college.

Muskie, Edmund

The family name of the Secretary of State was Marciszewski but when his father emigrated from Poland, he changed the name to Muskie.

Mussolini, Benito

The Italian Fascist dictator, named after Mexican revolutionary leader Benito Juarez, was an elementary school teacher in Gualtieri, Italy but left the profession to become active in the Italian revolutionary movement.

N

Nader, Ralph

After graduating magna cum laude from Princeton in 1955 and from Harvard Law School in 1958, consumer advocate Nader served six months in the United States Army as a cook at Fort Dix, New Jersey. In fact, one of his proudest moments was the time he substituted for an absent cook and baked banana bread for 2,000 soldiers. Also, at Harvard he managed a bowling alley for a while.

The only automobile that Nader has ever owned was a '49 Studebaker when he was attending law school.

Nader was a classmate of author David Halberstam at Winsted High School in Winsted, Connecticut. They and one other boy were the only three males to receive straight "A's."

Consumer advocacy is lucrative. Nader is one of the highest paid lecturers on the lecture circuit—he gets *$4,000 an hour.*

Naish, J. Carrol

The late character actor was the great-great-grandson of John Naish, Attorney General and later Lord Chancellor of Ireland.

Nash, Ogden

Although the witty poet was born in Rye, New York, he came from a distinguished southern family whose ancestors included a governor of North Carolina and a Revolutionary War general after whom the Tennessee city of Nashville was named.

Nasser, Gamal Abdul

The late Egyptian ruler had one of the largest funerals on record. Four million people crowded the streets of Cairo to witness his funeral in 1970.

Nast, Thomas

Born in Landau, Germany, Nast emigrated to the United States at age six with his mother. The cartoonist and illustrator invented the donkey and elephant symbols for the Democratic and Republican parties.

Nation, Carry

Had Carry Nation's physician husband not died of alcoholism at an early age, she probably would never have launched a career-long crusade against the vices of alcohol.

Negri, Pola

The silent screen star's real name was Apolonia Mathias-Chalupec. While recovering from tuberculosis at a sanatorium in Poland, Pola (short for Apolonia) read the poetry of Ada Negri, an Italian poetess and was strongly moved by her writing. Later, when Pola took up dramatics and was urged to take a stage name, she paid homage to the poetess by adopting her last name.

Nelson, Barry

Nelson was the first actor to play the role of James Bond. He appeared in 1951 on a Climax television series version of *Casino Royale*.

Nelson, Lord

The English admiral lost the sight of his right eye during the siege of Calvi, lost his right arm at Santa Cruz, but despite these handicaps led the British Navy to victory at Trafalgar in 1805 before dying from wounds suffered in the battle.

Nelson, Harriet

Born Peggy Lou Snyder, she adopted the stage surname of her parents, Roy and Hazel Hilliard, and added the name Harriet. When she married then bandleader Ozzie Nelson in 1935, she became Harriet Nelson.

Nelson, Ricky

Early in his singing career Ricky Nelson used the stage name Jerry Fuller.

Nerina, Nadia

Born Nadine Judd, she danced with the Sadler's Wells Theatre Ballet in London under the name Nadia Moore. Soon after, she adopted the name Nerina, which was her mother's first name.

Nero, Franco

The Italian movie actor (*Camelot*), born Carlo Spara*nero* in Parma, was an accountant for a public utility company before he became an actor.

Neruda, Pablo

When Pablo Neruda (real name Neftali Ricardo Reyes Basoalto), the Walt Whitman of Chile, was 17 years old, he published his first poems, using the name "Neruda" which he took from the Czechoslovakian short story writer Jan Neruda whom he admired. Fifteen years later, he officially adopted the surname.

Newcombe, Don

The great Brooklyn Dodger pitcher used to drink ten cans of beer (presumably Schaefer) in the clubhouse after every Dodger game and drank as much as two-fifths of liquor a day before becoming a teetotaler.

Newhart, Bob

The comedian has a fear of flying which he says is common among celebrities, especially comedians, because they abhor not being in control of a situation.

As a bored accountant with the Illinois State Unemployment Service, Newhart used to spend off-hours making lengthy but amusing telephone calls to a friend, Ed Gallagher, an advertising copywriter. The conversations were so zany that Newhart recorded them and eventually sold the idea to Warner Brother's Record division who booked him into the Tidelands nightclub in Houston, Texas. There six of his routines were recorded live and went into his first album, "The Button-Down Mind of Bob Newhart," which became an immediate hit in April of 1960. He was the first comedian to become famous not by working his way up the nightclub circuit but by making a record album.

Newman, Edwin

Edwin Newman self-deprecatingly claims that as a reporter he has a record of being in the right place at the wrong time. He is, however, not entirely wrong. Just after he left London in 1952, King George VI died. Six years later, after leaving Rome he found out that Pope Pius XII had just died.

Newman, Paul

Newman used to drink a couple of six packs of Coors beer a day until 1977 when Coors workers went on strike to protest the company's invasion of the workers' privacy. (They used lie detectors to screen out employees with health problems and possible "saboteurs.") Newman also protested by switching to Budweiser beer.

Everybody knows that Paul has beautiful blue eyes but few know that he is partially color-blind. In fact, this defect prevented him from going to flight school in World War II.

Appraising his own performance in *The Silver Chalice*, his first movie, Paul said that he "delivered his lines with the emotional fervor of a New York Central conductor announcing local stops."

Paul's first stage role was at age 11 when he played St. George in a grammar school play. He confessed later that he really wanted to play the dragon because he thought it was a better role.

Paul and his wife, Joanne Woodward, sleep in a huge bed that they bought from a New Orleans brothel when they were first married. In fact, when they were to appear on Edward R. Murrow's "Person to Person" television program, they wanted to tell the story about the bed but Murrow wouldn't let them.

Newton, Wayne

The engaging singer is the highest paid nightclub performer ever. He makes about $225,000 a week for 36 weeks for his Las Vegas nightclub act, grossing him $8 million, and for the rest of the year picks up another $2 million for other appearances.

He is the son of a German-Cherokee mother and Irish-Powhatan father.

Newton-John, Olivia

Olivia's grandfather on her mother's side was the Nobel Prize-winning German physicist Max Born.

Although "Livvie" is considered an Australian, she was born in Cambridge, England, where her father was a university don. She moved to Australia when she was five, when her father joined the University of Melbourne faculty.

Nichols, Mike

Born Michael Igor Peshkowsky in Berlin, Germany, he and his family fled the country in the 1930s because of Nazi oppression. They moved to New York City where Mike's father, a doctor, started a medical practice and adopted the new family name of Nichols.

Mike is the grandson of Gustav Landauer, once head of the German Social Democratic party and one of the early victims of Nazi extermination camps, and the grandson of Hedwig Lachmann, who wrote the German libretto of Richard Strauss's opera *Salome*.

Nietzsche, Friedrich

Nietzsche, the German philosopher whose preachings of the *superman* influenced Hitler, claimed to be descended from Polish aristocrats named Nietsky and once said, "Germany is a great nation only because its people have so much Polish blood in their veins."

In grammar school Nietzsche was so well-behaved that he was called "The Little Pastor."

Nightingale, Florence

The founder of modern nursing was encouraged by her wealthy English parents to make a "brilliant marriage" but at age 17 she heard the voice of God calling her to service and decided to become a nurse. It should be noted that at that time nurses tended to be drunken prostitutes so her career choice was not regarded very highly by her parents.

Nijinksy, Vaslav

The great Russian ballet dancer's career was ended when he was only 27 years old because he was declared insane and had to be institutionalized for the rest of his life (he died at age 60).

Nixon, Richard M.

At the age of three Nixon fell off a carriage, cracked his skull and almost died.

Nixon visited all 50 states during his presidency, the only president to do so.

At Duke University Law School Nixon was known as "Iron Butt" and "Gloomy Gus."

Nixon won the presidential election in 1968 by 510,000 votes, a small margin, but larger than the 120,000 votes by which he lost to John F. Kennedy in 1960. In 1972 Nixon's 60.7% of the popular vote was the highest percentage any Republican candidate had ever received and his 47,169,911 votes were the greatest number of votes any presidential candidate has ever received!

In a rare moment of humor and self-deprecation, Nixon joked, "I hear that whenever anyone in the White House tells a lie, Nixon gets a royalty."

Nixon was president when the first White House worship service to be conducted by a Jewish rabbi was held (June 29, 1969).

While he was president, his wife Pat traveled 131,723 miles.

The ex-president is a descendant of Edward III, King of England, according to *Burke's Presidential Families*.

During the tape sessions with David Frost, Nixon in a nervous attempt to establish some rapport with bachelor Frost asked him, "Well, did you do any fornicating this weekend?"

Nixon was the first U.S. vice-president to appear on the postage stamp of a foreign country. In 1958 Ecuador issued a 2-sucre stamp on which appeared a picture of Nixon and the flags of the United States and Ecuador.

Nobel, Alfred Bernhard

Most people know that Nobel was the founder of the Nobel Prizes but few people know how the Swedish philanthropist became so rich—he was the inventor of dynamite.

Noguchi, Isamu

The son of a Japanese poet and an American writer, Noguchi studied sculpture with Gutzon Borglum, the man who created the monument at Mount Rushmore, South Dakota.

Norell, Norman

The late designer's real name was Norman Levinson but as a student at Parsons School of Design in New York City, he was told to change his name to a fancier one if he wanted to make it as a theater costume designer, then his ambition. He not only changed his name to Norell but he also changed the direction of his career, choosing dress designing.

Normand, Mabel

The silent screen comedienne's real name was Mabel Fortescue.

North, Sheree

Sheree North's real name is Dawn Bethel but to avoid being confused with the similar sounding name of her brother Don, she picked an entirely different namé.

Novak, Kim

Kim's real first name was Marilyn but Columbia Pictures head Harry Cohn felt that there were too many Marilyns in Hollywood so he decided to name her Kim.

Novarro, Ramon

The Mexican-born silent screen star, a homosexual, was given a black lead Art Deco dildo by fellow actor Rudolph Valentino.

Nureyev, Rudolph

Nureyev moves well perhaps because he was born moving—he was born on March 17, 1938 on a train en route to Vladivostok where his soldier father was then stationed.

For their performance in Tchaikovsky's *Swan Lake* at the Vienna State Opera in October of 1964, Nureyev and Margot Fonteyn got 89 curtain calls.

Nyad, Diana

The marathon swimming champion was born Diana Sneed but her name was legally changed when her divorced mother married Aristotle Zason Nyad, a Greek real estate man. (The word "naiad" in Greek, coincidentally refers to water nymphs in ancient mythology.)

Diana was graduated Phi Beta Kappa from Lake Forest College in Illinois.

The swimmer once said, "Swimming bores me to tears."

Miss Nyad also does aerial work. She parachuted out of her dormitory window at Emory University in Atlanta, for which she was expelled.

O

Oakie, Jack

The vaudeville and movie comic actor, born Lewis Delaney Offield in Sedalia, Missouri, went to school in Oklahoma—after which he earned the name "Oakie."

Oakley, Annie

Annie's full name was Phoebe Anne Oakley Moses (later corrupted to Mozee).

After she was in a train accident, Annie Oakley's hair turned completely gray.

The Sioux warrior Sitting Bull called her "Little Sure-Shot."

Oates, Joyce Carol

The National Book Award winner (*Them*, 1970) was class valedictorian at Syracuse University in 1960 and graduated Phil Beta Kappa.

Oberon, Merle

Born Estelle Merle O'Brien Thompson, the actress was discovered by producer Alexander

Korda who changed her stage name from "Queenie" Thompson to Merle Oberon. Oberon sounds like a variation of O'Brien but actually is the king of the fairies in *A Midsummer Night's Dream* and in medieval folklore.

Obolensky, Serge

In World War II, Obolensky, then a major, was the oldest combat paratrooper in the United States Army—he was almost 53 years old when he parachuted into Sardinia carrying important dispatches from General Dwight D. Eisenhower.

O'Brian, Hugh

The star of the "Wyatt Earp" television series was born Hugh J. Krampe in Rochester, New York, but picked the stage name Jaffer Gray when he first started acting. He changed his name to Hugh O'Brian when he started a theater engagement at the Lobero Theatre in Santa Barbara, California.

O'Brien, Margaret

Born Angela Maxine O'Brien, the child actress took her new first name from her title role in her first movie *Journey for Margaret* (1942).

O'Brien, Pat

The veteran actor was born William Joseph O'Brien, Jr. but later took the name Pat in honor of his deceased paternal grandfather who, incidentally, was shot to death trying to break up a barroom brawl.

O'Brien attended Marquette Academy in Milwaukee where one of his classmates and friends was Spencer Tracy. In fact, they both joined the U.S. Navy together in 1918.

O'Casey, Sean

The Irish playwright's real name was John Casey. In the early 1900s, John Casey became involved in the Irish Revival movement and learned to speak, write, and read Gaelic, as well as learned to play the bagpipes. He published songs in 1918 as Sean O'Cathasaigh but later changed the name to Sean O'Casey when the Abbey Theatre accepted his first full-length play, *The Shadow of a Gunman.*

Odets, Clifford

The playwright's father, owner of a direct mail advertising agency, wanted his son to be an advertising copywriter and was disappointed when Odets avoided advertising to pursue writing poetry and plays.

Odetta

The folksinger is well known by only her first name was born Odetta Holmes but later became Odetta Felious when her father died and her mother remarried.

Ogilvy, David

Early in his career, Ogilvy worked for pollster George Gallup doing, among other things, consultant work for Hollywood movie studios. One of his services was to predict how many people would see a movie, based on a story synopsis, title, and cast. In fact, it was Ogilvy who suggested to Walt Disney that he make *Alice in Wonderland*. Ogilvy also told Selznick that a movie version of *Jane Eyre* would be a flop!)

The distinguished advertising man recently confessed in his latest book, *Blood, Brains and Beer*, that he scored 96 on an IQ test, ranking him with "the norm for ditchdiggers."

Ogilvy, whose mother's maiden name is Fairfield, is a cousin of British writer Rebecca West (whose real name is Cicily Fairfield).

O'Hara, John

The late novelist was once in a movie *The General Died at Dawn* which starred Gary Cooper and Madeline Carroll. (O'Hara was a friend of both the director, Lewis Milestone, and the scriptwriter, Clifford Odets. As a minor gesture to the author they named the Cooper character O'Hara.)

Olivier, Sir Laurence

While filming the movie *Wuthering Heights*, Sir Laurence Olivier developed a severe case of athlete's foot and was so disabled that he used crutches when he was off camera.

The cynical Humphrey Bogart used to call the knighted British actor Larry Oliver (no second "i") because he thought that the name Olivier sounded "phoney."

Onassis, Aristotle

Even in extreme cold weather Aristotle Onassis never wore an overcoat. His rationale was, according to writer Frank Brady: "Since I am known as a rich person, I feel I have to tip at least $5 each time I check my coat. On top of that, I would have to wear a very expensive coat, and it would have to be insured. Added up, without a topcoat I save over $20,000 a year."

The barstools on Onassis's yacht were covered with the skin of a whale's penis, according to reporter James Bacon, once prompting actress Betsy Drake to inquire, "You mean this is Moby's dick?"

Onassis, Christine

Aristotle's daughter was born in New York City on December 11, 1950.

Self-conscious about her God-given nose, Miss Onassis had plastic surgery done to straighten out and improve her profile.

O'Neal, Ryan

The movie actor was born Patrick Ryan O'Neal in 1941 but dropped his first name in the early 1960s to avoid being confused with the other actor Patrick O'Neal (born 1927) who, incidentally, is a third cousin to Ryan.

Ryan may have escaped a jail sentence in the movie *Paper Moon* but in real life he once spent 51 days in the Lincoln Heights jail in downtown Los Angeles after being arrested in a New Year's Eve brawl.

O'Neill, Eugene

Eugene O'Neill's family was constantly plagued by drug problems and suicides. His mother was a drug addict. His oldest son, Eugene O'Neill, Jr., a Greek scholar, committed suicide in 1950 and his other son, Shane, who was addicted to drugs, also committed suicide in 1977.

America's greatest playwright was expelled from Princeton University for throwing a beer bottle through the college president's window. The president of Princeton at the time was Woodrow Wilson, later to become president of the United States.

O'Neill, Tip

The Massachusetts Democrat and House majority leader, whose full name is Thomas Philip O'Neill, Jr., is said to have gotten his nickname "Tip" from a 19th-century baseball player also named O'Neill, who was famous for foul-tipping baseballs.

Orbach, Jerry

The popular stage actor (*Promises, Promises, The Fantasticks*), the son of a Jewish father and Catholic mother, was raised in the Roman Catholic faith.

Orbison, Roy

The rock 'n' roll singer has been beset by personal tragedies. In 1966 his first wife was killed in a motorcycle accident and two years later his two oldest sons were burned to death when their home caught on fire.

At North Texas State College, one of Roy's classmates was Pat Boone. It was Boone, who sent Orbison to record producer Sam Phillips (Sun Records) in Memphis, launching Orbison's career.

Orwell, George

In 1933 Eric Blair was about to publish a book which publisher Victor Gollancz suggested he entitle *Confessions of a Down and Outer*. Gollancz also suggested that Blair use the pseudonym "X." The writer didn't like the pseudonym so he wrote down four names from which he and Gollancz would select a mutually agreeable pen name. The four names were: P. S. Burton, Kenneth Miles, George Orwell, and H. Lewis Allways. They both liked the name George Orwell and so Eric Blair became George Orwell. The book title changed, incidentally, to *Down and Out in Paris*. (George V was the King of England at the time and Orwell was a river in Suffolk, England, possibly accounting for the origin of the pen name.)

Oswald, Lee Harvey

Among his other problems, the assassin of President John F. Kennedy was a dyslexic.

O'Toole, Peter

The bibulous Irish actor, born Seamus O'Toole, has a "thing" about emerald green socks and always wears them, even when he sleeps in the nude. In fact, O'Toole almost lost his role in the movie *How to Steal a Million* because director

William Wyler didn't want him to wear the brightly colored socks, but they reached a compromise—O'Toole did not wear the socks but kept them in his pocket.

O'Toole's father was a peripatetic bookmaker known as "Captain Paddy" and "Spats."

Peter has scars on his hand supposedly caused by convent school nuns who tried to correct his left-handedness by slapping him with a ruler.

Owen, Reginald

Owen was the only actor to have played both Sherlock Holmes and Dr. Watson in films.

Owens, Jesse

Although his full name was James Cleveland Owens, he was always called "J. C." as a child. When he enrolled in a Cleveland, Ohio grammar school a teacher misunderstood Owens's pronunciation of his name and wrote the name as *Jesse* Owens.

P

Paar, Jack

Not unlike Demosthenes, Jack Paar overcame a childhood case of stuttering by reading aloud with buttons in his mouth.

At Guadacanal in World War II Paar was a tentmate of actor Jackie Cooper.

Paderewski, Ignace

Paderewski's fame as a concert pianist obscured the fact that he was the Prime Minister of Poland from 1919 to 1921, and in fact was one of the signers of the Treaty of Versailles.

Having left a $5 million estate when he died, Paderewski is considered to be the highest paid concert pianist ever and once earned $500,000 in a single season (1922–1923).

According to *The People's Almanac #2*, the famous Polish pianist once played the piano in the St. Louis brothel "The Palace" in the 1890s.

Page, Patti

When Clara Ann "Katy" Fowler started singing on a Tulsa radio station, the program on which she appeared was "Meet Patti Page," sponsored by the Page Company, a local dairy. After the star of the show became ill, Katy Fowler took over and eventually became known as Patti Page—which was originally just a made-up name to strengthen sponsor identification.

Paige, Janis

After moving to Hollywood, Donna Mae Jaden adopted the last name Paige from a grandparent and took her first name from Elsie Janis (whose real name was Elsie Bierbauer!), a musical comedy star.

Paine, Thomas

Thomas Paine, the author of *Common Sense,* was an alcoholic.

Palmer, Bud

The lanky sportscaster and former basketball star, born in Hollywood, California, is the son of a silent movie actor who specialized in westerns.

Palmer, Lilli

The actress, born Maria Lilli Peiser in Posen, Germany, selected the stage name Palmer because it was the name of a British actress whom she admired.

Parker, Dorothy

When she married stockbroker Edwin Pond Parker II in 1917 the writer and poet, born Dorothy Rothschild, joked to friends that she married him for his name. She was not just kidding. As the daughter of a Jewish father and Scottish mother and sent to Catholic schools by her stepmother, Dorothy Parker had ambivalent feelings about her Jewish heritage and disliked the last name Rothschild. The marriage to Parker solved this name problem.

Parrish, Maxfield

Famous for his detail and intricate designs, Parrish painted the mural on the wall of the King Cole Bar at the St. Regis Hotel in New York City.

Parsons, Estelle

The Academy award-winning (*Bonnie and Clyde*) actress, a law school dropout, is the mother of twins.

Parsons, Louella

The Hollywood gossip columnist, born Louella Rose Oettinger, was named for a neighbor Louella Bixler who helped her mother during labor. She became Louella O. Parsons in 1905 when she married John D. Parsons, a real estate man and part-time reporter.

Parton, Dolly

The buxom country and western singer is only four feet eleven inches tall.

Pascal, Blaise

The next time you lose at roulette, blame it on the French mathematician—he invented the game in his quest for a perpetual motion machine.

Blaise Pascal also invented the hydraulic press and the adding machine, among other things.

Patton, General George S. Jr.

General Patton is buried in Hamm, Luxembourg at the American Military Cemetery.

General Patton was a dyslexic.

Pauling, Dr. Linus

Dr. Pauling is the only person individually to win two Nobel Prizes—one for chemistry in 1954 and the other the Peace Prize in 1962. (Marie Curie won twice also but shared her 1903 Physics Prize with her husband Pierre and Antoine Henri Becquerel.)

Pavarotti, Luciano

Although his mother wanted him to become an accountant, Luciano Pavarotti became an elementary school teacher after graduating from college but after two years of teaching he switched to selling insurance, which gave him more free time to practice his singing.

Pavlov, Ivan

The Russian physiologist's original experiment on conditioned responses was with a horse, not a dog.

Pavlova, Anna

A ballerina to the end, her last words were, "Get my 'Swan' costume ready."

Peale, Dr. Norman Vincent

Dr. Norman Vincent Peale's first job was as a newspaper boy selling the *Cincinnati Enquirer*.

The clergyman and author (*The Power of Positive Thinking*) was president of his fraternity, Phi Gamma Delta, at Ohio Wesleyan University.

After college Peale became a reporter for the *Detroit Journal* (now defunct) but within a year decided to enter the ministry.

Peck, Gregory

The movie actor's first name is Eldred! He was born Eldred Gregory Peck and has always hated the name.

Peck was grievously shocked in 1975 when his 30-year-old son, Jonathan, a former Peace Corps volunteer and then stringer for a Santa Monica, California television station, committed suicide.

Peerce, Jan

The Metropolitan Opera star, born Jacob Pincus Perelmuth, studied medicine for two years but dropped out to elope with his girl friend Alice Kalmanowitz.

Pei, I. M.

Regarding a drawback of his profession, Pei observed, "Doctors can bury their mistakes, but architects have to live with theirs."

Pele

As a child, Edson Arantes do Mascimento was nicknamed "Dico" but when he started playing soccer he was given the new nickname Pele. He says that the name does not mean or signify anything but it may have to do with his playing in *peladas*, or local soccer games on vacant lots, in his pre-professional days. (Pele is also known as *Perola Negra*, the Black Pearl, back in Brazil.)

Penney, J. C.

The chain store founder's full name fortold the making of money—he was named James Cash Penney.

Pepitone, Joe

Before Pepitone became a professional baseball player, he was almost killed in 1958 by a .38 caliber bullet accidentally fired by a schoolmate. The bullet narrowly missed his heart and spinal column but he survived surgery and made a speedy recovery.

Pepper, Claude

When Pepper was only ten years old he carved the following words in the bark of a tree at

385

Camp Hill, Alabama: "Claude Pepper, United States Senator." Twenty-six years later in 1936, he became the U.S. Senator from Florida, replacing Duncan Fletcher.

Perdue, Frank

Frank Perdue's favorite dish is chicken Verdicchio. The dish, which originated at Felicia's Restaurant in Boston, consists of breasts of chicken sautéed in white wine, with mushrooms, artichoke hearts, and garlic. It is excellent!

The chicken entrepreneur is a descendant of Henri Perdeaux, the explorer who left Europe to find Martinique but ended up on the Maryland shores. The same family is believed to have founded Purdue University.

Perelmann, S. J.

Sidney Joseph Perelman, using the pseudonym Sidney Namlerep, wrote the introduction to his own book *The Best of S. J. Perelman*. Namlerep, of course, is Perelman spelled backwards.

The humorist, famous for his Marx Brothers movie scripts, won an Academy Award in 1956 for his screenplay contributions to the movie *Around the World in Eighty Days*.

Perkins, Marlin

Perkins showed his fondness for animals in his early years. At military school he kept snakes in his closet.

Perot, H. Ross

When Perot's nine million shares of E.D.S. stock was going for $150 a share he became a billionaire on paper. However, he put this accomplishment in perspective when he made the following comment: "The day I made Eagle Scout was more important to me than the day I discovered I was a billionaire."

Perrine, Valerie

The movie actress's license plates read RATS or "star" spelled backwards, suggesting that she has stardom in her eyes.

Pescow, Donna

In her leaner days the actress (*Saturday Night Fever*) demonstrated cosmetics at Bloomingdales in New York and also sold Christmas tree ornaments.

Peters, Bernadette

Born Bernadette Lazzara, the buxom and bouncy singer got the inspiration for her stage surname from her father, *Peter* Lazzara, a bread route salesman in Queens, New York.

Phillip II, King of Spain

Of Phillip II's four wives, two were his cousins, one an aunt, and the other a niece.

Phillip III, King of Spain

Phillip III of Spain sired 32 illegitimate children.

Phillip, Prince

When asked what type of work he did, Prince Phillip tersely but accurately replied "I'm self-employed."

Phyfe, Duncan

Born in Scotland, the cabinet maker's family name was spelled Fife but he changed the spelling nine years after he emigrated to the United States.

Piaf, Edith

The French chanteuse's real name was Edith Giovanna Gassion but she was renamed by Louis Leplée, the owner of Gerney's, a fashionable Paris nightclub. He picked the name Piaf, which means sparrow in French, because she was small, delicate, and sang well. Also, prior to her adopting the name Edith Piaf she also sang under the name Huguette Elias.

Picasso, Pablo

Picasso was christened Pablo Nepomuceno Crispiniano de la Santissima Trinidad Ruiz y Picasso but was known as Pablo Ruiz by his friends. When the artist first exhibited his paintings he signed them P. Ruiz Picasso, using both his father's and mother's surnames. At age 20, though, he dropped the name Ruiz because it was too common a name and used the more unusual name of his mother, Picasso.

Picasso had a simplistic view of women, "There are only two kinds of women—goddesses and doormats," he once commented.

Pickford, Mary

Born Gladys Smith in Toronto, Canada, the actress was billed as Baby Gladys Smith as an eight year old touring the United States, but became Mary Pickford on Broadway in 1907 when David Belasco renamed her and cast her in the play *The Warrens of Virginia*.

Pierce, Franklin

All three of Pierce's sons, his only children, died in their childhood. After the third son, Benjamin, died at age 12 in 1853, Pierce's wife wore black every day she lived in the White House.

Pierce, an alcoholic, drank heavily after his wife died in 1863.

Pike, James

The late Episcopal bishop, born a Roman Catholic, was a highly successful lawyer before he entered the ministry. He was a graduate of the law school at the University of Southern California, and was a Sterling Fellow at Yale University where he received his doctorate of law in 1938. He became an attorney for the Securities and Exchange Commission from 1938 to 1942, during which he taught federal procedure at Catholic University and civil procedure at George Washington Law School. It was as a lieutenant in the U.S. Navy during World War II that Pike became interested in religion.

Pinkerton, Allan

Founder of the detective agency bearing his name, Pinkerton was the first director of the Secret Service Bureau and was appointed by Abraham Lincoln who started the Bureau in 1861.

The Glasgow-born detective agency founder was said to have gone "from cooper to copper" because his original trade was that of a barrel-maker.

Pinter, Harold

The Absurdist playwright came from a Sephar-dic Jewish family originally from Portugal where the family name was "da Pinta." When his family moved to Britain, however, the name was Anglicized to Pinter.

Pinza, Ezio

When Pinza was ten days old he still did not have any given name because his father, having had six children die shortly after their christen-ings, was afraid to tempt fate again. A friend told Pinza's father that if he named the baby Ezio he would be a great opera singer (the friend's younger brother Ezio had just signed a contract to sing with La Scala). The father liked the name and registered it with the local civil authorities but was rebuffed when he talked to his priest. The name Ezio, according to the priest, was the name of a pagan general who had massacred early Christians and for that reason the name had been banned by the Church for centuries. Pinza's family paid lip-service to the priest's advice by baptizing the boy Fortunato but they always called him Ezio and many years later he became a world-famous opera singer.

At age 18 Pinza wanted to become a professional bicycle racer but after two years switched to music and voice instruction, acknowledging that the lung power he developed as a bicyclist helped his voice projection.

Pleshette, Suzanne

The television wife of Bob Newhart on "The Bob Newhart Show" was once the real life wife of Troy Donahue, the "pretty boy" movie actor especially popular in the late 1950s and early 1960s.

Pocahontas

The Indian Princess's real name was Matoaka but she was nicknamed Pocahontas ("playful") by her father Powhatan. When she married English colonist John Rolfe in 1614, however, she adopted the Christian name Rebecca and became Rebecca Rolfe.

Pocahontas died while she and Rolfe were living in England and she, in fact, was buried on the banks of the Thames in an unmarked grave.

Poe, Edgar Allan

An alcoholic, Poe drank himself to death and was found dead lying in a gutter in Baltimore in 1849.

Poe is generally regarded as the creator of the first detective story. His "The Murder in the Rue

Morgue," published in *Graham's Magazine* in April of 1841 started a new genre in popular literature. Poe's stories inspired A. Conan Doyle, Agatha Christie, and scores of other people to write detective stories.

When Poe was 26 years old he married Virginia Clemm—who was only thirteen years old—half Poe's age!

Poitier, Sidney

Poitier has excellent diction but it has not always been that good. In his first attempt to become an actor, he was turned down by the American Negro Theatre in New York because of his thick West Indian accent.

Polanski, Roman

The Polish director (*Rosemary's Baby*) offered $20,000 for information leading to the arrest of the Sharon Tate killer but no one ever collected the money.

Polk, James Knox

Polk was baptized six days before his death, at the age of 53.

Ponselle, Rosa

The opera soprano's family name was originally Ponzillo.

Pope, Alexander

Alexander Pope was only four feet six inches tall and was a hunchback.

Porter loved to play practical jokes on people. He once had bearded actor Monty Woolley come to one of his cocktail parties with an elegantly dressed woman who also sported a beard. He also invented a couple, Mr. and Mrs. Fitch from Muskogee and fed gossip items about them to the newspaper columnists. When Porter heard from friends who said that they recently had the Fitches over for drinks, he decided to "kill" them in an auto accident.

Porter wore white socks because his skin was especially sensitive and he didn't want to risk getting infections.

Porter lived in the Presidential Suite on the 41st floor of the Waldorf Astoria Towers in New York City, previously the residence of Herbert Hoover and later the Duke and Duchess of Windsor.

People are surprised to find out that Porter wrote the song "Don't Fence Me In." He wrote it as a parody of the cowboy ballads popular in the 1930s.

At Harvard University in 1913 Porter roomed with Dean Acheson who later became Franklin D. Roosevelt's and Harry S Truman's secretary of state.

The lyricist and composer published his first song ("The Bobolink Waltz") when he was 10 years old.

After graduating from Yale, Porter enrolled at Harvard Law School but soon transferred to the school of music.

When Porter's first musical comedy, *See America First*, proved to be a failure in 1915, he got depressed and actually joined the French Foreign Legion.

Porter, Katherine Anne

The writer (*Flowering Judas*) was a distant cousin of O. Henry whose real name was William Sydney Porter.

Post, Charles W.

The breakfast food entrepreneur (Postum) committed suicide in Santa Barbara, California in 1914.

Post, Emily

Born Emily Price, her father, Bruce Price, was the architect who designed the beautiful Chateau Frontenac in Quebec, Canada, and also designed many impressive buildings in Tuxedo Park, New York, where the rich always practiced good etiquette. She became Emily Post when she married banker Edwin D. Post in 1893.

Post, Wiley

With the compensation money Wiley Post received for losing an eye in a drilling accident, he bought his first airplane.

Pound, Ezra

The poet and critic was a distant relative of another great poet, Henry Wadsworth Longfellow.

Powell, Jane

Jane Powell's real name is Suzanne Burce but she played a character named Jane Powell in her first movie, *Song of the Open Road* (1944) and used the name ever since.

Powell, Jody

President Carter's press secretary's full name is Joseph Lester Powell, Jr. but he was nicknamed Jody as a child after the young boy in Marjorie Kinnan Rawlings's book *The Yearling*.

The presidential aide was dismissed from the United States Air Force Academy for cheating on a final examination in his senior year.

Powell's father, a cotton and peanut farmer, after learning that he had terminal cancer, committed suicide in 1975.

Powell, William

Actor William Powell's middle name was Horatio.

Powers, Stefanie

The actress's real name is Stefanie Federkiewicz.

Power, Tyrone

Power was one of few Hollywood actors who actually had some hair on his head removed rather than added. His front hairline was too close to his brow, making him look like a monkey, according to the studio executives.

Although the handsome leading man had affairs with Lana Turner, Judy Garland, and Sonja Henie he was a bisexual, according to Hector Arce in a recent biography of Power.

Preminger, Otto

Early in his career, as an actor in Prague, Czechoslovakia, Preminger used the stage name Otto Pretori because the Preminger name was politically controversial. His father had prosecuted certain political leaders for treason during World War I.

He is the father of twins, Victoria and Mark.

The news that Otto fathered Gypsy Rose Lee's only child, Erik, was kept quiet until recently because "Gypsy didn't want anyone to know because she had an afternoon television show, watched by housewives, and she feared losing her audience," according to Preminger.

Preminger always wanted to go into theater work but his father, an attorney, encouraged him to go to law school which he did in fact do, getting an LL.D. from the University of Vienna in 1928. He did not, however, practice law.

As a director, Otto's best movie was *Laura* in 1944 but he wasn't the orginal director assigned to the movie. Reuben Mamoulian started to direct it but Darryl Zanuck didn't like Mamoulian's dailies so he hired Preminger to direct it.

Paramount Studio asked Otto to direct *The Godfather* but when Sinatra turned down the lead ("Ludvig, I pass on this."), Otto turned down the assignment, too. (Otto even volunteered to eliminate the character of the singer—who most people thought was supposed to be Sinatra—but Frank was adamant.)

Prentiss, Paula

The attractive movie actress attempted suicide during the filming of *What's New Pussycat* in 1966 and was hospitalized at New York's Payne Whitney Psychology Clinic for seven months.

Miss Prentiss's last name was originally Ragusa.

Presley, Elvis

Elvis ate meat loaf, mashed potatoes, gravy, and sliced tomatoes every night for two years.

Elvis apparently was strongly influenced by his tour in the U.S. Army. He knew General Douglas MacArthur's farewell speech by heart and also knew every word and scene of the movie *Patton*.

Elvis had a twin brother, Jesse, who died at birth on January 8, 1935.

According to his birth certificate, he was born Elvis Aron Presley but according to his tombstone at Graceland, he died Elvis Aaron Presley, an apparent acknowledgment that his middle name was originally misspelled.

Price, Leontyne

Miss Price's first name was originally spelled Leontine (with an "i").

To have sex or not to have sex is a controversial topic among opera singers. Miss Price's view: "A healthy sex life. Best thing in the world for a woman's voice."

Priestly, Joseph

The British chemist, philosopher, and theologian, best known for his discoveries of gases and carbonated water, was a pastor of Mill Hill Chapel, near Leeds, England, and lived next to a brewery where he first became interested in the fermentation process and the creation of gases.

Proust, Marcel

In his *Cities of the Plain* Marcel Proust wrote a sentence which contained 958 *words*.

Proxmire, William

Edward William Proxmire was called Edward until age six when he saw the cowboy movie star William S. Hart in a silent movie, and started using the name William.

His first marriage was to Elsie Borden Rockefeller, a great-grand-niece of John D. Rockefeller. They were divorced in 1955.

Proxmire's father was a well-to-do doctor in Lake Forest, Illinois whose patients included Adlai Stevenson and Jack Benny.

Pryor, Richard

Pryor grew up in a Peoria, Illinois brothel where both of his parents worked and his grandmother was the proprietress.

Pryor has a special talent for mimicking people because he has an almost perfect aural memory. In fact, he says that half of his comedy dialogues consist of things actually spoken to him at one time.

Pucci, Emilio

Coming from an old line of Florentine aristocrats, Emilio Pucci is an Italian Marquis. His title is the Marchese of Barsento.

In 1932 Pucci was a member of the Italian Olympic Ski Team.

Pucci has an unusual educational background: He studied two years at the University of Milan; went to the University of Georgia for one year; earned an M.A. in social sciences from Reed College in Portland, Oregon, in 1939; and was awarded a doctorate in political science from the University of Florence in 1941.

The designer was a fighter pilot and captain with the Italian Air Force in World War II.

Puccini, Giacamo

The great Italian composer was not necessarily a philanderer but his wife didn't take any chances. When attractive females (and presumably their husbands) were invited to dinner at the Puccinis', Mrs. Puccini would put camphor on her husband's trousers and put bromide in his coffee.

Pulitzer, Joseph

The newspaper publisher and philanthropist was superstitious about the number ten and justifiably so. He was born on April 10, 1847; he arrived in St. Louis after the Civil War on October 10, 1865; he took control of the *St. Louis Dispatch* on December 10, 1878; acquired the *New York World* on May 10, 1883; the *Evening World* began publication in October 10, 1887; he bought the site of the Pulitzer Building on April 10, 1888; the cornerstone of the building was laid on October 10, 1889 and the building was open for business on December 10, 1890. (He died on October 29, 1911.)

Pulitzer's wife, the former Kate Davis, was distantly related to Jefferson Davis, president of the Confederate States of America.

In 1884 Pulitzer became a Congressman from New York's ninth district but resigned before his term expired to devote all his time to publishing activities.

Pushkin, Alexander

The greatest Russian poet was of Negro descent. His mother was the granddaughter of Abram Hannibal, an Abyssinian sold as a slave in Constantinople and adopted by Peter the Great. In Pushkin's unfinished historical work *Arap Petra Velikogo* ("The Negro of Peter the Great") Hannibal is depicted.

Q

Queen, Ellery

The author of the famous detective novels was actually two people: Frederic Dannay (whose real name was *Daniel Nathan* and his favorite composer was *Frederic* Chopin) and Manfred B. Lee (whose real name was Manfred Leopofsky). Dannay, an advertising agency art director, and his cousin Lee, a movie publicity man, met one day for lunch and came up with the idea to enter a mystery story contest sponsored by a magazine. They collaborated to write *The Roman Hat Mystery* which they submitted under the name Ellery Queen. Ellery was the name of a school friend and Queen was picked because it went well with Ellery. They won first prize in the contest (but never received the prize money because the magazine went bankrupt!) and began a long and successful career writing the Ellery Queen stories.

Quinn, Anthony

A numerologist once advised the Irish-Mexican actor to change his name. In Quinn's words, "He said that I'd never get anywhere with a name like Anthony Quinn. He said that I'd have to change it to Bruce Quinn. For a while I even tried writing under the name of Arthur Andretti. But I always came back to the fact that I'd have to make it with the name I was born with." (*The Original Sin*)

Quinn used to donate his blood to John Barrymore whenever the ailing actor needed a transfusion.

R

Rabelais, Francois

In *Gargantua and Pantagruel* Rabelais contributed the following phrases to the language:
Come off scot free; How the other half lives;
Look a gift horse in the mouth; Moon was made
of green cheese; Plain as a nose on a man's
face; Rob Peter to pay Paul; Scared out of his
wits; Two peas in a pod; You have hit the nail on
the head.

Radner, Gilda

The talented comedienne ("Saturday Night
Live") lives in the fashionable Dakota apartment building in New York City.

Radziwill, Lee

One of Lee Radziwill's classmates at Sarah Lawrence College was Barbara Walters, the television newscaster. Barbara, incidentally, remem-
bers that Lee bit her fingernails but dressed
"superbly."

Raft, George

Movie actor George Raft turned down the lead in *The Maltese Falcon* because it was being directed by a man who had never directed a movie before—John Huston. Bogart took the role and he and Huston created a masterpiece in the genre of detective movies and went on to be a successful combination in many other movies (*Treasure of Sierra Madre, Key Largo, The African Queen,* among others).

Raft's last name was originally spelled Ranft. After playing baseball with the Springfield (Mass.) team in the old Eastern League, however, George returned to New York in 1914 and started using the last name Raft. He thought the new name was easier to pronounce and it sounded American whereas Ranft sounded too German.

Raglan, Lord

During the Waterloo campaign in 1815, Lord Raglan was wounded and had to have his arm amputated, but when the arm was being disposed of, he called to have it back to retrieve his wedding ring.

Rainer, Luise

The movie actress was in only nine movies but won Academy Awards for two of them—her second and third movies (*The Great Ziegfeld* and *The Good Earth*).

Rains, Claude

Despite "flunking" the screen test because of his looks, Rains won his role in *The Invisible Man* because director James Whale liked his sonorous voice. This was Rain's film debut but he was so sure the movie was going to be a flop that he left Hollywood. With the immediate box office success of the movie, however, Claude returned to Hollywood and started a successful and lucrative career. In fact, Rains was the first British movie star to get paid $1 million for one movie when he played Julius Caesar in *Caesar and Cleopatra* in 1945.

The Invisible Man was technically well done and full of optical tricks but it included one obvious goof. In the final minutes of the movie when the invisible man runs from the burning barn, his footprints in the snow appear as *shoe* prints rather than *foot* prints.

Raleigh, Sir Walter

Raleigh never laid down his cloak over a puddle for Queen Elizabeth I of England. The story is an apparent invention of historian Thomas Fuller who made it a practice to spice up facts with bits of fiction.

After Sir Walter was beheaded in 1618, his wife was reported to have carried around his head.

The English explorer is usually credited with introducing tobacco to England but he is also responsible for brewing the first beer in this country, at the Roanoke Island colony in Virginia in 1587.

Rampal, Jean-Pierre

The French flutist went to medical school for three years but discontinued his studies after being drafted into the armed services.

Ramses II

The Egyptian king was the first known left-handed person on record. He was always depicted throwing or holding a spear in his left hand.

Rand, Ayn

Ayn Rand's first name rhymes with "mine."

The objectivist author (*Atlas Shrugged*) was born in St. Petersburg, Russia (now Leningrad) and is a graduate of the University of Leningrad. She became a United States citizen in 1931.

Rand, Sally

The famous fandancer, born Helen Gould Beck, used to dance to the music of Ravel, Debussy, Brahms, and Chopin.

Randall, Tony

After being discharged from the army, Tony Randall became an insomniac and went 600 nights without sleep! He claimed that it was the sudden fear of being on his own that caused this problem.

The witty television personality and opera buff hates baseball, birds, and cats but loves women with big noses.

Rasputin, Grigori Efimovich

According to Maria Rasputin, the Russian mystic's daughter, Rasputin's penis was 13″ when fully erect. (How she knew is another story!?)

Rathbone, Basil

Basil Rathbone's full name was Philip St. John Basil Rathbone, and he was born in South Africa, not England.

Ratoff, Gregory

The Russian-born movie director (*All About Eve*) received a law degree from the University of St. Petersburg, Russia.

Ravel, Maurice Joseph

His *Concerto for the Left Hand* was composed especially for Victor Wittgenstein, a Viennese concert pianist who lost his right arm during World War I.

Raye, Martha

Born Margie Yvonne Reed, Martha started in show business at age three when she joined her parents ("Reed and Hooper") in their vaudeville act. She later took her new stage name from a telephone book when she joined the Benny Davis revue.

Reagan, Ronald

The conservative Republican leader and former actor was originally considered for the part of Laszlo, the antifascist leader, in the movie *Casa-*

blanca but lost out to Austrian-born Paul Henreid.

Ronald Reagan was not the first Hollywood actor to become a governor of a major state. John Davis Lodge, a leading man in Hollywood in the 1930s, was governor of Connecticut in the early 1950s.

Reasoner, Harry

In 1946 Harry Reasoner published a novel *Tell Me About Women* (Beechhurst Press) which was "warmly received" according to him. Eighteen years later, however, when it was reissued he commented: "I was only 20 years old then, and I wince a bit when I read some parts of the book today."

Reddy, Helen

When it comes to charity Helen is always ready —she donates one-third of her earnings to charity.

Miss Reddy comes from a show business family. Her father, Max, is a producer, writer, and actor in Australia and her mother, Stella Reddy, is an actress and former lead in one of the most popular soap operas on Australian television.

Redford, Robert

Despite Robert Redford's immense success as an actor, his original calling was art. At Van Nuys High School in Santa Monica, California, he won a *Scholastic* magazine gold key award for art. At the University of Colorado (on a base-ball scholarship) he was an art major until he left in his sophomore year to go to Europe. After living and studying in Paris and Florence, he had a sidewalk showing of his paintings in Florence to raise $211 to pay for his return ticket to the United States. At Pratt Institute in Brooklyn Redford continued his art studies but also attended the American Academy of Dramatic Arts. There his interest in acting became so strong that he abandoned his art career.

As a teenager in Santa Monica, Redford belonged to a gang that raced hot rods and occasionally broke into Bel Air mansions. Regarding the latter activity, he told a reporter, "We never stole anything much; we just did it for kicks."

Before Dustin Hoffman was offered the role of Benjamin in *The Graduate*, Robert Redford turned the role down.

Redford used to draw cartoons for his high school newspaper.

Redgrave, Vanessa

Actress Vanessa Redgrave was born on January 30, 1937, a night on which her father Sir Michael Redgrave and Sir Laurence Olivier were appearing together in an Old Vic production of *Hamlet*, with Olivier in the title role and Redgrave as Laertes. After the final act, in his curtain speech Olivier announced, "Tonight a lovely new actress has been born. Laertes has a daughter." Olivier's prophesy came true despite Redgrave's wanting daughter Vanessa to be a linguist or international airline stewardess.

Reed, Rex

On the David Susskind TV show, Rex's image soared when he said that he was once in bed with Farrah Fawcett-Majors before she became a star. However, Rex clarified the remark by saying that Farrah played his wife in the movie *Myra Breckinridge* and one scene required a shot of Rex and Farrah in bed together.

Reese, Della

Born Deloreese Patricia Early, the singer briefly used the name Pat Ferro (her husband's name was Taliaferro) in the early 1950s but soon changed her name to Della Reese which essentially was her real first name changed to two names.

Reeves, George

The actor who played the role of Superman in the 1950s television series wasn't exactly a muscleman in real life. He needed three men to help him get out of his costume.

Regine

Regine's first professional job was as a maid.

Reilly, Charles Nelson

Charles Nelson Reilly is one of few show business personalities who publicly admits that he wears a toupee.

Remick, Lee

In the movie *Anatomy of a Murder* Lee appears in a dress during a scene in the cafe but when she leaves the cafe she is wearing slacks. (The movie's director, Otto Preminger, occasionally allows this kind of inconsistency to avoid costly overtime shooting.)

Remington, Frederick

Frederick Remington, the artist famous for his western paintings, was on the football team at Yale (with Walter Camp who later became an expert on football and physical fitness).

Renay, Liz

The actress and stripper's real name is Pearl Elizabeth Dobbins. She changed her name to Liz Renay just before winning the title of "Miss Stardust of Arizona." As a stripper, she was billed as Liselle, Lonnie Lovejoy, and Exotica at various times.

Reston, James

The New York Times journalist is known as Scotty by his friends because he was born in Clydebank, Scotland. He came to this country at age ten and lived in Dayton, Ohio.

Rey, Fernando

The suave Spanish movie actor (*The Discreet Charm of the Bourgeoisie* and *The French Connection*), born Fernando Casado Arambillet, used to dub American movies in Spain, the first of which was for *Lloyds of London*—he was the voice of Tyrone Power.

Reynolds, Burt

Actor Burt Reynolds is often compared to Marlon Brando in looks but it is also coincidental to note that Reynolds was called Buddy as a child to distinguish him from Burt, Sr. and Brando was called Bud to distinguish him from his father, Marlon, Sr.

Reynolds raises horses and Black Angus cattle at his 180-acre Jupiter, Florida ranch once gangster Al Capone's hideaway.

From 1962 to 1965 Burt played the blacksmith Quint Asper on the television series "Gunsmoke."

The macho actor has hypoglycemia or low blood sugar, causing him to be a compulsive eater.

Reynolds, Debbie

Movie mogul Jack Warner wanted to change Franny (Mary Frances) Reynolds's name to Debbie Morgan because actor Dennis Morgan was popular at the time. Miss Reynolds didn't like the name but gave in on the name Debbie.

Revere, Paul

A Huguenot who emigrated to Boston, Revere's father was named Apollos Rivoire but the name was Anglicized in America.

As a skilled silversmith, Revere also made false teeth, surgical instruments, and spectacles.

After the Revolutionary War, Revere wore a war uniform every day until his death on May 10, 1818.

Rice, Elmer

Born Elmer Reizenstein, the playwright (*The Adding Machine*) changed his name because people kept mispronouncing it.

Richard, Little

The pioneer of rock 'n' roll, born Richard Penniman, is now a Bible salesman for Memorial Bibles International, Inc.

In his less religious days, Little Richard was using about $1,000 worth of cocaine a day.

His right leg is three inches shorter than the left one.

Richardson, Elliot

In World War II, Elliot Richardson got two Purple Hearts and a Bronze Star and was in the Normandy invasion. His service nicknames, incidentally, were "Lucky" and "Fearless Fosdick."

Rickover, Hyman

The "Father of the Atomic Submarine" and mentor of President James E. Carter spent the first six years of his life in Makow, Russia—now Poland—where he was born. He came to the United States in 1906 with his parents who settled in Chicago.

Riesman, David

David Riesman best known for the book *The Lonely Crowd*, which he wrote with Nathan Glazer and Reuel Denney, was once a lawyer. He clerked for Justice Louis D. Brandeis and later taught law at the University of Buffalo.

Ringling, Charles

The circus entrepreneur was originally a musician. He and his four brothers started a family orchestra that played at local concerts. The group became known as The Ringling Brothers Classic and Comic Concert Company and only after gradually adding other acts did they become known as a circus company.

The family name was originally Rungeling.

Ripley, Robert

Leroy ("Roy") Ripley was an aspiring semiprofessional athlete until he injured his arm trying out for the New York Giants. He then shifted his interests to writing sports cartoons. At the *New York Globe* (where they made him to use the more "athletic-sounding" name Bob L. Ripley), he was near deadline on his sports cartoon one day and came up with the idea of drawing cartoons of seven athletes who had set records for running backwards, hopping, broadjumping on ice, etc. and entitled the cartoon "Believe It or Not." The reader response was so great that Ripley continued to do the cartoon with sports oddities but gradually expanded to include any kind of oddity.

Believe it or not, Ripley is credited with getting Congress to make "The Star-Spangled Banner" the official national anthem after pointing out in his "Believe It or Not" column that it had never been confirmed officially.

Ripley was born on Christmas Day, 1893.

Ritchard, Cyril

When Cyril Trimnell-Ritchard dropped out of medical school in 1917 to become a chorus boy in a Sydney, Australia theater, he trimmed his last name to Ritchard so it could fit on the marquee. At the same time, he named his dog Trimnell, thus keeping the name in the family.

Rivera, Geraldo

At the University of Arizona, the future newscaster used the last name Riviera which his mother thought sounded "more European."

Rivers, Joan

Joan Rivers was not joking when it came to her academic life. She graduated Phi Beta Kappa from Barnard College at age 19.

The comedienne's real surname is Molinski.

Rivers, Larry

The painter was born Yitzroch Loiza Grossberg but when he was a saxophone player in the Catskills, a nightclub comedian introduced him and his combo as "Larry Rivers and his Mudcats" and he decided to keep the name.

Rizzuto, Phil

While broadcasting a Yankee game Rizzuto was informed that Pope Paul VI died, about which he commented on the air, "Well, that kind of puts the damper on even a Yankee win."

Robards, Jason

In an auto accident on December 8, 1972, Robards's face was damaged so severely that it took five operations for the face to be reconstructed.

Robards's first stage appearance was in October 1947 at the Children's World Theatre. He played the rear end of the cow in "Jack and the Beanstalk."

Robbins, Harold

Harold Robbins really loves his profession. He once remarked, "Next to masturbation, it's [writing] the most fun you can have alone."

Robbins is truly a best-selling author. His books have sold over 100,000,000 copies. The current selling rate of his books is 25,000 a day, earning him approximately $1,000,000 a year.

When he was a child, Robbins used to run errands for gangsters Lucky Luciano and Frank Costello.

At the age of 20 Robbins became a millionaire by buying and selling options on crops, before he wrote any best-selling books.

The hero of his first book *Never Love a Stranger* was named Francis Kane, which is Robbins's real name. (As an infant, Robbins was found abandoned at the doorstep of a Catholic orphanage in the Hell's Kitchen section of New York City. He was raised in various foster homes but his last foster home was with Harold Rubin, a New York druggist, and his wife. Kane adopted the name of his foster father but changed the last name to Robbins when he started writing because he thought it sounded better than Rubin.)

Roberts, Oral

When probed about the vast assets of his church organization, Roberts commented, "Christ has no objection to prosperity."

The healing evangelist is of American Indian descent.

Robertson, Cliff

Actor Cliff Robertson's playing John F. Kennedy in the movie *PT-109* was better casting than most people realized. As a 16-year-old seaman on a merchant ship in the Pacific when Pearl Harbor was raided, Robertson's ship was bombed and he was reported dead to his family back home in La Jolla, California. The report, of course, was greatly overexaggerated.

Robertson, Oscar

Basketball player Oscar Robertson's great-grandfather, Marshall Collier, born a slave in 1838, died at age 116 in 1954 and was allegedly the oldest person in the United States at the time.

Robeson, Paul

Paul Robeson's father was originally named Roberson but when he escaped from slavery he slightly altered the name given him by his former owner.

Robinson, Bill "Bojangles"

Bojangles was not only a great tap dancer but he also set the world's record for running 75 yards backwards in 8.2 seconds.

Robinson, Jackie

Robinson was not the first black to play major league baseball but was the first black in *modern-day* baseball. The first black was Moses Fleetwood Walker, of the Toledo Mudhens, then considered a major league team.

Robinson's middle name was Roosevelt.

Robinson, Sugar Ray

Sugar Ray is the only boxer to win a world title five times in the same weight class.

The boxer's real name is Walker Smith, Jr. but to qualify for a boxing match once when he was under age, he borrowed the birth certificate of another boxer whose name was Ray Robinson. He won the fight and decided to keep the name. He acquired the nickname "Sugar" later when a sports writer described Ray as "The sweetest fighter . . . sweet as sugar."

Rockefeller, John D.

The U.S. capitalist and philanthropist gave away a total of $750,000,000 in his lifetime.

Rockefeller, Nelson

By his first marriage to Mary Todd Hunter Clark, Rockefeller was the father of twins.

The late vice president was a dyslexic.

Three days before the late vice-president died, a cousin named Nelson D. Rockefeller passed away at his home in Los Altos, California.

Rockne, Knute

The great Notre Dame football coach was born in Voss, Norway in 1888 but emigrated to the United States with his family in 1893.

Rockwell, Norman

Rockwell was only 21 years old when his first *Saturday Evening Post* cover appeared. It was the May 20, 1916 issue and the painting featured a dutiful young boy pushing a baby carriage past his friends who were in baseball uniforms, about to play a game.

Rockwell appeared on the stage of the Metropolitan Opera next to Enrico Caruso in a production of *Aida*. Rockwell was an art student earning extra money as a spear-carrying extra.

Judging from his paintings, one suspects that Rockwell came from the Midwest but actually he was born in New York City and raised in nearby Mamaroneck, N. Y.

Rodgers, Bill

The shaggy-haired marathon runner smoked a pack of cigarettes a day in his early 20's but later gave up the habit.

Rodin, Auguste

Rodin's famous sculpture *The Thinker* is actually a portrait of Dante Alighierei, the Italian poet. It was originally conceived to be one of a series of bas-reliefs representing scenes from Dante's *Divine Comedy*.

Rodriguez, Chi Chi

Pro golfer Chi Chi Rodriguez was born Juan A. Rodriguez Vila but was nicknamed after his childhood *baseball* idol, *Chi Chi* Flores.

Rogers, Fred

Among Mr. Rogers's friends are Arnold Palmer, with whom he grew up in Latrobe, Pennsylvania, and actor Tony Perkins, with whom he attended Rollins College in Florida.

Rogers, Ginger

The movie actress's name sounds like it was inspired by a Hollywood talent agent but not so. Born Virginia McMath, she was given the nickname Ginger as a child and when her divorced mother married John Logan Rogers, she became

Ginger Rogers. (Note: In 1928 Ginger married Jack Pepper—a spicy combination if there ever was one.)

Rogers, Kenny

In the mid-60s the popular country and western singer was a member of the New Christy Minstrels singing group.

Roebling, John Augustus

The German-born engineer designed the Brooklyn Bridge but one week after the plans were approved his foot was crushed while he was surveying the pier area. The foot was amputated, gangrene developed and he died three weeks later. His son, Washington Augustus Roebling, continued the work but not without mishap—he developed "the bends."

Rogers, Will

The popular humorist used to say, "I don't make jokes; I just watch the government and report the facts."

Roget, Peter Mark

The famous lexicographer and creator of *Roget's Thesaurus* was a medical doctor by profession. Roget was a graduate of the medical school at Edinburgh, practiced in London, and did not start writing his *Thesaurus* until his retirement in 1840.

Roget was good at numbers as well as words. In 1815 he invented the "log-log" (vs. Mannheim) slide rule.

Romanoff, Mike

The colorful owner of Romanoff's restaurant in Hollywood, California claimed that he was the nephew of the last of the Russian Czars, yet he never bothered to learn even the simplest of Russian words.

Romanoff also claimed that he was the man who killed Rasputin.

Romberg, Sigmund

After emigrating to the United States in 1910, the Hungarian composer's (*The Student Prince*) first job was as a piano player in a New York City restaurant.

Romney, George

Romney was born on July 8, 1907 in Chihuahua, Mexico, where his American parents were living in a Mormon colony, and lived there for five years until Pancho Villa expelled all American families from the country.

Ronstadt, Linda

Her maternal grandfather was Lloyd Copeland, an inventor who developed the prototype of a microwave oven.

Rooney, Mickey

Mickey is still going strong in the marriage department. He married for the eighth time in July of 1979. His latest wife, Jan Chamberlin, calls him "Micker" and he calls her "Bunker."

For the record, Mickey is five foot three, three inches shorter than his eighth wife but 17 inches taller than Hervé Villechaize of *Fantasy Island*.

Roosevelt, Eleanor

F.D.R.'s fourth cousin and wife was probably one of the most active and "intellectual" wives of a U.S. president, but, in fact, she never went to college.

Although Eleanor gave birth to six children, she was known to dislike sex and, in fact, after the birth of the last child, never had sex with Franklin again.

According to James Roosevelt in *My Parents: A Differing View*, "Mother once confessed that she was completely naive about sex and had not even kissed father until they were married."

Roosevelt, Franklin D.

Roosevelt weighed ten pounds at birth.

Roosevelt is best remembered for all the legislation passed during his administration but like most home run hitters' striking out a lot, F.D.R. also vetoed 631 bills as president.

It is fairly well accepted now that Roosevelt satisfied his sexual needs with women other than his wife (who didn't like to have sex). Some of the women included Lucy Mercer, Eleanor's social secretary and Missy LeHand, his own private secretary, according to his son Elliott.

Roosevelt was a frustrated advertising man, as he indicated in a speech he gave to the Advertising Federation of America in 1931 when he was still governor of New York: "If I were starting life over again, I'm inclined to think that I would go into the advertising business, in preference to almost any other."

F.D.R. is credited with coining the word "chiseler."

Genealogists have determined that F.D.R. was related by blood or by marriage to eleven former presidents: Washington, John Adams, Madison, John Quincy Adams, Van Buren, William Henry Harrison, Taylor, Grant, Benjamin Harrison, Teddy Roosevelt, and Taft.

F.D.R. had minor literary ambitions. He once wrote a movie screenplay about the American frigate *Old Ironsides* but was not successful in selling it to the Hollywood studios. Also an avid reader of detective stories, he inspired the book *The President's Mystery Story* by posing the question, "How can a man disappear with five million dollars in negotiable form and not be traced?" Six different writers conjured up solutions and each solution became a chapter in the book which Farrar & Rinehart published and *Liberty* magazine reprinted in their November 1935 issue.

At Harvard College he was a "C" student but he was elected editor of the Harvard *Crimson* in his junior year.

He had two sons named Franklin, Jr. The first one was born on March 18, 1909 but died less than eight months later. The second Franklin Delano Roosevelt, Jr. was born on August 17, 1914.

He was the first president to ride in an automobile (a Columbia Electric Victoria in Hartford, Connecticut), fly in an airplane (in St. Louis, Missouri), and go in a submarine (in Long Island Sound off Oyster Bay).

On October 14, 1912 an assassination attempt was made on Roosevelt's life as he was about to make a campaign speech in Milwaukee, Wisconsin. He was shot in the chest but proclaimed, "I will deliver this speech or die, one or the other." He then proceeded to speak for 50 minutes, after which he went to the hospital to be treated.

Teddy originated the phrases "lunatic fringe," "muckrakers," and "my hat is in the ring."

He was the first president to visit a foreign country while in office. He visited Panama in November, 1906 and then visited Puerto Rico.

Valentine's Day in 1884 was a day of tragedy for Roosevelt. Both his mother and his wife died on that day.

While in the White House, Teddy kept a .44 caliber revolver near his bed.

Theodore Roosevelt lost two sons in two different wars. Quentin Roosevelt was killed on July 14, 1918, in France during World War I when his plane was shot down and Theodore Roosevelt, Jr. died of a heart attack in Normandy, France on July 12, 1944, while in the service.

Teddy lost sight in one eye because of a hard punch he received in a boxing practice session at the White House.

Franklin Delano was the Roosevelt who once said he wanted to get into advertising but it was Teddy Roosevelt whose words actually helped create one of the greatest advertising campaigns ever launched. After drinking a cup of Maxwell House coffee for the first time, Teddy was asked if he would like to have another cup. His response—"Will I have another? Delighted! It's good to the last drop." The line summed up the coffee's flavor so well that the company adopted it as their advertising slogan and has used it ever since.

On his 22nd birthday, October 27, 1880, Teddy Roosevelt married Alice Hathaway.

President Roosevelt once shook hands with a record *8,513 people* in one day, at a New Year's Day White House party on January 1, 1907.

At the age of 22, he wrote the book *The Naval War of 1812,* a well-regarded interpretation of that war.

Among the many books Roosevelt wrote were *Thomas Hart Benton* (1887), *History of New York City* (1891), *Oliver Cromwell* (1900), *Life Histories of African Game Animals* (1914; with Edmund Heller), and *Book-Lover's Holiday in the Open* (1916).

Rorem, Ned

The composer, writer, and critic once admitted that he watched the television panel show "To

Tell the Truth" "to see what Kitty Carlisle was wearing," according to *People* magazine.

Rose, Billy

William Samuel Rosenberg (his real name) was the "greatest natural writer in the history of shorthand" according to John Robert Gregg but he quit stenography after World War I to write songs. As a songwriter in Tin Pan Alley, he shortened his name to Billy Rose and produced such hits as "Barney Google," "That Old Gang of Mine," and "It's Only a Paper Moon."

Rosenberg, Julius and Ethel

The convicted spies were executed on June 19, 1953—their 14th wedding anniversary.

Ross, Betsy

Born Betsy Griscom, she became an upholsterer, the profession of her husband John Ross, after he died. It was John Ross's uncle George Ross who suggested to his friend George Washington that Betsy design a flag for the United States.

Ross, Herbert

The movie director (*The Turning Point, The Goodbye Girl*) used to pose in the nude as an artist's model when he was a ballet student in his teens.

Rossini, Gioacchino

The Italian opera composer kept his head warm in the winter by wearing three wigs at the same time.

Rosten, Leo

He originally wrote his book *The Education of H*Y*M*A*N K*A*P*L*A*N* under the pseudonym Leonard Q. Ross.

Rostow, Walter

During World War II Walter Rostow was an O.S.S. agent and was aboard the British tanker *Empire Mersey* when it was sunk by a German submarine. He was lucky enough to save his life but in the process lost his luggage. Five years later, however, Rostow persuaded his congressman to introduce a bill to reimburse him for the loss and on May 19, 1947, the bill was adopted —giving him $585.50 for his torpedo-sunken luggage.

Roth, Lillian

The stage and movie singer, born Lillian Rutstein, was named after Lillian Russell (whose real name was Helen Louise Leonard), the famous turn-of-the-century singer. "Roth" is a shortened version of her real last name "Rutstein."

Rowan, Dan

Dan Rowan was a fighter pilot with the Fifth Air Force in World War II, and received injuries in a crash landing.

Rubenstein, Arthur

During World War II the Polish-born pianist lived in Beverly Hills, California and worked as a "ghost" piano player for actors who played the roles of Schumann, Liszt, and Brahms. He "ghosted" in *I've Always Loved You*, *Song of Love*, and *Night Song* (and also appeared in person in *Carnegie Hall* and *Of Men and Music*.)

Rusk, Dean

The former U.S. secretary of state, born in Cherokee County, Georgia, was delivered by a *veterinarian*.

Russell, Bertrand

About chastity, the philosopher once said, "I gave it a good try once, but never again."

One woman said that Bertie's sexual advances felt like "dry leaves rustling up your thighs," according to Alistair Cooke.

Russell, Jane

Jane Russell's well-developed breasts inspired the name of two adjacent mountains in Alaska —they are called the "Jane Russell Peaks!"

The brassiere pitchwoman and former actress founded WAIF, a national organization for placing orphans. (The license plates on her Mercedes read WAIF 1.)

Her son Buck served nine months in prison on a manslaughter charge.

Russell, Rosalind

During a love scene in the movie *Under Two Flags* actor Ronald Colman refused to kiss Rosalind Russell on the mouth so she took a swig of mouthwash, put on some Arpege perfume, and kissed him until his face turned purple.

Miss Russell was named after the steamship S.S. *Rosalind.*

Ruth, Babe

Many baseball fans know that Babe Ruth was originally a pitcher but few people realize how good he was. In the 1916 and 1918 World Series Ruth pitched 29⅔ scoreless innings, setting a record, and in 1919 he was considered the best left-handed pitcher in the American League.

George Bernard Shaw once asked an American journalist, "Who's this Baby Ruth? And what does *she* do?"

As a student at St. Mary's Industrial School in Baltimore, Maryland, Ruth was trained to become a *tailor* but his incredible ability to wallop a baseball altered the direction of his career.

Contrary to popular belief, the candy bar Baby Ruth was not named after the Yankee home run slugger but after President Grover Cleveland's oldest daughter.

Rutherford, Dame Margaret

The British actress best remembered for her movies as Miss Marple, Agatha Christie's elderly sleuth, was a chronic late starter: She made her first movie at age 44, did not get married until she was 52 years old, was 71 years old when she won an Academy Award for best supporting actress in *The V.I.P.'s*, and was 74 years old when she became honored as Dame of the British Empire.

Ryan, Robert

When movie actor Robert Ryan was a student at Dartmouth College (1927–1931) one of his Psi Upsilon fraternity brothers was Nelson Rockefeller.

S

Sadat, Anwar

The dark callus in the center of the Egyptian leader's forehead is from years of praying five times a day with his head to the ground.

Sadat once wrote a political novel entitled *The Prince of the Island* but it has never been published.

Safer, Morley

The "60 Minutes" investigative reporter was born in Toronto, Canada, and is still a Canadian citizen.

Sagan, Carl

At Rahway High School, New Jersey, the astronomer and exobiologist was voted the most outstanding male student and most likely to succeed ('51).

Sagan, Françoise

Just before publishing *Bonjour Tristesse* in 1954, Françoise Quoirez took the pseudonym Francoise Sagan because she liked the sound of the name. She took the name Sagan from the Princess de Sagan in Proust's *A La Recherche du Temps Perdu*.

Sahl, Mort

Mort Sahl has a B.S. (Bachelor of Science!) degree in city management and engineering from the University of South Carolina. His thesis dealt with the subject of city traffic flow.

Saki

Writer Saki's real name, H. H. (Hector Hugh) Munro, is well known but how he got the name is not: When Munro was writing political sketches for the *Westminster Gazette* in England, he started using the pen name "Saki" which he took from the *Rubaiyat of Omar Khayyam* (in which Saki was the name of the cupbearer).

Sales, Soupy

Born as Milton Hines, the comedian was called "Soupbone" or "Soupy" as a child because Hines and Heinz (the maker of soups, among other things) sounded the same. Later, Soupy changed his last name at the request of a radio station manager who thought the name Soupy Hines sounded too much like a plug for Heinz 57 Varieties.

Salinger, J. D.

Recluse writer Jerome David Salinger once worked in a pig slaughterhouse in Bydgoszcz, Poland when he was 18 years old.

Salinger, Pierre

The former presidential press secretary was a piano prodigy at six years of age and gave his first major recital at the Canadian National Exposition in 1931. After six years of recitals, however, his parents ended his piano career because he was becoming too shy and introverted.

After enlisting in the U.S. Navy in 1942, Salinger served as a lieutenant in the Pacific and as a commanding officer of a submarine chaser, was one of the youngest men ever to command a U.S. Navy ship.

Salk, Dr. Jonas

In 1970 Dr. Salk married Françoise Gilot, once the mistress of Pablo Picasso.

Samuelson, Paul

The Nobel Prize-winning (1970) economist has an economy of scale in his home life. He is the father of six children, including triplets.

Sand, George

The French writer's real name was Amandine Lucile Aurore Dudevant (nee Dupin). When she published her first book the French public was still not ready to accept a novel written by a woman so she took the pen name George Sand. The name was inspired by Jules Sandeau, a French novelist and playwright, with whom she worked on the staff of the newspaper *Figaro* and with whom she was having an affair. Earlier they jointly wrote the book *Rose et Blanche* using the pseudonym "Jules Sand."

Sandburg, Carl

Poet and author Carl Sandburg applied for and received an appointment to West Point in 1899 but later decided to attend Lombard College instead.

The poet's wife was Lillian Steichen, sister of photographer Edward Steichen.

Sandburg once appeared on the television program "What's My Line."

At Lombard College in Galesburg, Illinois, the future Pulitzer Prize-winning biographer (*Abraham Lincoln: The War Years*) was captain of the basketball team and a member of the Poor Writer's Club.

Sanders, Colonel

The Kentucky Colonel is not originally from Kentucky! He was born near Henryville, Indiana in 1890 and didn't move out of the Hoosier State until 1929 when he opened a gas station in Corbin, Kentucky.

Through the help of restauranteur Toots Shor, who was a friend of John Daly, Colonel Sanders appeared on the TV show "What's My Line?" His line, of course, was that he made and sold his own fried chicken in a little shop in Kentucky. That nationwide publicity plus Sander's unique recipe gave the impetus Kentucky Fried Chicken needed to become the large fast-food chain that it is today.

Sanders, George

The stuffy Russian-born British actor was the brother of actor Tom Conway.

George Sanders became an actor by accident. He was in the textile business in London but his sonorous voice (heard at a cocktail party) prompted an offer to go on the stage and he accepted the offer.

Saroyan, William

Saroyan used the pen name Sirak Gorgan for his first published story "The Broken Wheel" which appeared in the Boston Armenian-American newspaper *Hairenik*.

The writer learned to read at age eight but started to write seriously only one year later. He wrote an essay "How I Spent My Summer," submitting 1,500 words instead of 50 words, much to the consternation of his teacher.

Saroyan submitted almost 100 pieces to magazines before anything was accepted for publication.

Saroyan was once an inveterate gambler and went to the racetrack every day.

The writer was awarded the Pulitzer Prize in 1944 for *The Time of Your Life* but rejected on the grounds that he was opposed to the patronizing of art by the wealthy.

Sarnoff, David

As a wireless operator for the Marconi Wireless Company on duty the night of April 14, 1912, when the S.S. *Titanic* hit an iceberg, Sarnoff was the first person to pick up the *Titanic's* S.O.S., and he stayed on duty for 75 hours straight in order to coordinate rescue operations. (Nine years later he became president of the National Broadcasting Company.)

Sartre, Jean-Paul

Jean-Paul Sartre's mother, Anne Marie Schweitzer, was a first cousin of the missionary and doctor Albert Schweitzer.

Sayers, Dorothy

At the age of seven Miss Sayers was taught Latin by her minister father. (She later majored in languages and took honors at Oxford. In fact, she was one of the first women to receive a degree from Oxford University, England.)

She had an illegitimate son who was raised by one of her cousins.

Scaasi, Arnold

Scaasi spelled backwards in the designer's real last name—Isaacs. (This type of name change was inspired by Serutan, a laxative spelled Nature's backward.)

Schaap, Dick

The sports writer and television newscaster originated the nickname "Fun City" for New York City.

Schippers, Thomas

Thomas Schippers, a piano prodigy at age six, was conductor of the Metropolitan Opera when he was only 25.

Schlesinger, Arthur Jr.

Born Arthur Bancroft Schlesinger, he changed his name to Arthur Meier Schlesinger, Jr. "At that point I wanted to be Arthur Schlesinger, Jr." (His mother was a descendant of George Bancroft, another distinguished American historian.)

Scholl, Dr.

The cornpad entrepreneur's motto was "Early to bed, early to rise, work like hell and advertise."

Schubert, Franz Peter

The Austrian composer was rejected for military service because of his short stature.

The only public concert Schubert ever gave was on March 26, 1828.

Schubert died of syphilis and typhoid fever.

Schulz, Charles

Charles Schulz's childhood nicknames foreshadowed his subsequent involvement in cartoons. He was nicknamed "Sparky" after the horse Sparkplug in the "Barney Google" cartoon strip. Years later he was also nicknamed "The Timid Soul" from another comic strip, H. T. Webster's "Caspar Milquetoast," but the name Sparky stayed with him for the rest of his life.

At St. Paul's (Minnesota) Central High School, Schulz not only failed Algebra, Latin, English, and Physics but also had his cartoons *rejected* by the yearbook staff.

One of cartoonist Charlie Schulz's friends at a school in Minneapolis was named Charlie Brown—which Schulz thought would make a good name for one of his cartoon strip characters. The real Charlie Brown gave him permission to use his name but when he saw the character he was disappointed because he didn't look like Steve Canyon.

After getting out of school, Schulz applied for a job as a cartoonist at the Walt Disney studios but was turned down.

Schweitzer, Albert

Albert Schweitzer, doctor and humanitarian, graduated from medical school at the age of 33.

Scorsese, Martin

Raised a Roman Catholic, the young movie director (*Taxi Driver, Mean Streets*) wanted to be a priest but eventually lost interest especially when he failed the entrance examination to Fordham University's divinity school.

Scott, George C.

George C. Scott, an aspiring writer, enrolled in the University of Missouri School of Journalism in 1949 but quickly became interested in dramatic arts after seeing a play produced by the Missouri Workshop Theatre. He tried out for their next production, *The Winslow Boy,* after memorizing every line and won the lead.

In 1962, Scott was nominated as Best Supporting Actor for his role in *The Hustler* but was the first actor to ever decline an award in advance of the ceremony. George Dewey Scott, George's father, however, did get an academy award that year. The senior Scott, as a vice-president of the Ex-Cell-O Corporation, had sponsored an industrial film entitled *Project Hope* and it won the award for the best short documentary of 1961.

George officially achieved his original ambition to be a professional writer in 1965 when *Esquire* published his article on the war in Vietnam. It was a serious, well-intended defense of America's involvement in the war but it was not Scott's finest moment nor was it *Esquire's* best journalism on the war.

Scott's tour de force performance in the movie *Patton* was so strong that it is hard to believe that Twentieth Century-Fox had first considered Burt Lancaster, Lee Marvin, and John Wayne for the role before giving it to Scott. (NOTE: Twentieth Century-Fox considered doing a Pat-

441

ton movie in 1951 with Spencer Tracy in the lead but the project was abandoned because it was felt to lack commercial potential!)

In the tradition of other great actors like John Barrymore and Douglas Fairbanks, Sr., George C. Scott is a heavy drinker and has been known to get into a bar brawl from time to time.

Scott, Sir Walter

When Walter Scott was 18 months old, he had a severe fever that caused paralysis in his right leg, leaving him lame for the rest of his life.

Scott coined the word "freelance" to refer to soldiers, equipped with lances, who sold their services.

Scourby, Alexander

The character actor and movie narrator (*Victory at Sea*, among many) suggests a British or Bostonian accent but actually he was born in Brooklyn, New York, of Greek immigrant parents.

Scull, Robert C.

The taxi tycoon and art collector's family name was originally Sokolnikoff before Ellis Island officials shortened it to Scull.

Sears, Richard Warren

The co-founder of Sears, Roebuck & Co. was originally a watch salesman. As a railroad worker, he bought the rights to buy an abandoned shipment of watches and sold them via mail order and advertising. Within a year he started the R. W. Sears Watch Company and soon teamed up with Alvah C. Roebuck, a watchmaker, whom he hired to fix watches being sent back.

Seberg, Jean

When the 17-year-old girl from Marshalltown, Iowa was chosen by Otto Preminger for the lead role in his movie *Saint Joan,* she was one of 17,799 girls supposedly screened for the part.

The late actress retained her real name but her family's name was originally Carlson. Jean's Swedish paternal grandfather changed it to Seberg.

Sedaka, Neil

The perennially youthful singer and songwriter is of Sephardic Jewish ancestry.

Segal, George

In college George Segal played the banjo and was the leader of "Bruno Lynch and his Imperial Jazz Band" and in the army he started another band, "Corporal Bruno's Sad Sack Six."

Segar, Elzie Crisler

In 1919 the cartoonist started the comic strip "Thimble Theatre" which featured the Oyl family and daughter Olive. It wasn't until ten years later that the muscle-bound, corn-cob smoking Popeye appeared and became the central character of the strip.

Segovia, Andrés

The 87-year-old classical guitarist has a son, Carlos Andrés, who is only ten years old.

Sellers, Peter

In 1964 the British comedian became the first male ever to appear on the cover of *Playboy* magazine. The rarely bestowed honor was also extended to Burt Reynolds in the October '79 issue of the magazine.

When Peter Sellers had his heart attack he was pronounced dead six times but was revived each time, thanks to special equipment at the Cedars of Lebanon Hospital in Los Angeles.

An automobile hobbyist, Sellers once owned 62 cars.

Selznick, David O.

Selznick, whose family's original name was Zeleznick, was never given a middle name by his parents so he decided to give himself one to justify a middle initial. After all, Mayer, his father-in-law, was Louis B., DeMille was Cecil B., Lasky was Jesse L.! David's instincts led him to the initial "O" and then he picked the name Oliver to back it up, after thinking of Oliver Thomas, a Ziegfeld girl who was appearing in his brother Myron's movies at the time.

After hearing Selznick's full name many people thought he was Irish—as in David O'Selznick!

At first, Selznick was not interested in making the movie *Gone With the Wind* because he knew that most movies about the Civil War, with the exception of *Birth of a Nation*, were not successful moneymakers.

Sennett, Mack

Born in Denville, Quebec, he was named Mickall (or Michael) Sinnott at birth but altered the name to Mack Sennett as a burlesque and circus performer in the early 1900s.

Sennett found the name for his Keystone movie company on a train schedule for the Pennsylvania Railroad whose logo was a keystone.

Sequoya

The Indian leader was the son of an English trader and a part-Cherokee mother. Although he was also known by the Anglo-Saxon name George Guess, he spoke no English.

Seuss, Dr.

Dr. Seuss recently revealed in *Parents* magazine that a few of the characters in his children's stories were based on real people. For example, Yertle in *Yertle the Turtle* is a caricature of Adolf Hitler, "a little domineering guy who pushes people around." In *Marvin K. Mooney, Will You Please Go Now* the puppylike creature constantly asked to "go" is ex-President Richard M. Nixon.

Dr. Seuss, whose real name is Dr. Theodore Seuss Geisel, received a big break when one of his cartoons in *Judge* magazine showed a knight using Flit insecticide to kill dragons. The cartoon caught the attention of a woman whose husband was an executive at Flit's advertising agency. The agency, McCann-Erickson, subsequently signed a contract with Geisel and for over ten years he created humorous cartoon-drawn advertisements ("Quick Henry! The Flit!") for Flit and other Standard Oil of New Jersey products.

Most of Dr. Seuss's stories are in verse not because he was a meter-obsessed student of poetry but because he once visited Europe on the liner *Kungsholm* and the rhythm of its engines (he obviously wasn't traveling first class!) gave him the idea to write a children's book based on the apparent meter of the ship's engines. The final product was his book *And To Think That I Saw It On Mulberry Street* which he published in 1937.

Seward, William Henry

Most people know that William Seward was responsible for the purchase of Alaska from Russia in 1867 for $7,200,000 which for years was called "Seward's Folly" (now considered one of the best purchases the U.S. ever made!) but few people know that on the night Lincoln was assassinated Seward was attacked by Lewis Powell, a cohort of John Wilkes Booth. He was stabbed severely while in bed recovering from an accident. Seward survived the attack but shocked by the event, his invalid wife died two months later. His only daughter died the following year.

Seymour, Whitney North

In his senior year at the University of Wisconsin, the future head of the American Bar Association ran for the class presidency but lost to a classmate named Frederick Bickel, who later became famous as actor under the name Fredric March.

Shaffer, Peter

British playwright Peter Shaffer and his twin brother, Anthony, once collaborated on two mystery novels, using the pseudonym Peter Anthony.

Shah of Iran

At Le Rosey boarding school in Switzerland, the Shah was captain of the tennis team.

Shakespeare, William

William Shakespeare was only 18 years old when he married Anne Hathaway, who was six years his senior.

Alert English students note that Shakespeare's first child, Susanna, was born only six months after his marriage to Anne Hathaway and immediately suspect a forced marriage. The fact is that in those days a betrothal was legally binding and any offspring born nine months after the betrothal were considered legitimate. Shakespeare and Anne Hathaway were betrothed sufficiently in advance for Susanna to be considered a legitimate child.

Shakespeare used 28,000 words in all his works but used 40 percent of the words only once, which is a statistical way of saying that he had a way with words.

The English playwright was the father of twins, Hamnet (not Hamlet) and Judith.

Shange, Ntozake

The black poet and playwright (*For Colored Girls Who Have Considered Suicide*) was born Paulette Williams in Trenton, N.J. She dropped her "slave name" in 1971. Her African first name means "she who comes with her own things" and her last name, the name of the man with whom she was living, means "who walks like a lion."

Shapp, Milton

The former Pennsylvania governor's real name is Milton Jerrold Shapiro but early in his career, as a salesman in Philadelphia, he noticed that no one ever returned a call when "Mr. Shapiro called," so prompting him to shorten his name to Shapp.

Sharif, Omar

The Egyptian actor and bridge fanatic, born Michael Shalhoub, is actually *Syrian* by blood but was born and raised in Egypt.

Sharif's first television commercial was for Stolichnaya vodka in Australia. He was asked to do the commercial because 82 percent of the Australian public identified him with Russia and vodka because of his performance in the movie *Dr. Zhivago*.

His first movie *The Blazing Sun*, a 1953 Egyptian production, featured the first kiss in an Arabic film. He played opposite Egypt's movie queen, Faten Hamama, whom he later married.

In Egyptian movies he appeared as Omar El Sharif.

Sharkey, Jack

Sharkey's real name was Joseph Paul Zukauskas. He adopted the name Jack Sharkey because his two favorite boxers were *Jack* Dempsey and Tom *Sharkey*. (In 1927 Sharkey fought Dempsey and was knocked out in the seventh round.)

Shaw, George Bernard

George Bernard Shaw won an Academy Award for the Best Screenplay of 1938 (*Pygmalion*) but called the Hollywood honor an insult when he found out that he won.

Shaw originally grew his long beard when he contracted smallpox and was unable to shave.

At age 29, Shaw became a music critic and adopted the pen name Corno Di Bassetto (which was the name of a musical instrument no longer in use). His reviews of operas and concerts were incisive and still can be appreciated today.

In the last years of his life, vegetarian Shaw had a bad case of body odor caused by digestive problems.

Shaw, Irwin

The author (*The Young Lions, Rich Man, Poor Man*) was expelled from Brooklyn College in his freshman year for failing calculus but was later re-admitted. He soon started writing a column for the college newspaper, thus beginning his writing career.

Shawn, Ted

While a student of theology at the University of Denver, Shawn caught diphtheria which partially paralyzed his legs. To help him recover, doctors recommended that he take ballet lessons to exercise his legs. Shawn liked ballet so much that he decided to become a dancer.

Sheen, Martin

The popular young actor was born Ramon Estevez in Dayton, Ohio, where his Spanish immigrant father and Irish-American mother met at a language school. He changed his name when he began acting and took his new surname from the popular Roman Catholic orator and spokesman, Bishop Fulton J. Sheen, whom he admired.

Shelley, Mary Wollstonecraft

The English writer and wife of poet Percy Bysshe Shelley wrote the novel *Frankenstein* at age 19.

Shelley, Percy Bysshe

The English poet's grandfather, Sir Bysshe Shelley, was born in Newark, New Jersey. Sir

Bysshe's father emigrated to the United States from England but after second thoughts returned to England.

Shelley was a vegetarian.

Sheridan, Ann

The ex-beauty contest winner, born Clara Lou Sheridan, was originally considered for the part of Ilsa in the movie *Casablanca*. (Swedish actress Ingrid Bergman won the part.)

Sherman, Roger

A signer of the Declaration of Independence and member of the First Continental Congress, Roger Sherman was a shoemaker and had a cobbler's shop in Milford, Connecticut earlier in his career.

Shore, Dinah

Born in Georgia as Frances "Fanny" Rose Shore, Dinah was stricken with poliomyelitis at age two years, seriously affecting her right leg. Exercise and massage, however, enabled her to fully recover and even now she plays a good game of tennis.

Although there are several stories about the origin of Fanny Shore's new name Dinah, most stories agree that it was her singing of the song "Dinah" (made popular by Ethel Waters) that gave her the identification with the name.

On some of her early recordings she is listed as Dinah Shaw because someone mispronounced her name and she was so nervous during the recording session that she didn't correct the pronunciation.

The name of Dinah's dog, Grunk, appears on her license plates.

Shute, Nevil

The author of *On the Beach,* whose full name was Nevil Shute Norway, was an aeronautical engineer by profession and he never really considered himself an author. Writing was his avocation.

Sills, Beverly

Born Belle Miriam Silverman, she received the nickname "Bubbles" at birth because she was born with a large bubble of saliva in her mouth and the doctor considered it a good omen. She was renamed Beverly Sills at seven years old because a friend of the family thought that the new name would look better than "Belle Silverman" on a marquee.

As a child, Miss Sills studied piano with Paolo Gallico, the father of writer Paul Gallico.

Beverly Sills in a soap opera? Yes, when she was 12 years old she appeared in the soap opera "Our Gal Sunday," playing the part of Elaine Raleigh.

She sang the Rinso White soap flakes song "Rinso White, Rinso White, Happy Little Wash Day Song" in commercials.

Silverman, Fred

Silverman is not the first person in his family to be in the television business. His father was a television repairman.

Silvers, Phil

Comedian Phil Silvers is not known for being a songwriter but he and Jimmy Van Heusen did write the song *Nancy* (with the Laughing Face...) which they wrote for Frank Sinatra's daughter Nancy.

Phil's family name was originally Silversmith but he used the name Silvers because several successful show business people had the name (Lou Silver, Al Jolson's conductor, and Sid Silvers, Phil Baker's Heckler) and he didn't think he should be any different.

Simenon, George

The creator of Chief Inspector Maigret, the fictional detective, was born on Friday, the 13th (February 1903) but his superstitious mother registered the birth as being on February 12th.

The Belgium-born writer is prolific, to say the least. He has written over 200 novels, including 88 Maigret detective books and has made love to 10,000 women, a statistic which he conspicuously did not deny, saying, "That's what I did most of the time since I was 13. . . . When you make love to them, you understand them better." Among the women was black singer Josephine Baker whom he almost married.

Simon, Carly

Carly Simon's father, the late Richard Simon, was co-founder of Simon and Schuster, the publishing company.

Carly and her sisters billed as The Simon Sisters, had a hit single record in 1964, "Winkin', Blinkin' and Nod."

Simon, John

The hypercritical critic strongly believes that actresses should at least look good if they can't act. Liza Minelli and Barbra Streisand unfortunately have not passed his criteria. Liza has "blubber lips" and a face "going off in three directions simultaneously" and Barbra has a "hypertrophic ego and bloated countenance."

Simon, Neil

Playwright Neil Simon, whose full name is Marvin Neil Simon, is nicknamed "Doc" not because he can "doctor up" or rewrite an ailing play but because he used to play doctor with a stethoscope when he was a boy.

Simon used to have a bad case of claustrophobia but psychoanalysis has almost completely cured him of this fear.

Simone, Nina

While Eunice Kathleen Waymon (her real name) was a music teacher in Philadelphia, she also moonlighted as a nightclub singer in Atlantic City. She took a stage name because she did not want her parents or students to know about her working at a nightclub. "Nina" came from her nickname *Nina*, Spanish for "little girl," and the "Simone" was added because it "seemed to go well with Nina."

Simpson, Adele

The four feet nine inch fashion designer's real name is Adele Smithline.

Simpson, O. J.

As a youthful football player O. J. Simpson was arrested three times and once spent six hours in jail for minor juvenile gang offenses.

Because he had rickets as a child, O. J. wore braces on his legs and is still pigeon-toed and bowlegged.

While a student at the University of Southern California, O. J. drove a truck for the local RC Cola bottler but was fired for sleeping on the job. Several years and one Heisman Trophy later, RC hired him to be a spokesman for a six-figure fee.

O. J. is a cousin of Ernie Banks, the former Chicago Cubs first baseman.

The "O" stands for Orenthal which was a name suggested by an aunt who said that "it was the name of some French or Italian actor."

Sinatra, Frank

Frank's nickname during his Hoboken days was "Slacksy" because he had so many pairs of slacks.

At Clark Gable's suggestion, Frank tested for the role of Maggio in *From Here to Eternity* and got it, despite Harry Cohn's favoring Eli Wallach for the part. (Incidentally, Frank was paid only $8,000 for being in *From Here to Eternity*.)

With his career revitalized after *From Here to Eternity*, Frank was supposed to play the part of Terry Malloy in *On the Waterfront* but eventually lost out to Marlon Brando.

Sinatra almost drowned once off the island of Kauai, Hawaii, but was saved by actor Brad Dexter.

When Frank's ex-wife Ava Gardner heard that he was getting married to actress Mia Farrow, she was quoted as saying, "I always knew Frank would end up marrying a boy!"

Skelton, Red

Red's full name was Richard *Red* Skelton, according to his biographer Arthur Marx. (Other sources list his full name as Richard Bernard Skelton.)

His father, who died two months before Red was born, was a clown with the Hagenback Wallace Circus and in absentia seemed to influence Red's career choice.

Although Red often portrays drunks in his comedy routines he does not drink. In fact, he is allergic to alcohol.

When Farouk was still King of Egypt, the Skeltons threw a dinner party for Farouk's mother but Red did not endear himself to the Queen

Mother when, according to reporter James Bacon, he asked her, "Queenie, do you know your son is 'farouking' Egypt?"

Slaughter, Frank G.

The author and physician was elected to Phi Beta Kappa at age 17, received a B.A. degree from Duke University at age 18, and was awarded an M.D. degree from Johns Hopkins Medical School when he was only 22 years old.

Slick, Grace

When asked about taking LSD the rock star admitted, "I stopped dropping acid for a while after my daughter was born. It's hard to keep an eye on the kid while you're hallucinating."

Smith, Howard K.

As a Rhodes scholar, the TV newscaster studied at Oxford University in England.

Smithson, James

The distinguished chemist and founder of the Smithsonian Institution (not Institute) in Washington, D.C. was never in the United States except after his death when his remains were brought to the Smithsonian in 1904 for reinterment.

Born in Paris, France, he was named James Macie until he was 36 years old. He was the illegitimate child of Elizabeth Macie, a descendant of Henry VII, and Sir Hugh Smithson, first

Duke of Northumberland. His name was changed in 1801 by assent of the Crown.

Smothers, Tommy and Dick

Singer-comedians Tommy and Dick Smothers were born on *Governors Island* off New York City where their father, Major Thomas B. Smothers, was stationed.

In World War II their father died on a Japanese prisoner of war ship en route to Japan.

Snowdon, Lord

In *The Book of Lists* Lord Snowdon was on a list of men who had vasectomies. This fact was interesting because Snowdon's second wife, Lucy Lindsay-Hogg, gave birth to a baby girl after the book was published.

Snyder, Tom

The television newscaster and late-night talk show host has a middle name that he hates—Malachi, a good Old Testament name which means "my messenger" or "messenger of the Lord."

Somers, Suzanne

Born Suzanne Marie Mahoney and later nicknamed "Bony Mahoney" because she was so skinny, the popular television actress ("Three's Company") became Suzanne Somers when at 17 years old and pregnant, she married her boyfriend Bruce Somers, then a law student at the University of San Francisco.

Suzanne was paid $136.72 for her small but memorable role in the movie *American Graffiti* —she was the blonde in the Thunderbird!

Somoza, Anastasio

The former president of Nicaragua, a 1946 graduate of West Point, likes to boast that only three West Pointers ever became presidents: Ulysses S. Grant, Dwight D. Eisenhower, and himself.

Sondheim, Stephen

The composer and lyricist's first job was writing a script for the television series "Topper."

Sontag, Susan

The writer and intellectual was graduated from high school (North Hollywood, California) at age 15 and from college (University of Chicago) at age 18.

Soo, Jack

The late actor, who played Sgt. Yemana in the television series "Barney Miller," was born Goro Suzuki in Oakland, California.

Sothern, Ann

Ann Sothern's real name is Harriette Lake. After studying music at the University of Washington, she joined her mother, who taught singing and diction in Hollywood. She made several movies under her real name until Harriette eventually got a contract with Columbia Pictures where they changed her name to Ann Sothern, and made her dye her hair from red to platinum for a role in *Let's Fall In Love* in 1933.

Sothern, Georgia

At Georgia Southern's request, H. L. Mencken coined the word "ecdysiast" in 1940 as a euphemistic title for a striptease dancer. (The stripper, born Hazel Anderson, re-named herself Georgia Southern because she was a *Southern* girl from *Georgia*.)

Spacek, Sissy

Born Mary Elizabeth Spacek and nicknamed "Sissy" by her brothers, the freckle-faced movie actress is not the first thespian in her family. One of her first cousins is actor Rip Torn.

Sissy was born on Christmas Day, 1946.

Spencer, Herbert

The English philosopher was a railway engineer from 1837 to 1846 in London and Birmingham, England.

Spillane, Mickey

Frank Morrison Spillane's first job was writing comic books to help pay his college expenses.

Spinoza, Benedictus de

The Dutch philosopher and metaphysicist could not live by philosophy alone. To support himself he was an expert lensmaker who ground and polished lens for microscopes, telescopes, and eyeglasses.

Spock, Benjamin

Dr. Spock is a descendant of a Dutch family named *Spaak*. They changed the spelling of their name when they settled in the Hudson River Valley.

As an undergraduate at Yale, Spock wanted to be an architect but changed his mind after working as a counselor at a summer camp for crippled children. At this camp he decided to become a doctor and minister to the needs of children.

Dr. Spock was in the 1924 Olympics. He was an oarsman for the Yale University crew team.

Stack, Robert

People associate Vincent Price with the first 3-D movie but it was actually Robert Stack who appeared in the first one, *Bwana Devil,* which was released in black and white in February of 1953, two months before *House of Wax,* with Vincent Price, was released.

Stalin, Joseph

Stalin's mother wanted him to be a priest and in fact young Stalin did attend the Tiflis Theological Seminary for three years before getting expelled for heresy when he questioned some of their beliefs.

The Russian dictator's real name was Joseph Vissarionovich Djugashvili but he assumed the name Stalin (meaning "steel" in Russian and signifying his toughness and tenacity) in his late twenties when he became deeply involved in revolutionary activity.

Stalin's first son, Yakov, died in a Nazi prison camp during World War II.

Stalin was born with the second and third toes on his left foot joined together and one of his arms was longer than the other.

Stallone, Sylvester

Sly and his ex-wife Sasha met when they were both ushers at the Baronet Theatre in New York City.

Stallone bought the Coldwater Canyon (Los Angeles) mansion of the late Ernie Kovacs.

Sly wasn't the only Stallone in his movie *Rocky*. His father was the timekeeper in the boxing scene, his brother Frank, Jr. was a street singer, and even his pet bull mastiff, Butkus, appeared on screen.

For the first two years of his life, Michael Sylvester Stallone was called "Binky" by his parents.

Stallone and his ex-wife took astrology seriously enough to make sure that their child would be born under the right sign. Sage was conceived so that he would be born under the sign of Taurus, with Libra moon and Leo rising—all of which would presumably make the boy very intelligent.

Stanley, Kim

Actress Kim Stanley's real name is Patricia Reid but because there was another Patricia Reid in her drama class at the University of New Mexico she adopted the stage name Kim Stanley.

Stanton, Frank

The former president of CBS majored in zoology at Ohio Wesleyan University and received his M.A. and Ph.D. degrees in psychology at Ohio State University. His Ph.D. thesis, entitled "A Critique of Present Methods and a New Plan for Studying Radio Listening Behavior," impressed CBS executives enough for them to hire him in 1934.

When Stanton became president of CBS in 1946, *The New Yorker* magazine wrote that he was "one of the few men to achieve success despite the handicap of a Ph.D."

Stanwyck, Barbara

Barbara Stanwyck's real name is Ruby Stevens (and she was born in Brooklyn, New York) but when she saw the listing "Jane *Stanwyck* as *Barbara* Fritchie" in an old *Playbill* adopted two of the names to create her own stage name.

Stapleton, Maureen

The actress used to model for the burlesque paintings of the late artist Reginald Marsh and appeared in the 1935 painting of *Minsky's Chorus*. She also posed for artist Raphael Soyer.

Starr, Ringo

Paul McCartney is not the only left-handed Beatle. Ringo is also a lefty.

Before replacing Peter Best on drums for the Beatles, Ringo (then Richard Starkey) joined a group named Rory Storm and the Hurricanes. They each decided to adopt American "cowboy" names, and the drummer selected the name, Ringo Starr.

Staubach, Roger

In an interview with Phyllis George, the former Dallas quarterback admitted that he probably liked sex more than Joe Namath liked it, but with only one woman—his wife.

Stein, Gertrude

As an undergraduate at Radcliffe, Gertrude Stein was a favorite pupil of psychology and philosophy professor William James. Once, after a late night of opera and partying, she wrote on an exam paper, "Dear Prof. James: I am so sorry, but I do not feel a bit like writing an examination paper on philosophy today." Being rational and sympathetic, James replied, "Dear Miss Stein. I understand perfectly. I often feel like that myself." And then gave her the highest mark in the class!

Gertrude Stein studied medicine for four years at Johns Hopkins University in Baltimore but left without taking a degree. She failed her exams, and rather than go to summer school, she went to Europe to visit her brother Leo, a painter.

She and Alice B. Toklas, her lover, called each other pet names. Gertrude was "Lovey" and Alice was "Pussy."

Steinbeck, John

John Steinbeck's family name was originally Grossteinbeck.

One of Steinbeck's early jobs after leaving Stanford University in 1925 was as a bricklayer in the construction crew building the old Madison Square Garden.

Steinberg, Saul

The artist, famous for his *New Yorker* magazine covers, was hired to play an unusual movie role in 1950. His hand was supposed to appear in the movie *An American in Paris* as the hand of Gene Kelly whenever he was shown painting but Steinberg quit after one day of filming.

Steinbrenner, George

The New York Yankee owner was president of the glee club at Williams College in Williamstown, Massachusetts, and studied voice, in addition to his regular studies, for three years.

Steinem, Gloria

At her high school senior prom in 1952 Ms. Steinem was voted "Best-Looking Girl."

Stengel, Casey

Stengel attended Western Dental College in Kansas City, Missouri and used to say that he quit because they didn't have any dental instruments for left-handed people.

Stephen II

Stephen II has the unfortunate distinction of being Pope for the shortest period of time—two days. He was made Pope on March 24, 752 A.D. but died only two days later.

Stevenson, Parker

After graduating from Princeton University, the actor appeared in TV commercials for products like Right Guard deodorant and Close Up toothpaste.

Stevenson, Robert Louis

When the Scottish novelist entered Edinburgh University, he was supposed to study lighthouse engineering, the family profession. Not wanting to be an engineer, he and his father agreed to compromise—he would prepare for the bar.

Stevenson was thought to have written the first draft of *Dr. Jekyll and Mr. Hyde* under the influence of cocaine and the story itself is thought to be a parable of cocaine's effect on one's mind.

Stewart, Jimmy

After graduating from Princeton where he majored in architecture, young James Stewart had no immediate career plans so he became an accordian player in a Massachusetts tea restaurant.

The stammering actor rarely makes rash decisions. For example, he did not get married until he was 41 years old.

His son Ronald was one of the 50,000 American servicemen killed in the Vietnam war. He died in June of 1969.

Stewart was made a Brigadier General in the Air Force Reserve despite protestations from Sen. Margaret Chase Smith who complained that he had only nine days of training since World War II.

Stewart, Rod

Rock groupies of the world will be interested to know what Rod's priorities are. According to *Us* magazine, Rod admitted, "My passions are soccer, drinking, and women, in that order."

Rod once worked as a grave digger.

Stewart likes soccer so much that he has his father send him videotapes of British games by airfreight every time there is a match.

Stiller and Meara

Before any guest appearances on television shows, the husband and wife comedy team eat Italian food—which is what they ate the time they won an audition with Merv Griffin's talent scout and got their first big break.

St. John, Jill

The actress (and former Henry Kissinger girl-friend) was originally named Jill Oppenheim.

St. Laurent, Yves

The popular couturier, whose real name is Henri Donat Mathieu, was born in Oran, Algeria.

Stockwell, Dean

Actor Dean Stockwell is the son of Harry Stockwell, the man who sang the role of the prince in Walt Disney's *Snow White and the Seven Dwarfs*.

Stoppard, Tom

The playwright's real name is Thomas Straussler. After his father was killed in Singapore by the Japanese in 1942, Tom and his family evacuated to India where his mother met and married Kenneth Stoppard, a British army officer. At that time both Tom and his brother adopted the last name of their new stepfather.

Strauss, Levi

When gold was discovered in California in 1849, Strauss left New York and headed for the gold fields. In the fields a miner friend complained that his trousers were not made durable enough. Strauss made some trousers from his tent canvas and they were significantly stronger than other makes of trousers. Strauss's product became popular so he gave up panning for gold and set up his new business making denim jeans.

Strauss, Robert

At Stamford High School in Stamford, Texas the presidential aide was voted "Wittiest Senior" and "Most Likely to Succeed" by his classmates.

Streep, Meryl

The talented movie actress was Homecoming Queen at her high school in Bernardsville, New Jersey.

Streisand, Barbra

While appearing on Broadway in *Funny Girl*, Barbra contemplated getting a nose job but decided not to after producer David Merrick advised her, "Don't. You'll be like everyone else."

Struthers, Sally

As a child, Sally was chubby and was nicknamed "Packy"—short for pachyderm—by her sister.

Stuyvesant, Peter

The last governor of the Dutch colony of New Amsterdam had a wooden leg to replace the one he lost in an attack on the island of St. Martin in the Caribbean.

Styne, Jule

The English-born composer's name was originally spelled Jules Stein but after frequently being confused with MCA head Jules Stein, the composer changed the spelling of his name.

Styron, William

The Pulitzer Prize-winning author (*Confessions of Nat Turner*) found two books to be very helpful while he was writing *Sophie's Choice*—Leo Rosten's *The Joys of Yiddish* and the *Encyclopaedia Britannica*, the latter for its section on anti-semitism and the former for its definitions of Yiddish words, conveying also their nuances.

Sullavan, Margaret

After signing a contract with Universal Studios in 1933, Margaret underwent the following cosmetic changes: A mole on her face was removed. Her hair was dyed blonde. Her right eyebrow line was raised. The top lipstick line was raised to make the distance between her mouth and nose smaller. The corners of her mouth were heightened with lipstick because her mouth sagged to the right. Other than those changes, she was pretty much the same old Margaret.

Sullivan, Ed

The late television personality had a twin brother, Daniel, who died in his first year.

Sulzberger, Arthur Ochs

Newspaper publisher Arthur Ochs Sulzberger got his nickname "Punch" at birth when his father wrote and illustrated a book to announce his son's arrival. In it he mentioned that his son had "come to play Punch to Judy's endless show"—Judy being his youngest daughter.

Sumac, Yma

Although Yma's name is Amy Camus spelled backwards, that is not her real name nor was she a relative of French writer Albert Camus. Her real name was Emparatriz Chavarri and she took her professional name from her Peruvian Indian mother, Imma Sumack Emilia Atahualpa.

Sundance, Kid, The

Born Harry Longbaugh, the sidekick of Butch Cassidy acquired his nickname after he robbed a bank in Sundance, Nevada.

Susann, Jacqueline

Jacqueline Susann had a son named Guy who was conspicuously never talked about. Supposedly he is "asthmatic" and is living in Arizona.

Susskind, David

The name Talent Associates, Ltd., Susskind's talent production agency, which he co-founded with Alfred Levy, was inspired in part by a pack of cigarettes—which was made by a British company using the "Ltd." after its name. Susskind and Levy thought it gave the agency name a nice ring.

Suzuki, Pat

Actress Pat Suzuki's real given name is Chiyoko which means "a thousand times good" in Japanese, but she was nicknamed Chiby ("Squirt") by her family. She was given the name Pat by a neighborhood grocer who had trouble saying her real name.

Swados, Elizabeth

The eclectic composer and writer has been beset with personal tragedies. Her grandmother, a violinist, had a lobotomy and her mother committed suicide in 1954.

Swanson, Gloria

The movie actress's real name is Josephine May Swenson.

Swift, Jonathan

The next time it rains a lot, think of Jonathan Swift. He created the phrase to "rain cats and dogs" in his dialogue "Polite Conversations."

Swit, Loretta

Upon arriving in Hollywood, Loretta was told by an agent to change her name because it "sounded like a bad nose job looks." She kept her real name and does not seem to have suffered for it.

T

Taft, William Howard

Taft once said, "The nearer I get to the inauguration of my successor, the greater the relief I feel."

Taft was the first president to throw out the baseball on the first day of the season—on April 14, 1910. It was a game between Washington and Philadelphia. The attendance was 12,226—then a record.

Weighing as much as 350 pounds, Taft needed a special-sized bathtub installed in the White House so that he could bathe in comfort.

In 1921 Taft was appointed chief justice of the Supreme Court, the only president to become one. He was in fact an excellent Chief Justice, prompting Justice Louis Brandeis to say, "It's very difficult for me to understand how a man who is so good as chief justice could have been so bad as President."

Dwight D. Eisenhower is the president who is most identified with the game of golf but Taft was the first president to ever play the game.

Because Taft was so tone deaf, he could barely recognize "The Star-Spangled Banner" and in fact had to be nudged by his secretary to stand up whenever the anthem was played at public functions.

Talmadge, Norma

Norma Talmadge, the silent screen actress, was the first person to have her footprints implanted at Grauman's Chinese Theatre. Sid Grauman was showing her the progress of the theater construction and the actress accidently stepped into the freshly poured cement. Sid knew a good thing when he saw it and started a new Hollywood tradition.

Tati, Jacques

The French movie comedian's real name is Jacques Tatischeff. He is the grandson of Count Dmitri Tatischeff, once an attaché at the Russian embassy in France, who married a French woman. For professional reasons, Jacques shortened his name to Tati.

Tati was trained and apprenticed as a picture framer. His maternal grandfather owned a picture framing shop in Paris and was said to have framed paintings for Toulouse-Lautrec.

Taylor, Elizabeth

Most people think that "Elizabeth Taylor" is a stage name but Liz was in fact born Elizabeth Rosamond Taylor in London, England, of American parents. (Her mother was Sara Warmbraten, an actress, who used the stage name Sara Southern.)

Once, in defending her honor and reputation, Liz said, "I've only slept with the men I've been married to. How many women can make that claim?"

Liz was affectionately called "Lizzie Schwartz-kopf" by Mike Todd, her third husband, and "Fatty" by Richard Burton, her fifth husband.

She was supposed to accompany Mike Todd on the night of the plane crash that killed Todd in March, 1958. Liz stayed home because she had a bad virus infection.

The public calls her Liz Taylor, but she hates the name Liz.

Miss Taylor met her current husband, John Warner, on a blind date. It was a dinner party in Washington, D.C. at the British Embassy in honor of Queen Elizabeth and Gerald Ford.

Taylor's phone bill has been as high as $10,000 a month.

Taylor, Robert

At Doane College in Nebraska, Taylor played the cello in a string quartet to earn extra spending money. After transferring to Pomona College in Claremont, California, where his music teacher took a new job, Taylor started acting in college plays and was discovered by MGM casting director Ben Piazza.

Taylor's real name was Spangler Arlington Brugh (his mother read a novel in which the hero was named Arlington and decided to give her son the name!) and he was called "Arly" by his family and friends. He was given the name Taylor by Ida Hoverman, Louis B. Mayer's secretary, and the name Robert by Mayer himself. (Taylor wanted to use the last name Stanhope which was his mother's maiden name and the name of a character he was playing when he was discovered, but Mayer wanted a more all-American sounding name.)

Taylor, Zachary

Taylor, the 12th president of the United States, was guilty of not exercising one of his basic rights. He never voted in any election.

Taylor was a second cousin of James Madison.

Taylor was late in acknowledging his nomination for the presidency because the letter was delivered postage due and he refused to pay for it.

Tchaikovsky, Peter Ilyich

Tchaikovsky, strongly attached to his mother and surrounded by many female relatives, was a homosexual.

Tchaikovsky attended law school and clerked for two years before he decided to study harmony and composition at St. Petersburg Conservatory.

Suffering from acute nervous disorders and hallucinations, the composer would sometimes have a morbid fear that his head would roll off his shoulders while conducting a symphony.

Temple, Shirley

The average doctor (the highest paid profession in the U.S.) probably makes his first million by age 45 but Shirley made her first million dollars by age 10.

Terry-Thomas

The British actor, born Thomas Terry Hoar-Stevens, once used the stage name "Mot Snevets" which spelled backwards is the name Tom Stevens. He also tried ·the name Thomas Terry but he was often confused with the theatrical Terry family, so he reversed his given names and became known as Terry Thomas. Although he refuses to close the gap in his teeth he did close the gap in his name by adding the hyphen for "box office appeal" around 1947.

Thackeray, William Makepeace

William Makepeace Thackeray had a huge head and at age six could fit into an adult male's hat. When he was taken to a doctor for examination the doctor remarked, "He *has* a large head but there's a great deal in it."

Thalberg, Irving

Although Irving Thalberg was an influential Hollywood producer for about 15 years, his name appeared on the movie screen only once —in the credits of *The Good Earth* (1937) which was released after his death. The movie was dedicated to him and the inscription was as follows: "To the memory of Irving Grant Thalberg, we dedicate this picture, his last great achievement."

Thatcher, Margaret

The British prime minister is the mother of 26-year old twins. Daughter Carol is a reporter in Australia and son Mark is a businessman in London.

Prime Minister Thatcher majored in chemistry at Oxford and worked as a research chemist from 1947 to 1951.

Thumb, Tom

Charles Sherwood Stratton, better known as Tom Thumb, weighed an above-average nine pounds and two ounces at birth. At age four, however, he was only twenty-five inches tall and was signed up by showman Phineas T. Barnum. Barnum immediately gave Stratton the name of Tom Thumb after the tiny knight at King Arthur's court. He advertised Tom Thumb as being 11 years old and from England, knowing that it would increase his drawing power. Barnum soon added the title "General" because of Thumb's preference for military uniforms. (Note: Tom Thumb's wife Lavinia Warren was born Mercy Lavinia Bump, but Barnum changed her name because he believed that no one would pay to see a person named Bump!)

When Thumb and Lavinia Warren were married on February 10, 1863, President and Mrs. Lincoln gave them a set of Chinese fire screens as a wedding present and were among the 2,000 guests at the wedding.

Thurber, James

Thurber lost the sight of his left eye when he was six years old, after one of his brothers accidentally shot him with an arrow.

Thurmond, Strom

Thurmond won his 1954 senatorial bid as a write-in candidate, getting 139,106 votes vs. the 80,956 received by Edgar Brown, the regular Democratic candidate on the ballot.

The South Carolina senator is a second cousin of Herman Talmadge, the Democratic senator from Georgia.

In 1957 the senator, then a Democrat, filibustered against the Civil Rights Bill for 24 hours and 19 minutes, interrupted only once for the swearing in of a new senator.

Thomas, Danny

Just before his opening at the 5100 Club in Chicago, Amos Jacobs changed his name to Danny Thomas, which he devised by using the first names of his two brothers, Danny and Thomas.

Thomas, Dylan

At age 12, Dylan Thomas sold his first poem— which he had plagiarized from a local newspaper.

Thomas, Lowell

The author and radio-television commentator during a wartime broadcast referred to British cabinet minister Sir Stafford Cripps as "Sir Stifford Crapps," a classic spoonerism.

Thomas, Michael Tilson

The young orchestra conductor is a nephew of the late actor Paul Muni, for whom his father worked as a writer.

Thomas, Norman

The noted American Socialist Party leader was a graduate of Princeton University where he was valedictorian of the Class of 1905.

Norman Thomas, son of a Presbyterian minister, was a graduate of Union Theological Seminary and was ordained as a Presbyterian minister. His interest in socialism developed from his experiences as a minister for the East Harlem Church in a poor section of New York City. There he realized that the two major political parties were not recognizing the needs of the poor.

Tierney, Gene

The former movie actress almost committed suicide in 1958 by jumping off the 14th floor ledge at her mother's New York City apartment. According to Miss Tierney, vanity was the only thing that stopped her—she didn't want to die looking "like a scrambled egg."

Titian

The Venetian painter was 99 years old when he died.

Tito

The late Yugoslavian leader was born Josip Broz but changed his name to Tito in 1934 for political reasons after spending five years in prison for illegal communist activities. He took the name Tito because it was a popular name in his native district—a well-known Zaforje writer in the late eighteenth century was named Tito Brezovacki and the father of a great Croatian writer (Ksaver Sandor Gjalski) was also named Tito.

Tomlin, Lily

Lily was a home economics major at Cass Technical High School in Detroit, Class of '57.

At a 1978 auction of Judy Garland's possessions Miss Tomlin, through an agent, bought the loaded dice from the movie *Casablanca*, given to Garland by her neighbor Humphrey Bogart. The auction price of the dice was $1,200.

Miss Tomlin recently bought W. C. Fields's Hollywood home—for a bargain $500,000.

Tone, Franchot

The actor's full name was Stanislas Pascal Franchot Tone.

Franchot lived up to his screen image. He was rich (his father was president of the Carborundum Company) and smart (he graduated Phi Beta Kappa from Cornell University in 1927).

Torme, Mel

The "Velvet Fog" has earned over a million dollars for his Christmas Song ("Chestnuts roasting on an open fire . . .") which he wrote with Bob Wells.

Torn, Rip

The actor's real name is Elmore Torn, Jr. but he used the name Rip because he thought Elmore was too "prudish . . . and undramatic." However, when he got his first big break to appear on the *U.S. Steel Hour*, Rip was asked by the producers to use the name Eric Torn which was felt to be a more believable name. For the appearance he did use the name Eric but when he convinced everybody that he was a serious and good actor, he again used the name Rip.

Toscanini, Arturo

Addressing members of his orchestra, the Italian symphony conductor announced, "After I die, I shall return to earth as a gatekeeper of a bordello and I won't let any of you—not a one of you —enter!"

Toulouse-Lautrec, Henri de

The French artist and lithographer, an alcoholic, was sent to a sanitarium in 1899 after having a nervous breakdown. It was in this asylum that he painted his famous series *The Circus*.

Although Lautrec was only four feet tall, he was not a dwarf. The growth of his legs was stunted at age 14 when he broke them, but the rest of his body continued to grow normally.

Tracy, Dick

Chester Gould's cartoon strip was originally called "Plainclothes Tracy" but Captain Joseph Medill Patterson of the *Chicago Tribune* syndicate thought the name was too long. He suggested the name Dick—which was the slang word for detective.

Gould once admitted ". . . because Sherlock Holmes is the greatest detective of them all, I decided to make Tracy look like Holmes: straight aquiline nose, square chin, generally sharp features."

Tracy, Spencer

Actor Spencer Tracy was a devout Catholic (his middle name was Bonaventure!) and attended mass every Sunday. It was because of his strong religious beliefs that he never obtained a divorce from his wife, Louise Treadwell, to marry actress Katharine Hepburn, his longtime and close friend.

Spence was a childhood friend of actor Pat O'Brien and, in fact, they both joined the Navy together in 1917.

Spencer Tracy was the only actor to win an Academy Award for Best Actor two years in a row: in 1937 for his role as a Portuguese fisherman in *Captains Courageous* and in 1938 for his role as Father Flanigan in *Boys Town*.

Katharine Hepburn used to call Tracy her "dipsomaniac"—acknowledging his extreme fondness for alcohol.

Spencer's Oscar for *Captains Courageous* was erroneously engraved "Dick Tracy."

Tracy was nominated for an Academy Award nine times, more than any other actor.

One of Tracy's first stage acting roles was as a *robot* in the Theatre Guild's production of *R.U.R.*

Traver, Robert

The author of *Anatomy of a Murder* was a retired judge whose real name was John Voelker.

Travolta, John

Travolta made his film debut in the horror movie *The Devil's Rain* (1975). He wore a mask and uttered the lines, "Blasphemer! Get him, he is a blasphemer!"

Trevino, Lee

On his right forearm Lee Trevino has a tattoo of the name "Ann," which refers to a girl he dated when he was in the Marines. The bad news is that the girl eventually sent him a "Dear John" letter. The good news is that his present wife's middle name is Ann and his daughter's name is Lesley Ann.

One of Trevino's favorite golf clubs was made from an adhesive-taped Dr Pepper bottle. He used it to hustle golfers at Hardy's Pitch-n-Putt par-3 course in Dallas and could hit a golf ball *100 yards* with it.

Trippe, Jean

The founder of Pan American Airways was so quiet as a student at the Hill School in Pottsdown, Pennsylvania that his classmates called him "The Mummy."

Trollope, Anthony

In addition to being a novelist, Anthony Trollope was also a post office inspector and was credited with inventing the mailbox on a pillar that is placed at streetcorners.

Trudeau, Gary

Trudeau's popular cartoon strip "Doonesbury" is named after one of its original characters, Mike Doonesbury, whose last name was formed by combining "Doon," Yale slang for a good-natured fool, with "sbury," the second part of Pillsbury, the name of one of Trudeau's college roommates.

Trudeau, Margaret

The unconventional wife of the Canadian prime minister does not let politics interfere with her sexual preferences. In her book *Beyond Reason*, she commented, "Castro is the sexiest man I've ever met."

Truman, Harry S

Truman's middle initial did not stand for any name and did not have a period after it because his parents did not want to show any favoritism toward his paternal grandfather (Shippe Truman) or his maternal grandfather (Solomon Young). But it is interesting to note that his daughter's biography of him was entitled *Harry S. Truman* (with the period!) and in fact Truman sometimes inadvertently put the period after the "S."

Of all the U. S. Presidents, Truman is believed to have been the worst speller.

In a 1956 *Look* magazine article, Truman was quoted as saying, "I never gave them hell, I just tell the truth and they think it's hell."

Truman is the only twentieth-century president who never went to college.

Truman was a 33-degree Mason of the Supreme Council of the Scottish Rite.

Truscott, Lucian IV

The author (*Dress Gray*) graduated 658th in a class of 800 at West Point.

Tschombe, Moise

The late African leader's first name means "beloved of Moses," a name introduced to the Congolese by Arabic slave traders in the nineteenth century.

Tucker, Sophie

Although Sophie's family name was Kalish, her father took the name of a dead Italian friend, Charles Abuza, in order to emigrate to the

United States. The immigration officials didn't notice that Sophie's father spoke only Russian and Yiddish—a remarkable talent for an "Italian"—so Sophie became Sophie Abuza. Sixteen years later she eloped with Louis Tuck, became Sophie Tuck, and then changed it to Tucker in 1906 when she worked on *Tin Pan Alley*.

Turcotte, Ron

The Triple Crown-winning jockey, now paralyzed from a racing accident in 1977, won a total of $28,746,073 in purses in 16 years as a jockey.

Turgenev, Ivan

When the Russian writer (*Fathers and Sons*) died in 1883, an autopsy revealed that his brain weighed about 4½ pounds—one of the heaviest brains on record.

Turner, Lana

Lana Turner's real name was Julia Jean Mildred Frances Turner (she was called Judy) but was given the name Lana by Mervyn Le Roy, the movie director, when she arrived in Hollywood.

Lana's first screen appearance was not her famous "rear-shot" walk-away in *They Won't Forget* (1937) but in a crowd scene in the 1937 version of *A Star is Born*.

Turpin, Ben

Turpin had the honor of receiving the first custard pie in the face—thrown by Mabel Normand in a Mack Sennett comedy.

Tutankhamen, King

The 14th-century B.C. King of Egypt, whose tomb was discovered in 1922 was nine years of age when he was married and was only 18 years old when he died.

Twain, Mark

Although Mark Twain was from Hannibal, Missouri, he wrote his three most famous books (*The Adventures of Tom Sawyer, Life on the Mississippi,* and *Huckleberry Finn*) in Hartford, Connecticut, where he lived for 17 years.

Twain was also an inventor and a shrewd businessman. He had a patent on a steam engine, invented an automatic type-setting machine, and as a publisher, induced Ulysses S. Grant to write his memoirs—a venture which made Grant over $500,000 and made Twain almost as much.

Twain predicted that just as he was born in the year of Halley's Comet (1835) so would he go out with it. He was right; he died in 1910, a year in which Halley's Comet also appeared.

Twain's popular book *Tom Sawyer* was the first manuscript submitted in typed form by an American author.

Tweed, William Marcy "Boss"

The corrupt New York politician was named after a U.S. senator from New York, William Learned Marcy, who first uttered the phrase "To the victor belong the spoils of the enemy" in a senate speech defending then-senator Martin Van Buren.

Tweed was born in a house on Cherry Street, New York City, a fact significant only because the house was the nation's first White House and residence of George Washington.

Twiggy

The British model and aspiring actress, born Leslie Hornby, was originally called "Sticks" during her school days but was given the nickname "Twiggy" by Justin de Villeneuve (real name is Nigel Davies), her boyfriend and promoter.

Tyler, John

Of all the U.S. presidents Tyler had the most children—15. By his first wife, Letitia Christian he fathered 3 sons and 5 daughters and by his second wife Julia Gardiner, he had 5 sons and 2 daughters.

After William H. Harrison died, Tyler became the 10th president of the United States and the first vice-president to become president.

Tyler married Letitia Christian on March 29, 1813, on his 23rd birthday.

When Tyler married his second wife, Julia Gardiner in New York City on June 25, 1849, he was the first president to be married during his term of office.

Tynan, Kenneth

Writer and critic Kenneth Tynan's real name is Kenneth Peacock. He adopted the family name of his mother, Letitia Rose Tynan, when he found out that he was the illegitimate child of Sir Peter Peacock.

Tyson, Cicely

The Emmy-winning actress (*The Autobiography of Miss Jane Pittman*) was raised so strictly by her devoutly religious mother that she was never allowed to go to the movies because her mother associated movies with sin.

U

Udall, Morris

The Arizona politican lost the sight in his right eye in an accident when he was six years old.

Uggams, Leslie

Actress and singer Leslie Uggams is of Negro, Scotch, Irish, Cherokee, and Seminole Indian heritage and her last name is derived from an Indian word meaning "sweet one."

The letters on her license plates are SMAGGU —which is Uggams spelled backwards.

Ullman, Liv

Actress Liv Ullman was born in Tokyo, Japan where her Norwegian father, an aircraft engineer, was working at the time.

Updike, John

As a youth, writer John Updike was nicknamed "Ostrich" by a local boy because he thought Updike looked like Walt Disney's Ollie Ostrich.

The writer was a classmate of Sen. Edward M. Kennedy and lawyer F. Lee Bailey at Harvard College, Class of 1954.

Updike always wanted to get published in *The New Yorker*, but not as a writer. His ambition was to become a cartoonist (at Harvard College he contributed many cartoons to *The Lampoon*) and he also wanted to be an animator for Walt Disney.

Uris, Leon

The name Uris is from the Hebrew word "Yerushalmi," meaning "Man of Jerusalem."

At John Bartram High School in Philadelphia, Uris failed English three times but later pointed out that "English and writing have little to do with each other."

The author (*Battle Cry, Exodus, Trinity*) began writing at age seven when he wrote an operetta about the death of his dog.

Ustinov, Peter

When actor Peter Ustinov tested for the part of Nero in the production of the movie *Quo Vadis* he was only 28 years old and was considered too young for the part. He did a little research and found out that Nero died at age 31 so he cabled the studio to say that if they didn't give him the role soon that he would be too old for the part. The studio's reply read: HISTORICAL RESEARCH HAS PROVED YOU CORRECT STOP THE PART IS YOURS.

Utrillo, Maurice

Utrillo's mother Marie-Clementine Valadon, was a model who posed for such great painters as Renoir, Degas, and Toulouse-Lautrec, and became a painter herself, using the name Suzanne Valadon.

Utrillo's father was named Boissy but when Maurice started painting he signed the canvases "Maurice Valadon," then used "Maurice Utrillo-Valadon" (at age eight he was adopted by Spanish art critic Miguel Utrillo) and finally settled on the name "Maurice Utrillo, V."

The French painter was born on Christmas Day in 1883.

V

Vadim, Roger

The French film director's full name is Roger Vadim Plemiannikov.

Vallee, Rudy

Rudy Vallee joined the U.S. Navy at age 15 but served only a few weeks before he was discharged for being under-age.

The singer's full name is Hubert Prior Vallée but as an aspiring young saxophonist he adopted the name Rudy in the 1920s after Rudy Wiedoeft, a popular saxophone player whom he greatly admired.

Vallee was a Spanish major at Yale.

The former crooner was one of the guests on "The Tonight Show" on October 1, 1962, when Johnny Carson took over as host of the show.

Van, Bobby

In his early movies song-and-dance man Bobby Van (born Robert Stein) can be seen as he looked before he had some plastic surgery done on his nose.

Van Buren, Abigail

When Pauline Friedman's twin sister (see Landers, Ann) was hired by the *Chicago Sun-Times* to write the Ann Landers column, Pauline decided that she would like to do the same kind of work. She adopted the name Abigail Van Buren —Abigail being a nice Old Testament name good enough for the wives of two U.S. presidents (Adams and Fillmore) and Van Buren having the solid ring of a Dutch settler or U.S. president. She then sold her "Dear Abby" column to the *San Francisco Chronicle*, was soon nationally syndicated, and is now as well-known and well-read as her sister "Ann Landers."

Van Buren, Martin

Van Buren was the first president born an American citizen and not a British subject.

In his autobiography Van Buren never mentioned his wife Hannah.

Van Cleef, Lee

The villainous-looking actor (*The Good, the Bad and the Ugly*) lost his left kneecap in an auto accident in the late 1950s.

Vanderbilt, Cornelius

Born and raised in Staten Island, New York, Vanderbilt quit school at age 11. Five years later he bought a sailboat and ferried people between Staten Island and New York City. It was the start of a career in shipping and railroads which earned him millions of dollars.

Van Druten, John

The playwright (*I Am a Camera*) earned a law degree at London University.

Van Dyke, Dick

After being discharged from the Air Force in 1946 Van Dyke and a friend, Wayne Williams, started an ad agency in Danville, Illinois. Bankrupt a year later, however, Van Dyke teamed up with another friend, Philip Ericson, to do a pantomime comedy act called "The Merry Mutes," later known as "Eric and Van."

Dick Van Dyke is an excellent cartoonist and caricaturist and used to draw caricatures of Morey Amsterdam, Mary Tyler Moore and the rest of the cast during "The Dick Van Dyke Show" script-reading sessions.

The actor-comedian is a reformed alcoholic.

van Gogh, Vincent

Why did van Gogh cut off his ear and what did he do with it? It seems that a prostitute, whom he and Gauguin visited one pre-Christmas evening, teased van Gogh about his large ears so in an irrational fit he cut off an ear and sent it to the prostitute as a Christmas present.

Van Heusen, Jimmy

The composer's real name is Edward Chester Babcock. As a teenager, he didn't want his father to know that he had a job as a disc jockey so he used the name Van Heusen, which his boyhood friend, Ralph Harris, suggested, after seeing an outdoor poster for Van Heusen collars. The first name, James, was added because it went well with Van Heusen. (Note: Frank Sinatra, for whom Van Heusen has written many songs, calls him Chester.)

In 1928 Van Heusen was expelled from Central High School in Syracuse, New York for playing the song "My Canary Has Circles Under Its Eyes" before the school assembly.

The composer was a test pilot for Lockheed Corporation during World War II.

Van Heusen's grandmother claimed that he was a direct descendant of Stephen Foster.

Velasquez, Diego Rodriguez de Silva

The great Spanish painter was left-handed. Look at his painting *Maids of Honor* ("Las Meninas") and you will see a self-portrait of Velasquez in the painting. Assuming he painted himself by looking in a mirror, the brush in his right hand is in fact his left hand.

Vera-Ellen

The actress and dancer's full name is Vera-Ellen Westmeyr Rohe. She received the name Vera-Ellen after her mother saw the hyphenated name on a marquee in a dream she had a few nights before the future dancer was born.

Verdon, Gwen

Gwen Verdon and Carol Haney did the audio track shoe tapping for Gene Kelly's dance routines in the movie *Singing in the Rain*.

Verne, Jules

As his novels and stories showed, Jules Verne had an incredible imagination and an extraordinary ability to look into the future. In 1865 he wrote a story in which the states of Florida and Texas were competing to be the launching site of rocketships bound for the moon. This story has the hero and rocketship blasting off in Florida. Verne wrote that in 1865!

Victoria, Queen

Victoria was brought up in a very protective environment. Until she became queen, she always slept in her mother's bedroom and she was not allowed to speak to any grown-up unless her mother, the Duchess of Kent, or governess, Louise Lehzen, was present.

The British queen's menstrual cramps were so painful that her doctors prescribed cannabis (hashish) to ease the pain.

She was not called Victoria by her family but was called Drina, short for Alexandrina, her real first name. Victoria was her middle name.

Vidal, Gore

When writer Gore Vidal ran for Congress in 1960, he was not the best man but he did very well. Although he lost to a Republican in a predominantly Republican district in upstate New York, he received more votes than any other Democrat in 50 years and even garnered more votes than presidential candidate John F. Kennedy received in the district.

Vidal was born at the United States Military Academy at West Point, New York, where his father was an instructor in aeronautics. Gore benefited by his father's instruction and could pilot a plane when he was only ten years old.

Vidal is the godfather of Kenneth Tynan's son Matthew. When Vidal was given the news he wired back to Tynan, "Always a Godfather, never a God."

Villa, Pancho

After killing a man for molesting his younger sister, 16-year-old Doroteo Arango ran away from home and lived as a cattle rustler and bandit, using the name Francisco "Pancho" ("Frankie" in Spanish) Villa.

Villa and his banditos looked so photogenic that a Hollywood movie company went down to Mexico and hired them for $25,000 to appear in a movie. When the footage was screened back in California, however, it was considered too unconvincing and had to be reshot on the studio lot.

The Mexican revolutionary was married 9 times.

Villechaize, Hervé

Height is a matter of relativity. Hervé is 14 inches taller than Kenny Baker, the man who played R2D2 in the movie *Star Wars*.

Vinton, Bobby

Singer Bobby Vinton's full name is Stanley Robert Vinton, Jr., but the family name was originally Vintula.

Vinton became a chaplain's assistant in the U.S. Army because of his ability to play the church organ.

Voight, Jon

Voight was paid only $17,000 for his excellent performance in the movie *Midnight Cowboy*.

He made his Broadway debut in the play *The Sound of Music* in which he introduced the song "I am Sixteen."

Von Furstenberg, Diane

The dress designer's maiden name is Diane Simone Michelle Halfin.

Miss Von Furstenberg's mother spent 14 months in a German concentration camp and was lucky enough to survive the experience.

Diane's perfume, Tatiana, was named after her nine-year old daughter Tatiana.

Vonnegut, Kurt Jr.

The author studied biochemistry at Cornell for two years, studied anthropology at the University of Chicago for another two years, and was a public relations man for the General Electric Company in Schenectady, New York.

W

Wade, Adam

Before Adam Wade became a singer, actor, and quiz show host, he studied biochemistry at the University of Pennsylvania, after graduating from Virginia State College, and once worked as a research assistant to Dr. Jonas Salk, the polio-vaccine pioneer.

Wagner, Richard

In an attempt to alleviate the pain of his severe headaches, the German composer used to cut his hair.

Wagner was Franz Liszt's son-in-law.

Walcott, Jersey Joe

Walcott's real name was Arnold Raymond Cream but he changed his name in 1936 to honor a famous welterweight, Joe Walcott, whom his father admired in the early 1900s. When Jersey Joe "creamed" Ezzard Charles on July 18, 1951, he became the oldest man to win the heavyweight title—he was 37 years, 5 months and 18 days old.

Walker, James J.

The New York mayor, sometimes called the "Night Mayor" because of his fondness for night life, wrote the song, "Will You Love Me in December as You Do in May?"

Walker, Nancy

Christened Anna Myrtle Swoyer, the diminutive actress was the granddaughter of Roxy Swoyer, an acrobat and clown with the Ringling Brothers Circus, and the daughter of Stuart Swoyer who, as Dewey Barto was a member of the Three Bartos vaudeville team. She became Nancy Walker during a casting rehearsal when she was mistakenly introduced as Miss Walker.

Wall, Art

Between the years 1936 and 1966, the champion golfer hit 35 holes in one.

Wallace, De Witt

Wounded at Verdun in World War I, Wallace was sent to an army hospital to recuperate. At the hospital, the young sergeant, after reading many magazines, noticed that most articles were too long and conceived a new kind of magazine which would contain tight, well-edited articles from other magazines. The result of his idea was *Reader's Digest* magazine.

Wallace, Irving

The prolific writer (120,000,000 copies—*The Chapman Report, The Prize, The Fan Club,* et al.) used to ghost-write stories for celebrities like W. C. Fields, Boris Karloff, and Bob Hope for *Liberty* magazine. (During a W. C. Fields's interview the heavy drinking comedian passed out!)

Wallace, Lew

Lew Wallace is best remembered for writing *Ben Hur,* but he was also a major general in the Union army during the Civil War, a judge at the trial of the Lincoln conspirators, was a governor of New Mexico Territory (1878–1881) and a minister to Turkey (1881–1885), and also presided at the Andersonville trial of Henry Wirz.

Wallace, Mike

The "60 Minutes" reporter, whose family name was originally Wallik was born Myron Leon Wallace in Brookline, Massachusetts.

Wallace once did commercials for "Super Circus," the popular children's television show, and even earlier in his career was an announcer on the "Sky King" radio program.

Wallace made his Broadway debut in October, 1954, playing a young art dealer in the comedy *Reclining Figure.* About his performance, Walter Kerr wrote that "Wallace makes the transition from radio to Broadway with ingratiating ease."

Walsh, Raoul

Walsh was the director of the first full-length movie to be shot outdoors—*In Old Arizona*, which was shot at national parks in Utah and California, but not in Arizona.

Walters, Barbara

In an article Barbara wrote for *Family Weekly* in 1971, she listed Richard Nixon as one of ten men she found most appealing and even described him as being "rather sexy."

Barbara Walter's family name was originally Volters but her grandfather, a London tailor, Anglicized the name to Walters.

Barbara's first television appearance was as a model in a fashion show on "The Today Show." At the time, she was a writer but when a model (who wore size eight clothes) was not able to show up, Barbara (also size eight) volunteered and got the job.

Wanger, Walter

Born Walter Feuchtwanger, the movie producer (*Stagecoach*, 1939; *Invasion of the Body Snatchers*, 1955), once spent four months in jail for a fatal assault on an agent who was allegedly threatening his marriage.

Warhol, Andy

Andy's real name is Andrew Warhola.

Andy's distinguished-looking silver hair is really a toupee, according to an ex-Factory cohort of his.

Warhol's latest art innovation is to paint with copper-based paints and have his dog, Amos, urinate on the canvas, creating some unusual effects with the color green.

Warren, Earl

The late chief justice's family name was originally Varran but was Americanized when his father came to the United States from Stavanger, Norway.

Warwick, Dionne

Singer Dionne Warwick's last name was originally *Warrick* but it was misspelled in an early recording contract and she decided to keep the new spelling.

Washington, George

It is doubtful that George Washington ever chopped down a cherry tree. The only account of it was in Mason Locke Weems's *Life of George Washington* and the story did not appear in the first edition of the book. He claimed that a former Washington household employee told him the story but did not reveal her name. (Weems was known to add apocryphal anecdotes to his books, as with his *Life of William Penn* in which he created a treaty between the settlers and the Indians, but such a treaty never existed.)

George and Martha Washington never had any children but Martha had four children by a previous marriage to Daniel Parke Curtis.

Presidents have had libraries, dams, streets, and schools named after them but Washington is the only president after whom a state was named.

Winston Churchill and George Washington were eighth cousins, six times removed, according to *Burke's Presidential Families*.

During his two terms in office he bowed before people rather than shake their hands. Evidently because of a lack of precedents he adopted the royal court custom.

Washington's false teeth were made of everything but wood. In fact his favorite set was made from *hippo* teeth set in gold!

George was the only president who never lived in Washington, D.C.

Because Washington was always shown wearing a white wig, it hid the fact that his hair was sandy-brown and reddish.

Waters, Ethel

At age 17, Miss Waters as billed as "Sweet Mama Stringbean" at the Lincoln Theatre in Baltimore.

Watson, John

After resigning as professor of psychology at Johns Hopkins University because of a divorce scandal, the noted behavioral psychologist became a vice-president of the J. Walter Thompson advertising agency.

Waxman, Franz

The two-time Academy Award-winning screen composer (*Sunset Boulevard, A Place in the Sun*) originally spelled his last name Wachsmann but simplified it to Waxman when he went to Hollywood in the mid 1930s.

Wayne, David

Actor David Wayne (born Wayne McKeekan) was erroneously reported killed in action during World War II when Tobruk fell to the Germans.

Wayne, John

The late actor revealed his acting technique while on the set of *The Shootist:* "The only method I learned to use was to take a pause in the middle of a sentence. That made the audience keep their eyes on me, wondering what the son of a bitch is going to say next."

For his epitaph Wayne selected the Spanish phrase *Feo, fuerte, y formal,* which in Wayne's words mean "He was ugly, he was strong, and he had dignity."

In his last movie, *The Shootist*, Wayne played a gunslinger who was dying of cancer.

It is no wonder that John Wayne developed cancer—he used to smoke five packs of cigarettes (Camels) a day or six packs when he was up late drinking.

Wayne was an excellent poker player and once won the Hollywood dog *Lassie* from its owner and trainer, Rudd Weathersway. (He did not keep the dog, of course.)

Weaver, Dennis

Weaver may not seem that old but he and his wife Geraldine have been married for 39 years. (He's 56 years old.)

Weaver, Robert

Robert Weaver's maternal grandfather, Dr. Robert Tanner, a Harvard graduate, was the first Negro in the United States to be given a doctoral degree in dentistry.

Webster, Daniel

The next time you stand while the National Anthem is being played, think of Daniel Webster—he was the person who started the practice.

The persuasive lawyer and U.S. senator rehearsed his speeches by pretending a tree was his audience.

At Dartmouth College, Webster's nickname was "Black Dan" because of his swarthy complexion.

Webster, Noah

After graduating from Yale in 1778, Webster studied law and was admitted to the bar in 1781 but later made his mark as a lexicographer whose name is now synonymous with "dictionary."

Weicker, Lowell Jr.

The Republican senator from Connecticut was born in Paris, France. At the time his father was manager of foreign operations for E. R. Squibb & Sons (of which he later became president).

At six feet six inches tall, Weicker is the tallest U.S. senator.

Welch, Raquel

The actress not only had a nose job but Hollywood make-up artist George Masters once said that the five feet six inches tall actress was all plastic from the nose down.

Welch, Robert H. W. Jr.

Robert Welch, the founder of the John Birch Society, has an interesting educational background: he graduated from high school at age 12 and college at age 17; he attended Annapolis for two years but dropped out to become a reporter; and then enrolled at Harvard Law School, before leaving to start his own business.

The business that Welch started after leaving Harvard was the Oxford Candy Company—which introduced Sugar Daddy, the hard caramel lollipop, to the world.

Weld, Tuesday

The actress' full name is Susan Ker Weld and she was not born on a Tuesday but on a *Friday*. The name Tuesday evolved from her childhood nickname "Too-Too," which was babytalk for "Susan."

Miss Weld legally changed her name to Tuesday on October 19, 1959, which was a *Monday*.

Welk, Lawrence

Although Welk was born in the United States he has a good reason for speaking English with such a strong accent. He was raised by his Alsatian immigrant parents in an Alsatian immigrant town (Strasburg, North Dakota) and he didn't speak English until he was 21 years old.

The colorful bandleader's license plates read A1ANDA2, an obvious reference to the cue he gives his band when he starts conducting music.

Welles, Orson

Although George Orson Welles briefly attended the Chicago Art Institute, he never attended a college or university.

The accomplished director and actor is remotely related to the late Adlai Stevenson and Sumner Welles.

Wellington, First Duke of

The British statesman and military leader had a very small vestigial tail and had to have a special hole made in his saddle because of it.

Wells, H. G.

The British writer once used the pen name H. G. Wheels for a magazine article on bicycling in the country.

His first marriage was to his cousin Isabel Mary Wells.

Werner, Oskar

As Oskar Joseph Beschliessmayer, Werner was born next door to the house in which Johann Strauss once lived.

Werner was drafted into the German Wehrmacht in 1941 and although he avoided combat duty, he was injured in an American bombing raid.

Wertmuller, Lina

Movie director Lina Wertmuller's full name is Arcangela Felice Assunta Wertmuller von Elgg Spanol von Braucich-Job.

The Italian movie director owns 2,000 pairs of those distinctive white harlequin eyeglass frames. It was the minimum order the factory would take and she doesn't want to run out of the frames.

Wesley, Charles

The co-founder (with his brother John) of the Methodist movement in the Church of England wrote almost 9,000 hymns in his lifetime or almost three hymns every week of his adult life.

West, Dame Rebecca

Born Cicily Fairfield, the popular novelist began her career as an actress and in the brief career she once played the role of Rebecca West in Ibsen's *Rosmersholm*. When she later became a book reviewer for the publication *Freewoman* in 1911, she decided to use the name Rebecca West as a pseudonym.

West, Jessamyn

The author of *The Friendly Persuasion*, a collection of stories about Quaker farmers in Indiana, is related to Richard Nixon. Her mother was Grace Ann Milhous and ex-president Nixon is a descendant of Miss West's great-uncle, Frank Milhous. In fact, Miss West used to babysit for Nixon when he was a child, and she also attended Whittier College, Nixon's alma mater.

West, Mae

Mae West, who is about 87 years old, attributes her relatively youthful appearance to her not smoking or drinking and especially to her *lower colonics*, which she says remove harmful substances from her body.

The eternally sexy movie actress once made love to a man ("Tex") for 15 straight hours.

To keep her breasts firm Mae massages them with cocoa butter every night.

What does Mae West have in common with Calvin Coolidge, Franklin D. Roosevelt, Winston Churchill, and Howard Hughes? They all like or liked Poland Spring mineral water. (Mae recently made her television commercial debut in a Poland Spring commercial.)

The first time Mae West appeared in vaudeville she was dressed in a tuxedo and appeared as a man.

Mae once spent eight days in a New York City prison on Welfare Island after her play *Sex* was closed by police because of complaints from the Society for the Suppression of Vice. (Note: the raid occurred after the 375th performance of the play!)

West, Morris

Morris West, author of *The Devil's Advocate* and *Shoes of the Fisherman,* published his first novel, *Moon in My Pocket,* in 1945 under the pen name Julian Morris.

West, Nathanael

Born Nathan Weinstein, he began signing his name "Nathaniel von Wallenstein Weinstein" at Brown University, creating a romantic notion of himself. "Wallenstein" was his mother's family name and adding "von" the new name created an image of nobility to the aspiring writer. Several years later, before going abroad he legally changed his name to Nathanael West, preferring the distinctive "ael" ending to the first name.

Wharton, Edith

Edith Wharton, born Edith Newbold Jones, was the first woman to ever receive an honorary doctorate from Yale University.

Whistler, James Abbott McNeill

Whistler's famous portrait of his mother is the only painting by an American at the Louvre in Paris. The painting is popularly known as "Whistler's Mother" but the official title is "Arrangement in Gray and Black."

Son of Major General George Washington Whistler, James Whistler attended the United States Military Academy at West Point, New York, but dropped out and then became a draftsman and map engraver for the coast and geodetic survey bureau in Washington, D.C.

Whitman, Walt

The great American poet began his working career as a printer's assistant in Brooklyn, New York.

Whitman had a sexual preference for uneducated working class men and in fact praises these men in the "Calamus" section of *Leaves of Grass* and in some of his other poems.

Wicker, Tom

Early in his reporting career Tom Wicker published three "thriller" novels under the pen name Paul Connolly: *Kingpin* (1953), *So Fair So Evil* (1955) and *The Devil Must* (1957).

Wiesenthal, Simon

Nazi-hunter Simon Wiesenthal lost his father and 88 other members of his and his wife's families in Nazi extermination camps.

Wiesenthal summed up his dedication to Nazi hunting in the following sentence: "When history looks back I want people to know the Nazis weren't able to kill 11,000,000 people and get away with it."

Wilde, Oscar

Wilde's full name was Oscar Fingal O'Flahertie Wills Wilde.

Wilder, Gene

Born Jerome Silberman in Milwaukee, Wisconsin, Gene took his stage name from *Eugene* Gant in Thomas Wolfe's *Look Homeward Angel* and from Thornton *Wilder*, the playwright.

Wilder, Thornton

As a child, Wilder lived in Chefoo, China for several years where his father was in the U.S. foreign service.

Wilhelm, Hoyt

In his first two times at bat in the major leagues the famous relief pitcher and knuckleballer hit a home run and a triple, a remarkable accomplishment especially for a pitcher. He never hit a homer or triple again!

Williams, Anson

Born Anson William Heimlick, the young television actor studied physical education at Pierce Junior College before assuming the role of Potsie on "Happy Days."

Williams, Esther

On her calling card appears a line drawing of a wave and the words "Yes, I still swim."

Williams, Robin

Before Williams won the Mork role on "Mork and Mindy" he used to do white-faced mime comedy in front of the Metropolitan Museum of Art in New York City, making as much as $75 a day. His current salary is $15,000 an episode for "Mork and Mindy" and going higher.

One of his pet lizards is named Truman Capote because "it has no neck."

At Redwood High School in Tiburon, California Robin's classmates selected him "Most Humorous" but the "Least Likely to Succeed"!

Willig, George

In May of 1977, using mountain climbing equipment George Willig climbed up one of the World Trade Center buildings in New York City. The City "fined" him $1.10—a penny for each floor, after withdrawing a $250,000 suit—but as he humorously pointed out later, it would have cost him $1.80 to go to the observation deck by elevator.

Wilson, Dick

Who is Dick Wilson? He is one of the most familiar faces in the United States. He plays Mr. Whipple in the Charmin toilet paper commercials.

Wilson, Woodrow

He was the first U.S. president to visit Europe while still in office. He made two trips in 1919 to expedite the peace negotiations following World War I.

In a story about Woodrow Wilson taking his fiancee to the theatre, the *Washington Post* reported, "... the President spent most of his time *entering* Mrs. Galt." Of course, the newspaper meant "entertaining"! (Or did they?)

Most U.S. presidents (29) attended college but Wilson has been the only president to have received a Ph.D.

Wilson appeared on a special $100,000 gold certificate bill issued in 1934 by the U.S. Treasury. The bills were not in mass circulation but were used for bank transactions.

Although Wilson was a Princeton graduate, he spent his freshman year at Davidson College in North Carolina.

Wilson's second wife, Edith Galt, was distantly related to Pocahontas, the American Indian princess.

The twenty-eighth President of the United States Woodrow Wilson was a dyslexic.

Winchell, Walter

Although Walter's real name was often reported to be Lipschitz, Hirschfield, or Weinshield, the truth was that his paternal grandfather was named Chaim Winechel and when one of

Chaim's sons (George, who later became president of the New York Curb Exchange) changed his name to Winchel, the rest of the family followed. Walter got the other "l" in his last name when he went into vaudeville and a careless electrician misspelled his name as Winchell on the theater marquee.

Contemplating his legacy, Winchell said, "If only when my epitaph is readied, they will say 'Here is Walter Winchell—with his ear to the ground—as usual.'"

Winkler, Henry

Winkler's role of Fonzarelli was not in the original pilot of the popular television series "Happy Days." (Later the script called for Fonzarelli to wear a cloth coat and loafers but Henry, who appeared with Sylvester Stallone in the 1974 movie *The Lords of Flatbush,* suggested the leather jacket and boots.)

After graduating from Yale Drama School in 1970, Winkler went to New York City and did commercial work. Some of the commercials in which he appeared were for American Airlines, Chief Boyardee Frozen Pizza, Close-up toothpaste, Schick shavers, and Travelers Insurance. Regarding commercial work, Henry acknowledged that it taught him how to work in front of a camera and said that he took the commercials as seriously as he took Shakespeare in college.

With his fan mail costing $3,000 a month to answer, Winkler started charging $5 a month for a membership in the Fonz' Fan Club.

Winter, Johnny

The blues singer and guitarist like most albinos, is legally blind, as is his brother Edgar Winter.

Winters, Jonathan

The comedian once admitted that he was an alcoholic at age 18. He has not been drinking for over 15 years.

"The Jonathan Winters Show," the night of October 23, 1956, on station WRCA in New York was the first video taped television program ever aired.

Winters, Shelley

Shelley Winters, born Shirley Schrift, decided to take the stage name Shelley Winter while attending acting classes at the New Theatre School. The last name was taken from her mother's stage name (Rose Winter) and her new first name was a slight embellishment of the name Shirley. In 1947 she added the "s" to "Winter" supposedly to avoid being called "Chilly Winter."

Wodehouse, P. G.

The novelist and playwright's full name is Pelham Grenville Wodehouse (pronounced "Woodhouse.")

Wolfe, Tom

At Washington and Lee, writer Tom Wolfe was a varsity pitcher on the baseball team. After graduation he tried out for the New York Giants but didn't get an offer. Baseball's loss is journalism's gain.

Wonder, Stevie

The singer's real name is Steveland Judkins Morris.

Stevie, born a premature baby, made the following statement regarding his blindness: "I have a dislocated nerve in one eye and a cataract on the other. It may have happened from being in the incubator too long and receiving too much oxygen."

Wood, Grant

The woman and man in the artist's famous painting *American Gothic* are Wood's sister Nan and her friend Dr. B. H. McKeeby, a dentist. The Gothic-style house in the background, incidentally, was later found out to be a brothel.

Reflecting upon his work, Wood said, "I suddenly realized that all the good ideas I ever had came to me while I was milking a cow."

During World War I the painter worked as a camouflage artist for the U.S. Army.

Wood, Natalie

Movie actress Natalie Wood is the daughter of a Russian-born movie set decorator who specialized in miniature sets and her real name is Natasha Gurdin. Just before her first major movie (*Tomorrow is Forever*, 1946) was released, her name was changed to Natalie Wood by production executives Leo Spitz and William Goetz who used the name "Wood" to honor their friend Sam Wood, a director.

Miss Wood is just under five feet tall.

Woodward, Joanne

At the 1957 Academy Awards ceremony, Joanne Woodward received the biggest compliment when she won the Best Actress Award for her strong performance in *The Three Faces of Eve* but she also got the biggest "pan" when Joan Crawford remarked that "Joanne Woodward is setting the cause of Hollywood glamour back 20 years by making her own clothes."

Wordsworth, William

At age 73, the Romantic poet became the Poet Laureate of England—the oldest man ever to receive the honor.

William Wordsworth had a love affair with his sister Dorothy.

Wright, Frank Lloyd

The pompous architect wore elevator shoes and darkened his graying hair by rubbing graphite into it.

Wright once commented that ugly buildings made his teeth hurt.

In a moment of self-examination, Wright admitted, "Early in life I had to choose between honest arrogance and hypocritical humility. I chose honest arrogance and have seen no occasion to change."

Wright once stormed into a ladies' rest room to point out one of his lesser-known inventions—the wall-hung toilet bowl.

Wright, Teresa

The veteran stage and movie actress adopted the name Teresa because her real first name Muriel was already being used by Muriel Wright, another member of Actors' Equity.

Wynn, Ed

As a teenager, the comedian, born Isaiah Edwin Leopold, ran away from home and surfaced in a New York vaudeville act *Wynn and Lewis* with Jack Lewis. He created his new stage name by splitting up and re-spelling his middle name *Edwin.*

Wyeth, Jamie

The third-generation artist quit school after the sixth grade to devote all of his time to painting.

When he was only 14 years old, Wyeth had a 23-year-old mistress.

Y

Yale, Elihu

Elihu Yale, the eponymic patron of Yale College, made his money in the black pepper trade and is considered to have been the first American millionaire.

Yarborough, Cale

The stock car racing champion learned to fly an airplane before he got his automobile driver's license and now has his own twin-engine Piper Aztec for business trips.

Yeats, William Butler

The Nobel Prize-winning poet was a dyslexic.

Young, Andrew

Andrew Young's father was a New Orleans dentist and Andrew himself had intended to become a dentist. He was a pre-med student at Howard University, where he got his B.S. degree in 1951. After graduation, however, Andrew changed his mind and studied for the ministry.

Young, Alan

The movie and television comedian's real first name is Angus but he dropped the name in favor of Alan when he and his sister, Harriet, teamed up to do a comedy act in the early 1930s.

Young, Brigham

Young's fame for having many wives overshadowed the fact that he started the country's first department store—Zion's Co-operative Mercantile Institution in Salt Lake City.

Young, Burt

As an aspiring writer, the Italian-American movie actor (*Rocky*) submitted a short story "Sicilian Love Potion," to *Playboy* magazine but it was rejected.

Young, Loretta

While filming the movie *Naughty But Nice*, actress Gretchen Michaela Young was advised by actress Colleen Moore to change her first name to Loretta (the name of Colleen's patron saint) after First National Pictures' publicity department announced that the name Gretchen "sounded too Dutchy." Loretta later complained, "The first time I knew they'd changed it, I read it in the paper."

Loretta Young's career started when she mistakenly answered a studio return call that was meant for Polly Ann Young, her older sister.

Her sister Betty Jane acted under the name Sally Blane. She appeared in the movies *I Am a Fugitive from a Chain Gang* and *Charlie Chan at Treasure Island*, among others.

Youngman, Henny

The king of the one-liners, whose father, Yonkel Jungman, changed his name to Jacob Youngman, was born Henry Youngman in London, England, but changed his first name to Henny 18 years later while appearing in a Coney Island act. In his autobiography he explained the reason for the change: "All my life the guys used to call me 'Hen,' short for Henry. It wasn't until I saw it in print like that I realized it was a bad name for anyone in show business. A hen can lay an egg, so I changed it to 'Henny.' With a name like that you could only lay a little egg."

Z

Zappa, Frank

The eccentric rock composer wanted his fourth child to be named Clint Eastwood, but it was a girl because his wife named her Diva. Their other three children are named Moon Unit, Dweezil, and Ahmet Emuukha Rodan.

Zanuck, Darryl F.

Although D.F.Z. eventually became head of Twentieth Century-Fox movie studios, his first job in Hollywood was with Warner Brothers, as a writer for *Rin Tin Tin* movie scripts in 1924.

Unlike most movie moguls, Zanuck was not born in Eastern Europe and was not Jewish. He was born in Wahoo, Nebraska, and was of Swiss decent.

Zeffirelli, Franco

The Italian opera and movie director was born out of wedlock and has neither his father's nor his mother's last name. According to Zeffirelli, in those days (1923) illegitimate children could not be named after their parents and names had to be made up. Zeffirelli explained further in an interview with Tom Buckley, "For some reason the name had to begin with a certain letter of the alphabet that changed in rotation each day. I was born on February 12, 1923, and by chance, the letter that day was 'Z.' My mother picked the name Zeffirelli because it was part of the title of a favorite arietta of hers, from an opera either by Mozart or Rossini—I'm not sure which. It was 'Farfallie Zeffirelli,' that is, 'butterflies and little breezes.' I'm the only person in the world, as far as I've been able to determine, who has that name."

Zeppelin, Count Ferdinand von

Count Zeppelin is usually credited with inventing the dirigible but, in fact, he bought the patents from the widow of the real inventor, David Schwartz, an Austrian engineer, who literally died from excitement when he found out the German government was interested in producing his dirigible.

Zimbalist, Efrem Jr.

Actor Efrem Zimbalist's family name is derived from the profession of a Hungarian forebear who played the gypsy musical instrument *zymbal.*

Zimbalist went to Yale to study engineering but was expelled for "high jinks and low marks," and then decided to become an actor.

Zorina, Vera

When 16-year-old Eva Brigitta Hartwig accepted an offer to join the Ballet Russe de Monte Carlo, she was told that she would have to change her name. Given a list of Russian names, she picked the name Vera Zorina because it was the only one she could pronounce.